mother & SON

mother & SON

THE RESPECT EFFECT

EMERSON EGGERICHS, PhD

W PUBLISHING GROUP

AN IMPRINT OF THOMAS NELSON

Published in Nashville, Tennessee, by W Publishing Group, an imprint of Thomas Nelson.

Author is represented by the literary agency of Alive Communications, Inc., 7680 Goddard Street, Suite 200, Colorado Springs, CO 80920, www.alivecommunications.com.

Thomas Nelson titles may be purchased in bulk for educational, business, fund-raising, or sales promotional use. For information, please e-mail SpecialMarkets@ThomasNelson.com.

Unless otherwise noted, Scripture quotations are taken from the New American Standard Bible®. © 1960, 1962, 1963, 1968, 1971, 1972, 1973, 1975, 1977, 1995 by The Lockman Foundation. Used by permission.

Scriptures marked CEV are taken from the Contemporary English Version. © 1991, 1992, 1995 by the American Bible Society. Used by permission.

Scriptures marked THE MESSAGE and otherwise quoted as such are taken from *The Message*. © by Eugene H. Peterson 1993, 1994, 1995, 1996, 2000, 2001, 2002. Used by permission of Tyndale House Publishers, Inc.

Scriptures marked NIV are taken from the Holy Bible, New International Version®, NIV®. © 1973, 1978, 1984, 2011 by Biblica, Inc.® Used by permission of Zondervan. All rights reserved worldwide.

Scriptures marked GW are taken from *God's Word*®. © 1995 God's Word to the Nations. Used by permission of Baker Publishing Group. All rights reserved.

Scriptures marked KJV are taken from the King James Version. Public domain.

Names and facts from stories contained in this book have been changed, but the sentiments expressed are true as related to the author through personal conversations, letters, or e-mails. Permission has been granted for the use of real names, stories, and correspondence.

ISBN 978-0-7180-7958-1 (ITPE)

Library of Congress Cataloging-in-Publication Data

Names: Eggerichs, Emerson, author.
Title: Mother & son : the respect effect / Emerson Eggerichs, PhD.
Other titles: Mother and son
Description: Nashville, Tennessee : W Publishing Group, 2016.
  | Includes bibliographical references.
Identifiers: LCCN 2016001064 | ISBN 9780849948213
  (hardcover : alk. paper)
Subjects: LCSH: Mothers and sons—Religious aspects—Christianity.
  | Mothers and sons. | Respect for persons.
Classification: LCC BV4529.18 .E35 2016 | DDC 248.8/431—dc23 LC record
  available at http://lccn.loc.gov/2016001064

Printed in the United States of America

16 17 18 19 20 RRD 6 5 4 3 2 1

I dedicate this book to Sarah, my wife, who gave voice over the years to those who attended our Love and Respect Conference: "Had I known earlier about the Respect Effect on sons, I would have been a far better mother to my sons."

Though as a mother she was twenty-five times better than I was as a father, the Respect message, nonetheless, deeply affected her, and she in turn affected our sons, who have voiced their appreciation. It worked!

I also dedicate this book to my mother, now in heaven, who always showed me respect, even into adulthood when I pastored a church—she attended all four services each weekend! Sarah says, "I think that's why you have endearingly and regularly said since 2001, 'I miss my mother.'"

Contents

Introduction

A Testimony

As I've traveled the world over the last two decades, exploring the dynamic of healthy family relationships, one thing has become abundantly clear.

A boy needs his mother's respect.

Not only her love but also her respect. That's the message of this book, and I believe that it will transform your relationship with your son in ways you've only dreamed about. It won't be because of my writing. In fact, I'll try hard not to get in the way. It will be because the principle is life-changing in its simplicity, and it cuts straight to the deepest part of a boy's soul.

When it comes to respect between a mother and son, the point that most make is that a mother needs her son's respect. And to this point, I wholeheartedly agree. A boy does need to be respectful. In fact, I wrote a whole book about the need of a father and mother for the respect of their children, called *Love & Respect in the Family*. But it's only half of the equation, especially when you move from the parents as one unit into the highly unique and beautiful relationship between a mother and her son.

I explored this relationship briefly in "Parenting Pink and Blue," one of the chapters of *Love & Respect in the Family*. There, I briefly tell mothers that their "blue" sons need respect in the same way their "pink" daughters need dad's love. Yes, sons and daughters equally need love and respect, but I show that the felt need during stress and conflict differs among males and females. Research bears this out. Males filter their world more through the respect grid.

Fascinatingly, moms zeroed in on this teaching immediately and began sending me hundreds of stories and testimonials surrounding this revelation. With great excitement, they applied respect talk to their sons, whether they were four or forty. Judging from the letters, many of which you'll read in this book, they experienced astounding results.

Let me share one such testimony with you in this introduction to set the stage. This mother read the "Parenting Pink and Blue" chapter and applied it to her daily interactions with her son. Here is the Respect Effect. She wrote:

I had finally concluded—although I wasn't ready to completely believe it—that my seven-year-old son just had one of those moody, depressed personalities, and I had better just accept it, instead of wanting him to be happier. I should try to teach him to be grateful for all his blessings.

But after applying respect in the way you suggested, he changed. For example, he came up to me the other evening, with an unusually happy, calm demeanor, and said, "I feel so happy," in the most contented, almost sentimental tone. This was profound for me! This was my child, who according to his consistent behavior since birth would have been labeled melancholy/choleric. He would often tell me—and this breaks my heart—that he was "sad and didn't know why." I would try to talk to him about things, work through things, and prayed for him and with him regularly. But he usually only seemed really happy when something exciting was going on, a trip to the zoo or if he went with me to visit friends, but then on the way home would say he was "bored" (I think he was just trying to express unhappiness).

When I began the respect principles, he seemed calmer, less frustrated, less internally agitated (my respect seemed to release his internal tension), and more loving. . . . He has been coming up to me, and instead of acting out for attention, he will hug me, look right into my eyes, smile the sweetest, happiest smile, and say, "You're the best mom in the world!" Wow! Nothing quite that wonderful has ever happened between us before. Being respectful to him has triggered his affection for me. . . . [I am] seeing beautiful and meaningful results.

He has come up again recently and said, "I don't know why, but I'm so happy!" And I thought, *I know why, my little sweetheart. Because I have learned to show you the respect you didn't even know you were crying out for, that I didn't even know you needed.* He has been far more calm and content. He has been more willing to mind and has had little or no talking back to me. His affection for me has increased greatly; he comes up to me throughout the day and hugs and kisses me. I am beginning to enjoy the rewards of parenting on a much deeper level. It's like we are friends now, instead of always in a power struggle.

I long to be able to learn even more practical ways on how to show him respect. I am navigating unfamiliar waters . . . stepping out and doing what the book says even though it makes no sense to my "pink" brain. . . .

It has been much more challenging learning how to show respect in parenting because I still want my strong-willed, type A, firstborn little man to know that he is not the boss.

I have also been trying to take time each day to stop what I am doing and look at him and really listen to him, giving him my undivided attention when he wants to tell me something, rather than multitasking so much.

It's like a little miracle—the connection and affection I longed to have with my son have finally come. He finally feels respected (oh, how I wish I had known how to do this sooner!) and his happiness shows. I can't mourn over the many difficult years we had; I have to "forget those things which are behind, and press on" because God has many more good years ahead for us and our blossoming relationship.

My mom commented on how much calmer my son was when we went to visit a few days ago. She told my sister, who has five sons, about the wonderful transformation my son and I are enjoying. I will keep spreading the word! God bless!

Is this testimony too good to be true? You will have to decide as you read this book. I can tell you this: other moms chime in with equal enthusiasm. You will hear from them throughout as we proceed with the following:

- Why This Book?
- Understanding What Respect Looks Like to Boys
- A Game Plan: Mom G.U.I.D.E.S. with Respect
- Seeing the Man in the Boy: His Six Desires: C.H.A.I.R.S.
- Conquest: Respecting His Desire to Work and Achieve
- Hierarchy: Respecting His Desire to Provide, Protect, and Even Die
- Authority: Respecting His Desire to Be Strong and to Lead and Make Decisions
- Insight: Respecting His Desire to Analyze, Solve, and Counsel
- Relationship: Respecting His Desire for a Shoulder-to-Shoulder Friendship
- Sexuality: Respecting His Desire for Sexual Understanding and "Knowing"
- An Empathetic Look at the Motherly Objections to Respecting a Boy
- Forgiveness

Sarah, my wife, has said for many years, "If I had known this information when my sons were little (they are now in their thirties), I would have been a better mother."

This does not mean Sarah's love was insignificant. Mother-love is vital. In fact, mother-love is the epitome of altruism.

"But, Emerson, I have to ask: aren't *love* and *respect* synonymous? Using the word *love* should work just fine, right?" No, it won't work just fine. These are not two words with the same meaning. A husband doesn't give to his wife a card that says, "Baby, I really respect you!" These words are not synonymous. A mother can love her son but not respect him, just as a mother works outside the home for a boss that she respects but does not love. When a mother thinks about it, she knows these words differ.

I can tell you this: a boy knows his mom loves him, but he can lack assurance that she *respects* him. Sarah, along with me, has observed the Respect Effect among hundreds of mothers who stand in utter amazement, like the mother of the seven-year-old boy. Here are some quotes that I've pulled from letters in the last few months:

- What a difference.
- I was totally amazed.
- It kind of blew me away.
- To me that was awesome.
- He has never initiated saying, "I love you."
- It was life-changing.
- It spoke to their hearts.
- My relationship with my son improved overnight.
- These things make my son smile like I have never seen.
- I was slightly in a state of shock and euphoria at the same time.
- I could hear in his voice and see in his e-mails that he seemed to be more confident in his maleness.
- No lie! He saw me taking the trash out of the can, and he took it from me and said, "I'll take it outside for you, mommy." Then he came in and offered to pick up the toys and take them to his room. I about fell over.

Are you ready to find out more? Sarah wants you to know, "As a mother, it is never too early and never too late to apply this message of respect. A boy is never too young and never too old."

1

WHY THIS BOOK?

A woman responds to love. The woman is in a girl. Therefore, a girl responds to love.

A man responds to respect. The man is in a boy. Therefore, a boy responds to respect.

The first syllogistic statement receives an affirming nod from every mother. For some, the second statement is a bit more difficult to grasp.

I often scratch my head in bewilderment over the lack of understanding of mothers about their precious baby boys. They love their sons more than they love their very lives, but they readily confess ignorance and confusion.

A mom wrote:

I have been really struggling with my nearly four-year-old son lately. Now I understand why every mother wants a daughter . . . because we "get" them! When my sixteen-month-old daughter throws a fit about something, I know what angle to come from because I understand why she's upset. When my son does something, I'm like, "Why did he just do that?" *Again!*

1

Every mother recognizes the woman in the girl and her longing for love. In the movie *Notting Hill* (1999), Julia Roberts's character emotionally expresses, "I'm also just a girl . . . standing in front of a boy . . . asking him to love her." The feminine need and traits ring loud and clear to all women. For example, none miss the nurturing nature of women and little girls. All the research bears out the caregiving traits of the feminine soul, but who needs research to tell us this? We see it every day. No one is ever surprised when a little girl walks down the street with her baby doll, then stops to nurse it with a plastic bottle as she affectionately communicates her love. We observe the woman in the girl. We don't need research to educate us.

XX and XY Chromosomes

Yet as I talk to mothers and tell them there is a man in the boy, some respond with curiosity about who that man might be. Yes, they know their sons are "all boy." As one mother said, "He can be 'all boy' one second and the other the sweetest little thing ever." But note her negative contrast. The "all boy" is not sweet to her. These mothers admit they are a bit in the dark on God's virtuous design of testosterone, unlike the way they intuitively grasp the purity of estrogen. One mom quipped (about her son), "We love these kids, but Lord help us; if they don't have the same XX or XY chromosomes that we do, it can be like navigating a foreign country without a map."

To some moms the boy is an alien. But he is not from outer space. God created him male in his gender. When it comes to the boy, this book explains the attributes of the masculine soul. This book helps the mom hear a precious and endearing message: "I am just a boy, standing in front of his mother, asking her to respect him."

Both research and the Bible reveal the male's need for respect. This is a simple and revolutionary insight into the heart of a boy that we have overlooked—and shockingly so. This book is about a mother going beyond her love and applying respect to the heart of her son. But in addition to the research and the Scripture, every mom will begin to see for herself this need in her boy.

Do Not Beat Yourself Up

When you see his need for respect firsthand, you will find your love and compassion for your son providing you with the natural interest and energy to meet this need. So do not shame yourself. Please hear me. Relax. Do not beat yourself up as your mind races to those moments when you feel you may have failed. Some moms tend to torture themselves, then run to the hills to avoid this topic. But let your love motivate you to switch gears when this stuff about respect per se does not motivate you.

Let me say, I was unchurched growing up; so if you view yourself as secular or unchurched, please keep reading. Though I pastored for years, which enables me to bring the biblical perspective, I have a PhD in child and family ecology that enables me to highlight what we know about male behavior and what I have researched. In addition, I have collected hundreds and hundreds of e-mails from moms. You need to hear their testimonies. You owe it to yourself. You owe it to your son.

Research

As for the research, Shaunti Feldhahn has found that respect is extremely important to men. If men were forced to choose between feeling "alone and unloved in the world OR [feeling] inadequate and disrespected," 74 percent would rather give up love if they could keep respect, with just 26 percent saying they'd give up respect in order to be loved.[1]

Men and boys are far more sensitive, vulnerable, and reactionary to feeling inadequate and disrespected. Sadly, some have profiled these sentiments as rooted in narcissism. But moms know their sons are not egotistical maniacs any more than their daughters are prima donnas for longing to be special, noticed, and loved. A prudent mom gives the benefit of the doubt to her boy. He is a man in the making.

Though we all need love and respect equally, there is a statistically significant gender difference. I asked seven thousand people, "When in a conflict with your spouse, do you feel unloved or disrespected?" An overwhelming 83 percent of the men said disrespected, and 72 percent of the women said unloved. In other words, quite often during the same conflict, she filters his reaction as unloving and he interprets her reaction as disrespectful.

What Does a Boy Need?

Your son feels the same way. But did you know he feels this way?

During a conflict, if you do not filter the event as he does, you will miss the extent to which he feels disrespected. Because you do not intend to be disrespectful, you could dismiss his feelings. You might say, "He should know that I love him and am trying to help him be more loving. He needs to stop feeling disrespected." In like manner, I suppose it is okay for a dad to tell his daughter to stop feeling unloved.

As Louann Brizendine wrote in *The Female Brain*, "Males and females become reactive to different kinds of stress. . . . Relationship conflict is what drives a teen girl's stress system wild. She needs to be liked and socially connected; a teen boy needs to be respected."[2] Did you catch that? *A teen boy needs to be respected.*

When a mother and son get into a conflict—a very stressful event to both—the son feels far more disrespected than he feels unloved, and he craves respect more than love. But how many mothers detect this, and if they do, how many know what to say or do? Who has coached a mom to ask, "Is what I am about to say going to sound respectful or disrespectful to my son?"

Every mom needs to recognize and accept that her son filters the stress with her through the respect grid. He is not wrong for this, just different. In the same way, a daughter is not wrong, just different for wanting to be liked. A dad must not say to his daughter, "Quit worrying about being liked at school." The good news is that once mom sees this need in her boy, she can use this information with prudence. She need only say, "I am not trying to show you disrespect when I confront your misbehavior." Just using the word *disrespect* eases his stress.

The Crazy Cycle

If mothers do not use Respect-Talk like this, they spin on what I call the Crazy Cycle with their sons: without respect a son reacts without love, and without love a mother reacts without respect. This baby spins. Can you relate? Whatever the issue that first created heated fellowship between mother and son, it has now been relegated to second place. The root issue to the boy is the disrespect he feels, and the root issue to mom is the lack of love she feels, not to mention her feeling disrespected as the parent. It gets really crazy, really quick. He doesn't see his lack of love because he is feeling disrespected, and mom doesn't see her disrespect because she is feeling both unloved and disrespected.

To stop this craziness, every mom can use Respect-Talk. Though it is more than verbal and sounds abnormal at first, using the word *respect* is the starting point for a mother. To stop the crazy moments, she need only clarify, as I said above,

> "Look, I am not using this topic as an opportunity to send you a
> message that I don't respect you. I am not trying to dishonor you.
> I am seeking to address the issue at hand, okay? Let's take five
> minutes to calm down and revisit the matter respectfully."

This is the native tongue of a boy. He hears it loud and clear, then calms down.

Is this hard for a mom to do? No. A mother loves to use words and communicate. Research has found that women are expressive and responsive. What better way to commence than to learn a few vocabulary words of respect that energize, motivate, and influence the heart of a boy? What could be more thrilling to a mother than to speak words that soften the spirit of a son and trigger a desire in him to connect with her? She imagines this kind of relationship with her son but never seems to experience it as she hopes—not after age four for many moms.

As the mother said in the introduction, "It's like a little miracle—the connection and affection I longed to have with my son have finally come."

The Respect Effect

Respect-Talk ignites affection and endearment in a boy. Let me illustrate this between a father and a son to help you see this from another angle. A dad wrote:

> One weekend a few months ago, we traveled as a family up to Prague. We had read your book prior to this trip and so some of the concepts were still fresh in my mind. I spent my weekend helping my brother-in-law build a tree house for his children and then we made a zip line. While my nephew was too frightened to be the first to try the new line, my son volunteered. After that the boys went down the line several times.
>
> About the third or fourth time [my son] let go for some reason. He fell about fifteen feet to the ground. This is what happens when you leave two dads home alone with the kids. My son got the wind knocked out of him but had no broken bones. When the mothers arrived home they were less than happy, but I took the opportunity to show great respect for my son. I began to tell of this escapade and called him a warrior and a hero. These words resounded so much with my son that for the next three days he was glued to my side.
>
> Since the incident I have told the story often, always within earshot [of my son], and I have noticed how he will always stick around long enough to hear me call him a warrior hero, and then he will be on his way. After our return [from your conference], I shared with him that I was able to tell this story in front of 350 people, and that brought a huge broad smile across his face. I know I fail my son often; I know I have

much to learn as a dad, but there are times when I get to tell this story and he knows he is a knight in shining armor.

Note that the dad used Respect-Talk with his son by referring to him as a warrior and hero, resulting in the boy's staying glued to his dad's side for three days. Respect-Talk created affection and a desire to stay close and connect. I want every mom to pay attention to this. The boy bonded in a deep and profound way with his father, and the same can happen between mother and son when she uses Respect-Talk.

A mom wrote:

One night while putting our sons to bed, my five-year-old, in the midst of my monologue about how much I loved him, looked at me sadly and said, "Mom, are you proud of me?" Shocked, I expressed immediately that I was, of course, proud of him. He asked forlornly, "Then why don't you ever tell me so?" Ever since then, I have worked to hold back on my desire to grab him up off the floor and smother his cheek with kisses, and, instead, I practice putting one hand on his shoulder and telling him I'm proud of him. He responds to that simple gesture by puffing out his chest and replying, "Thanks, mom," with a nod of his head. And he walks away feeling more valued than if I'd kissed his cheek for a year.

Respect-Talk is not to be left to the dads. This boy needed his mother's honor and respect, and he told her so.

By the way, this ignites a new appreciation in a mom for the relationship her husband has with her boys. A mom told me,

I've begun to understand my husband's relationship with our boys. We have three boys, thirteen, ten, and five, and one girl of two years of age. I've been critical of my husband's way of communicating with the boys. This series of Love and Respect has explained the language between males. My boys spend hours talking with my husband about their interests, which include weapons, the military channel, World War I, World

War II, and girls. You must know that my husband is a cop by profession so their conversations are actually very interesting to a point. I've come to understand why they speak this language and how the respect between each other has developed.

The conversations between my sons and husband [are] about honor, respect, wisdom, tactical strategies, and how to apply them to everyday life. But I must say that the content of the conversations is not the only thing interesting to me but also the stern tone of voice my husband uses with them. If he were to use that tone with me or my daughter, we'd probably break down crying. On the other hand, my boys seem to thrive on it. They seek my husband's companionship and always want to seek his conversation.

There we have it. The boys are glued to the dad.

Connectivity

Respect-Talk creates the kind of connectivity every mother yearns to have with her son. Of course, we are not asking mom to put on combat boots, smoke cigars, harness a weapon, and lower her voice. She need not attend the police academy. We are not promoting the idea that a mother becomes a male. Instead, this mother's testimony highlights the importance of *not* passing judgment on this respect message simply because a mother feels uncomfortable with it. As this mother stated, she initially judged her husband's way of communicating as wrong when, in this instance, it was not wrong. A mother must not judge this language as unacceptable but embrace this as part of God's design. She will value this when her nineteen-year-old saves her life against a home invader.

Truth is, the conversation between this father and these boys represents some of the best of Respect-Talk. I am certain their discussions included such virtues as honor, integrity, caution, loyalty, bravery, prudence, service, and sacrifice. I predict these boys will turn into the kind of men that other men follow and women adore.

I invite moms to stop and ask, "Why do boys respond to a football coach? Why do boys join the Marines and subject themselves to a drill officer?" Many mothers declare, "I have no idea." These male leaders are attesting to these boys, "I believe in you. I admire who I believe you to be. But do you see this in yourself? Do you have what it takes to become what I believe you to be?" This has been a major slogan of the US Army: "Be All That You Can Be!" Boys dream of joining.

Respect-Talk also helps a mother as she connects a son with his father:

> The material from the book has been especially helpful with how I am able to support my husband in his relationship with our son and has allowed me to encourage a healthier, more respectful relationship between father and son. Here's how I have used what I learned from *Love and Respect* when speaking to my son about his father's wishes and encouraging behaviors that my husband desires.
>
> For example, my husband does not like the kids climbing on furniture. When my son does so, I gently remind him that "we need to respect how hard dad has worked to be able to buy things for our family and his desire to take good care of them." My son responds well to this. I suppose he understands this language better than hollering, "Dad says to get off the couch!" . . .
>
> I am able to tell my son, "Your dad thinks you should (fill in the blank). Because he wants what is best for you, we need to respect his wishes." It seems my son can understand this need to respect his father (even better than me!) and can rise to obedience out of pure respect.

Mothers Have an *Aha* Moment

What fascinates me is that many mothers who have attended our Love and Respect Marriage Conference began to e-mail me their testimonies of enlightenment. In our conference we teach Ephesians 5:33. That scripture commands husbands to love their wives and wives to respect their husbands; 1 Peter 3:1–2 also address respect. In my marriage book, *Love and Respect*, I guide wives to experience power and influence by putting on respect toward the spirit of their husbands while addressing unrespectable things. This respectful demeanor in the wives ends up motivating the husbands to be more loving and respectable.

After the conference these women start thinking, *Hey, doesn't this apply to my son? He's a male.*

A woman wrote, "I came from a family of all girls, and your information on respect toward my husband was all new to me. It really got me to thinking about how that could also translate to raising my boys, ages nine and eleven."

Mothers intuitively sensed that if respect worked on the masculine souls of their husbands, then respect would work on the masculine souls of their sons. They tried it and wrote me with the mind-blowing results. "This respect thing really worked with my boy; it blew me away."

Mothers began asking for more help on how to apply respect to their circumstances with their sons.

"What about my four-year-old? What should I envision doing
toward him in these early years?"
"How do I respect my teen son when he should be respecting me?"
"What if I have disrespected my adult son for too many years? Is it
too late to change?"

As I relayed ways to apply respect, it proved revolutionary to these moms. This opened up a whole new world to mothers toward their sons, and they shot back e-mails to me that contained story after story of the Respect Effect that left them in shock and awe—no matter the age, no matter the former mistakes.

As these mothers told me their stories, I became intrigued by the maternal refrain, "Why has no one told us this information before? This is incredible! I want to learn more. Do you have a book about mothers and sons?"

A Sense of Urgency

When I told them that I did not have a book but planned on writing one, they exclaimed, "Please hurry up, and sign me up for that book on mothers and sons. I want it! No, I need it! Now!"

What made this all the more urgent is that moms were coaching fathers to love their daughters, but no one was teaching moms how to show respect to their sons. All realized that little girls needed daddy's love, but who strongly promoted the truth that little boys need mommy's respect?

One day as I thumbed through the indexes of some leading books about boys, not one index listed either of these words: *respect* or *honor*. None declared that boys need to feel respected for who they are as men in the making. No wonder mothers feel left in the dark on this topic. Who pinpointed respect as central to the core of a boy?

The president of an NBA team invited me recently to address this topic of honor and respect to the team, coaches, and trainers. I was the only inspirational speaker he's ever invited to speak to one of his teams, and he himself is known as one of the greatest motivational speakers in this century. Why would he invite me? Because he recognized the uniqueness of the masculine soul and the power that exists when it is allowed to flourish. The need in an NBA all-star's soul is the same need in the young boy who wants to be that star someday.

Pixie Dust?

Having said all this, I do not wish to overpromise. This is no absolute formula. Your son is not a robot, nor are you. This is more art than science. Also, respect is not a theory to try out for a day or two. Your son is not a lab rat for you to test this on, and then conclude it doesn't work if he does not become perfectly sensitive, sentimental, sensible, and sensational overnight. This is a commitment to meet a son's need until the son dies— hopefully not from letting go of a zip line.

There is no pixie dust for a mom to sprinkle on her son's head that will magically influence him to obey her every wish and command. There is no tricky technique for creating a perfect son any more than there is a three-step process for turning a woman into a perfect mother. Neither mom nor son will ever walk on water.

But neither do I intend to downplay the power of Respect-Talk, just as I would never downplay expressions of love from a father to his daughter. When a mother does what I set forth in this book, even when she and her son have bad days, her son will respond less negatively. I acknowledge that things may not be as positive as she hopes and prays, but they will be better.

The Respect Effect has joyfully stunned many people. The responses of the sons put some folks back on their heels with giddy delight. So if all of this hinges on understanding respect, what exactly *is* respect? How do we define it in relatable terms? That's where we'll go in the next chapter.

2

Understanding What Respect Looks Like to Boys

What Is Respect?

A mom expressed,

> I live with a house full of male testosterone, and we even have a male dog. I am having conflict with my almost twelve-year-old and it is driving me nuts. My other two are fifteen and thirteen. . . . How do I show my boys that I can see [with] blue glasses and [hear with] blue hearing aids? . . . I am trying to figure out this respect thing and am finding it kinda difficult. Getting a handle on this is something I want to do, but I am not sure how. I even had to look up *respect* to see what it really meant. I am in prayer about this.

Mothers are humble and teachable. They long to give the best to their priceless boys. Yet they stumble about in the dark on the definition of *respect*. They echo what this mother mouths: "What in the world does respect look like?"

Here's a simple definition: a mother's respect is her positive regard toward her son, no matter what he does.

"But Emerson, how can you say no matter what? Everyone knows respect must be earned. My son needs to earn my respect. In fact, he needs to respect me! Besides, how can I have positive regard when I feel so negative about him because of his disobedience?"

I hear you loud and clear. But please hear me. I am not saying that your son *deserves* respect. I am saying he will not respond to your negativity and *disrespect*—not in the long term. He will resist or rebel against what he perceives as your contempt for him.

Sadly, some conclude, "Since respect must be earned and my son has not earned it, I have license to show my son disrespect when he disobeys." But no human being feels love and affection toward a person he thinks despises him. Who responds to a rude person?

My Son Does Not Deserve Respect

"Well, Emerson, I guess I agree that I don't have license to be rude. As you said, no human responds to contempt. But he doesn't deserve respect. Is there a middle ground here?"

No. Either a mother will show respect and positive regard toward the spirit of her son while confronting his wrongdoing, or she will show disrespect and negative regard toward the spirit of her son while confronting his sinful choices. There is no third option.

The secret here is recognizing two dimensions in your son. Do you recall what Jesus said to His disciples who fell asleep on Him in the Garden of Gethsemane? "The spirit is willing, but the flesh is weak" (Matt. 26:41). Jesus expressed disappointment at the disciples falling asleep. He did not sanction or honor their failings. But He honored the disciples for their deeper desires to do what was right. He honored their willing spirit. Jesus did not show disrespect toward their spirit while disapproving of their weak flesh.

There are two parts to your son: the spirit and the flesh. In your son's flesh he fails, and you must address his unrespectable conduct. But that's a separate matter from saying to him, "I have contempt for who you are as a human being—for your inner spirit. You are despicable."

Understand this foundational truth: showing respect toward the spirit of your son does not sanction and respect the sin of his flesh. A mother can say, "I do not respect your wrong choices. I am angry about those choices, and you will be disciplined for them." But then she can add, "I believe in your deepest heart. I respect the person God made you to be, and we will get through this moment."

Do not step over a line and condemn his spirit because he failed due to the weakness of his flesh. Imitate how Jesus responded to the disciples. Respectfully confront the inadequate behavior while showing positive regard toward your son's spirit, no matter what he has done.

Mom's Look

"But Emerson, I never speak words of disrespect to my son." Excellent. But what do you look like to him when you are displeased with him? Does he interpret your "look" to mean you have scorn and loathing toward him? I am not saying that you in fact do. I am asking, "Does he feel that you do from your 'look'?" Though you never intend to communicate disrespect toward the spirit of your son, do you unintentionally?

Admittedly, I am generalizing a bit here, but when upset, a woman can appear disrespectful to men. Her eyes darken. Her face turns sour. She rolls her eyes in disbelief. She sighs with disgust as she shakes her head. She scolds with her pointed finger. Perturbed, she puts her hands on her hips as she stares down the culprit. And when she speaks, her voice is shrill. As estrogen kicks in, her words of disrespect roll off her lips so quickly she surprises herself, and some of those words could sober a drunken sailor. Her weapon of choice is verbalized contempt.

Though much of this erupts from hurt, frustration, and fatigue because she gives, gives, and gives, she cannot excuse the look of contempt any more than a dad can excuse a look of anger and hostility toward his daughter. A mom must maintain positive regard toward the spirit of her son no matter what.

Common sense tells us that a contemptuous look never energizes, motivates, or influences a son's heart. Even secular humanists recognize the importance of unconditional positive regard.

Scholarship

Scholars on the topic of respect found, "Relational success is often dependent on being able to communicate respect and avoiding the communication of disrespect. Sometimes communicating respect is simply viewed as a means to an end, but the key is for the respected to perceive an unconditional respect rather than feeling manipulated."[1] Though it may be complicated to convey a message of unconditional respect, the result is almost always positive when the communication is successful.[2]

When secularists get this, all the more must a mother who loves Christ. After all, Jesus loved us while we were yet sinners and intends to glorify us throughout eternity as an absolute gift, freely given (Rom. 5:8–11). This is respect on steroids! More than anyone else, Christ-followers should appreciate and apply unconditional positive regard. We have an eternal and substantive reason. Every mother should see the image of God within her son and honor that image. Every mother should see her son as Jesus sees her son: a willing spirit but weak flesh.

Unconditional Positive Regard

Unconditional positive regard does not come naturally. Who naturally desires to be respectful while confronting a disrespectful son? What mom enjoys putting on positive regard toward the spirit of her son when he negatively disregards her heart? This is not about doing the easy or fair thing but the right thing. Kids are immature and obnoxious. But this is the way forward.

Some mothers prefer the easier way, especially when it accomplishes their goals. Many mothers have seen firsthand the power of their disrespect. That's why it's so dangerous and misleading. It works! When a boy feels his mother's disdain, he does what she expects. She comes to adhere to the Disrespect Effect. But long term that is as effective as a dad who believes in harshness and anger toward his daughter as the method to motivate her. Even though it may work short term, he loses her heart long term. The same thing will happen with your son. Hostility and contempt eventually lose the child's heart.

Bottom line, unconditional respect toward the spirit of a boy is the moral equivalence of unconditional love of a father toward the spirit of a daughter. The dad does not love his daughter's sinful, fleshly choices. He loves her spirit in spite of that behavior. So, too, a mom does not respect her son's sinful, fleshly choices. She respects his spirit in spite of that conduct.

What About Trust?

Does this mean you should unconditionally trust your son? Absolutely not, given he has broken trust by lying, stealing, or cheating. Respect is not blind trust. That kind of blind trust is enablement. When a boy does wrong in this way, he must suffer the consequences and re-earn trust. But mom can show positive regard toward the spirit of her son while enacting discipline.

A mother must confront the unrespectable transgressions and have the courage to do so. She is not running a popularity contest with him. But she shows respect toward the spirit of her son while informing him that he is grounded for three weekends due to doing things behind her back. She says,

> "I respect who God made you to be. I respect your deepest heart. You are my son. But when you break trust you must reestablish trust. Through this grounding you will become wiser, and I hope you will make the decision to stay true in the future. Men of honor stay true."

She lives independent of his behavior and opinion of her. His bad behavior cannot coerce her into becoming a contemptuous and undignified woman. Her response is her responsibility. But neither does his bad behavior manipulate her into passive silence. She confronts and corrects him.

Is Unconditional Respect a Biblical Idea?

The apostle Peter set forth the idea of honoring and respecting other people regardless of their behavior. Just as we love people independent of their unlovable actions (Matt. 5:46), so we are to put on respect in our demeanor toward the spirit of others regardless of their unrespectable actions.

Peter penned, "Honor all people." He continued, "Servants, be submissive to your masters with all respect, not only to those who are good and gentle, but also to those who are unreasonable" (1 Peter 2:17–18).

Respect an unreasonable person? Yes. He even instructed wives to put on "respectful behavior" to win a disobedient husband (1 Peter 3:2). Clearly this means showing respect toward a person who does not deserve respect.

Such respect is not toward the wrongdoing of the other person but toward the spirit of the person doing the wrong. We are to act honorably though they are not honorable. We are respectful though they are not respectable. We do not lose our dignity though they lose their dignity.

Unconditional respect means there's no condition, situation, or circumstance that can force us to show contempt. In the case of a mom, her son cannot turn her into a disrespectful woman. That's her choice for herself. He cannot control her inner spirit. God made mom free. This does not mean she loses all feeling. The range of amoral emotions pulsates in her heart, from grief to sadness, to gratefulness and happiness. But disrespect and rudeness is her choice since her response is her responsibility. She will never say to her boy, "You make me a disrespectful person." This is about mom being in charge—in charge of her tone of voice, word choice, and demeanor as she interacts with her priceless progeny.

Anger

What about anger?

A mom can say with controlled anger, "I love and respect you, but what you have done is not lovable or respectable. I am angry at you, very angry. But I see this as a teaching moment for you. I don't say this to shame you but to challenge. There are consequences to what you've done, but this is part of helping you become an honorable man."

Let him know in your anger that you are not seeking to show him disrespect. Go on record about having respect for him, for believing in him. Never assume he knows. This is Respect-Talk with anger. Demonstrating positive regard does not run at odds with anger. You can show positive regard while you show anger. The Bible says to be angry but do not sin (Eph. 4:26).

There is a line over which a mom must not allow her anger to step, and that would be when her anger causes her son to feel disrespected. A mom wrote, "I have found with my boys that anger and control enrage them, and bottom line, they feel disrespected. Even though they are at such an early age, I can see that this is what they have asked of me. When I am encouraging, patient, accepting of their mistakes, and gentle in correction and building them up in character, I have a much more peaceful home. . . . I am trying not to tear my house down with my tongue."

What Are Boys Experiencing When Respect Is Applied?

1. Research tells us that boys filter their world through the respect grid.

I am not arguing that girls do not need respect or that we can treat them with disrespect. I am highlighting the mind-set difference between men and women. We've never heard this line in a movie, "I'm just a girl . . . standing in front of a boy . . . asking him to respect her." Furthermore, there is not one card in the whole greeting card industry from a husband to a wife that says, "Baby, I really respect you." There is something in the female that speaks a different language—the language of love—and she wants to hear that language spoken to her. In the same way a male speaks a different language—the language of respect—and wants that language spoken to him.

I am calling you as a mother to become an expert in the language of respect that your son speaks. Not only because it will bless and energize your son but also because it will enable you to show him how to be a respectful person. How odd that so many mothers tell me, "I have no idea what this respect thing looks like," yet they expect their sons to treat them and others with respect.

How can a mom demand of her son to display respect while she pleads ignorance of what Respect-Talk to her son looks like?

I suppose the explanation is that, to her, respectfulness toward others can be reduced to two words: be nice. "Be nice, like I am nice." For some mothers, that is the extent of her mastery of respect and the basis of her moral appeal. I am not trying to trivialize the mother's acumen related to respect, but I want to accentuate where her depth resides. Her sophistication of the language of love knows no limits when it comes to eye contact, listening, empathy, care, burden-bearing, saying, "I am sorry," writing notes, sending cards, buying flowers, bringing gifts, talking about relationships, thinking of the person all day long—the list goes on. For this reason, she struggles with my teaching that a mother must learn the language of respect. That's not her mother tongue.

She does not process human interaction through the respect grid, not in marriage and not in the family. It feels unnatural to go beyond the idea of niceness to an expansive view that entails a gamut of information she never imagined.

But her love for her son compels her to find out if this is true. I believe it is important to help her discover this truth and give her the information that enables her to develop a proficiency in Respect-Talk. When she becomes proficient, she positions herself to lead her son in becoming a respected man of God.

Of course, she must decide if she will stay the course and keep this as her second language. Will she decide that her son must be a man of love who loves others and speaks the language of love, or will she accept another side of her son that he feels deeply? He intends to be a man of honor who honors others, and he speaks the language of honor.

Will she subscribe to the idea that God made her son a clean slate, and she can write on his being the language she wishes for him to speak, like the literal languages we learn? Indeed, English, French, or Spanish is learned from the mother. Allegedly the Holy Roman Emperor Frederick II in the thirteenth century deprived infants of human interaction to discover the natural language a child would speak. Would it be Hebrew, Greek, Latin, Arabic, or what? He never found out. As legend has it, the infants died due to lack of loving interaction.

You and I know children learn their mother's tongue. But what many of us do not consider is that deep in the soul of a boy is the XY chromosome, there by birth; and it has nothing to do with his mother's conscious and willful input. A chromosome is found in the nucleus of the cell and is an organized package of DNA. When I look at the sophistication, complexity, consistency, predictability, sequence, order, rhythm, and language of the twenty-three pairs of chromosomes in humans, one pair of which is the sex chromosomes, I worship in wonder at God's majestic design.

Though her words model a literal language, a mother's speech with her son has less to do with putting information into her son and more with drawing that information out of him. Language ability is already there in the DNA. It is a combination of imparting a literal language to him while discovering the language within him.

Boys and girls are equal, but they are not the same. Genetically, they differ. Neuropsychiatrist Louann Brizendine, who is both a researcher and a clinician, wrote in her book *The Female Brain*, "Out of the thirty thousand genes in the human genome, the less than one percent variation between the sexes is small. But that percentage difference influences every single cell in our bodies—from the nerves that register pleasure and pain to the neurons that transmit perception, thoughts, feelings, and emotions."[3]

Inherent in your son are Respect-Perceptions, Respect-Thoughts, Respect-Feelings, Respect-Morals, Respect-Volitions, Respect-Interactions, and a Respect-Soul. Your son will have thoughts and feelings about respect and disrespect where you do not. He will have moral convictions about the honor code that cause him to react to dishonor in ways you do not imagine. He will have a willful determination to pursue issues of honor and avoid dishonor in ways that are outside the scope of what drives you. He will interact with people based on matters of respect and disrespect in a way you do not filter socially. He will have a spiritual bent—matters of the soul—toward God's honor and glory and being a respected man of God; whereas, you lean toward loving God and seeing your son become a beloved man of God. He will have moods, a temperament, a personality, a disposition, and motivations based on respect and disrespect when your life revolves more around love.

Am I pushing this too far? Think of the sentimentality of women. Most men are not as sentimental as women, and the card and gift industry knows it. Or think of women's nurturing nature and the ongoing care-giving they provide within the family and among friends. Yes, men also care, but it differs as blue differs from pink. Look at the tears shed among women when happy, sad, or frustrated. Men do not cry the way women cry. Observe the fears women express that men do not have.

Generally speaking, neither of you are wrong—just different. Yes, there is crossover due to our common humanity, created in God's image, but this very same God created us male and female.

Will there be moments when your son feels disrespected even though no disrespect was remotely intended? Yes. He will misinterpret just as you have. You feel unloved at times, only to find out later that you felt hurt and offended over something that did not happen as you felt. Though your son will be imprudent in his interpretation, it is the better part of wisdom to give your son the benefit of the doubt. You can defuse his mistaken think-ing by saying, "Hey, I can see why you felt disrespected, and I feel bad for you, but no disrespect was intended, okay? I apologize. No disrespect was meant."

What happens if mom replies, "Grow up! That's ridiculous and arrogant. No one was trying to show you disrespect"? She will provoke him. She will lose his heart. She is unwittingly cursing in his true mother tongue. She crushes his heart in a comparable way a father crushes the heart of his teen daughter when he screams, "Stop crying like a big baby! You get too emotional. Who cares if you lost that note that boy at school wrote to you? Have him write another note." Of course, she runs to her room crying; whereas, the son clinches his fists in frustration toward his mom and purses his lips. Later the daughter seeks reassurance from her dad that he loves her, but the son keeps his distance with his mother.

2. Boys tend to personalize the appearance of disrespect.

Girls need respect but do not personalize maternal conflict through the respect grid, generally. When a mother complains and criticizes, her daughter instinctively knows mom intends to connect because she cares even though she reacts negatively. Moms have said, "I intentionally provoke my daughter, knowing she needs to talk." The daughter knows what mom is doing, and they end up sitting on her bed, talking for a half hour about their concerns. Women feel comfortable in the ocean of emotion.

But when this same mom provokes her son to get him to talk, he generally pulls away. He withdraws and stonewalls. Boys tend to personalize more through the respect grid, which explains why he shuts down. When a mother complains and criticizes, her son filters this through a blue lens in a way that a daughter does not see through her pink lens. This can leave mom feeling rejected, unloved, and disrespected. But she needs to ask herself: *Does he filter my approach to him through the respect grid while my daughter interprets me through the love grid?* A seventeen-year-old boy might say to a confidant, "My mom loves me, but she doesn't respect me."

Adding to the difficulty between mom and son, boys don't cry as often, so mom can misread the lack of emotion as arrogant disregard, especially when he refrains from saying he is sorry. Between mother and daughter, mutual negative venting takes place, but then, "I am sorry" is said. The "I am sorry" brings closure. The "I am sorry" says all is okay until the next conflict.

Unlike her daughter, her son tends to steel himself against the provocations. He says, "I am sorry" far less. So mom ups the disrespectful comments to get through to him so they can talk, but he closes off more or gets really angry. In attempting to break through, she finds her female approach backfiring.

One approach when observing him shut down is to say,

> "Look, I am coming at you this way not because I am trying to disrespect you. My goal is to honor you, not dishonor you. But I feel boxed out here. I care about you and want to make sure we are on the same page. My goal is not to put you down. That would be disrespectful. I'm just feeling that when you close off, you are feeling 'dissed,' as they say. I am only trying to address the issue, not attack you as a person."

He may not talk, but you can remove from his thinking the erroneous impression that you do not respect him. This modus operandi better energizes, motivates, and influences him.

3. Boys are quieter about their need for respect.

Many moms have been left in the dark about talking to a boy with Respect-Talk. Girls will be more expressive about love and more responsive to love. Girls tend to openly display their desire to experience love, as seen in notes with red hearts and XOs. Love is the topic among females, and they dominate the conversation.

Boys, on the other hand, are less openly expressive about respect and less openly responsive. But that desire is every bit as real, as we have seen from the testimonies about boys beaming with joy. Despite that, boys tend not to openly display their desire to experience respect as often as girls communicate their desire for love. For one, girls know they are to be loved unconditionally and can ask, "Do you love me?" Boys risk asking, "Do you respect me?" lest he hear, "You don't deserve my respect. You have not earned my respect."

Does research confirm this withdrawing tendency? The University of Washington studied two thousand couples. They found the two basic ingredients for a successful marriage were love and respect. But gender differences surfaced: 85 percent of those who stonewalled and withdrew were men. The women could not imagine withdrawing, and interpreted this as an unloving or hostile act. But women did something different during conflict. They complained and criticized. The ongoing criticism that the men received led them to believe that the women had contempt for who they were as men.

I have tried to help women understand that most men and boys withdraw not as an act of hostility but as an act of honor. He seeks to de-escalate the conflict by dropping it and forgetting it. He wants to move on—no harm, no foul. No big deal. I have tried to help men understand that women criticize not as an act of contempt but an act of care. Women care about the relationship and want to resolve the matter and reconcile. She wants to keep the relationship up-to-date and to make sure that he is not mad at her but loves her.

A girl has the right to ask, "Do you love me?" She can say, "Because I feel unloved, you are unloving." But when it comes to the need in a boy for respect, he will mention this need a couple of times until he is met with flat-out rejection. From there, he'll rarely open up again about his deepest need. Think about it. Who would allow and appreciate a son saying, "Do you respect me? Why don't you tell me that you respect me? You need to respect me." He could never, ever say to his mother and definitely not to a group of women, "You are disrespectful, and I feel disrespected."

Men have an understanding when one says to the other, "You are dissing me; knock it off. Quit being so disrespectful." A female might respond to the man who utters this, "Who do you think you are to talk to me this way? You don't deserve respect. You are not respectable. I refuse to be a doormat."

So if your son's need for respect has been dismissed, do not conclude he is no longer in need of it.

4. Mom *defaults to love and ignores respect.*

My son Jonathan heard a mother on the radio share that her son had an assignment that involved writing his own epitaph. He wrote, "A Respected Man of God." He envisioned those descriptive words on his gravestone. In learning of her son's sentiments, the mother objected. She gave voice to her differing preference. She told him that he should inscribe these words on the grave marker: "A Beloved Man of God."

Why the different epitaphs between son and mother? Why did he focus on respect and she on love?

The secret—hidden in plain sight—is that as boys grow and move into manhood, they filter their world through the respect grid. On the other hand, moms tend to see their sons through the love grid. Mothers love to love and want their sons to love to love. Mothers yearn for their sons to be loving and, thus, be beloved. A mother has a propensity to obsess over her boy's need to see the world through the love grid far more than the honor grid. Consequently, mom may ignore what he is saying from the core of his being because it does not matter to her. For her, love alone matters.

Mom needs to be intentional about unconditional respect since she defaults to love. A woman noted, "As a mother, my tendency is to love my teenage son. What I believe to be true is that he is changing from needing unconditional love to needing unconditional respect. The trick is to be able to move back and forth as he grows."

In becoming a mother, a woman places the child she loves at the center of the cosmos. The essence of mothering is other-centeredness, and she does not regret this. The feelings of love she has for her boy overwhelm her, especially as she walks down memory lane. The tenderness of a mother is immeasurable. But mother-love consumes her to the extent that she neither thinks about showing respect nor considers the ways she appears disrespectful to her son.

The good news is that most mothers can achieve more quickly through respect what they wish to achieve through love. A mom wrote:

> I finally tried it with my almost thirteen-year-old. We were about to play backgammon. I checked the rules and realized we had been lining up the pieces way wrong. (My brother spent all day learning how to play with my son, then my son taught me. So I knew this was delicate.) My son got very agitated and down and snappy as I began to rearrange the pieces. I started saying soothing things and ideas to make him feel better. He got snappier. Finally I said, "I am a female, so when I hear you upset, I feel a need to help you fix it or at least make you feel better. I realize I can't do that for you." He stopped, looked up, and said, "Thank you, I appreciate that." He unconsciously "loved" me. We both felt better, and I was in awe (and just a TAD proud of myself).

This exchange is subtle but powerful. To him, it felt too lovey-dovey when she tried to console him, tried to make him feel better. When she spoke the truth respectfully and said she could not fix it for him because she did not have that ability with him anymore, he heard loud and clear: "You are your own man." As odd as that exchange sounds to some women, she acknowledged and honored his independence from her, and he stopped to thank her.

Yes, this takes thoughtfulness. A mom wrote, "I generally don't understand if it's a discipline issue, a respect issue, or *what*. Having a son involves all the same pink versus blue issues, except it's with someone who can't even tie his own shoelaces yet!"

When we understand the way God designed our boys, we can better navigate the mother-son relationship. I believe that when a mom understands a son's need for respect, she will experience an improvement. She will better connect with him, motivate him, meet a need in his soul, understand his reactions, appreciate his boyishness, deal with conflict, and reestablish the relationship.

A mom shared her belief: "The more you respect your teen's growing sense of independence, the more he will feel loved."

Another mom told me,

The purpose of this message was to say you have given me hope with my boys. I'm on my fourth pregnancy with my third boy. I've been feeling a loss not having my second girl and thinking that I'll never be able to relate and bond with my boys like I do with [my daughter]. That is probably true, but I have hope that if I can learn to respect those boys, there might even be a tighter bond because I'll be the main woman in their lives, edifying who they are. Thank you for that.

One last thought. When a mom feels loved by her son, she needs to see this as an opportunity to use Respect-Talk—not just get caught up in the wonderful feeling she is experiencing from her son's Love-Talk.

A mother wrote to me about a conversation she had with her eight-year-old boy. What we notice is Love-Talk from her son but not Respect-Talk from mom. Listen to what she said:

I was sick for about a week. He asked me why I was crying, and I responded, "Someone told me I look like a mess." He responded: "That person is not nice. Why don't you do your hair? I have money if you want." I cried even more. He asked, "Did I say something wrong?" I said, "No, honey, that was beautiful, and you make sure you say that to your wife someday if she's ever tired or sick." He responded, "Okay, mom, and I promise never to say that other thing that was rude and hurt your feelings." He's only eight years old!

What is going on in this conversation? Like many mothers, she feels overwhelmed by the loving tenderness of her boy. She will never forget that conversation and will repeat it to all of his girlfriends.

But let's interpret this through the boy's eyes. He sees his mom crying and asks why. She tells him. He offers to help her. When he does, her emotions kick into high gear, and she cries more. His first thought? He thinks he did something wrong. Clearly, he does not understand. She tells him he did nothing wrong but did something beautiful (the closest she got to Respect-Talk). However, in a nanosecond, she jumps to a brief lecture on how her son ought to treat his future wife when she is tired or sick. The boy then promises not to hurt mommy's feelings.

My gut tells me this boy felt more anxiety than she imagined, which is what prompted him to make a promise to his mom not to be rude. What if she had added a few more respect words? Would she have affirmed her son for certain?

"Son, your words powerfully touched my heart. I am really proud of you. Please know that I cried from my happiness caused by you, though it didn't look like I was happy because I was crying. Many women cry when happy, not just when they are sad. Yes, I was sad about my messy hair, but your words helped me be happy. It also made me happy when you offered to give me money to redo my hair. Wow! I really respect your kindness and generosity. You are becoming a strong man of honor. Thank you. High five."

Mothers are good at words. Words flow from the hearts of mothers. But if they do not incorporate such vocabulary words, these moms will journal such exchanges and believe that a deep connection had been made. But Respect-Talk would have made her son feel much better.

When an exchange with her son feels loving, which puts mom's tenderness into overdrive, a mom needs to ask herself, *Are there words of respect I can add to this interaction?*

5. Modeling respect enables mom to request respect toward herself and others.

What is one of the side effects of using Respect-Talk with your son? A mother can appeal to her son to speak respectfully to others as she speaks to him. Does he get it? Listen to how one mom addressed this with her son.

As you read, notice the boy's inherent recognition of respect, as though this language resides within his DNA, coded by God in the womb. She stated,

> I understand that respect is a core need of his. I bring it up often when discussing how he needs to relate to others. We have discussed some aspects of what respect looks like—owning our choices and failures, choosing words carefully, trusting the other person's ability to make decisions, using a pleasant tone and attentive body language. I am able to talk with him about respecting someone even if one doesn't agree with them or like them. We talk about respecting God, friends, sisters, parents, and grandparents. He understands this language. I also talk to him about how others should treat him with respect and how to address them respectfully if they do not do so. We talk about the need to be respectful despite one's emotions, such as anger or frustration.
>
> This seems to work much better than talking to him about being "nice." For instance, if I tell him to rephrase something "nicely" to his sister, it comes out somewhat irritated with a "please" attached to the request. Whereas, if I ask him to say something respectfully, he may say it very directly (or even firmly), but it is always kinder and more heartfelt. Also, when he is whining or sassy toward me, I ask him to address me respectfully, and his tone typically changes immediately. He seems to just "get it" when I use the word *respect* in association with relationships.

When you feel your son is disrespectful, you can appeal to your son to show respect. You are a moral model. Putting it in the negative, showing disrespect to a disrespectful son undermines your appeal to him to show respect when he does not want to show respect. Think about it: since you don't want to show respect to your son, why would he want to show respect?

God commands a son to honor his father and mother. Your Respect-Talk shows him how to do this. Though he is responsible to obey God's command to honor father and mother independent of you, your Respect-Talk creates the best environment to motivate him to choose to obey God. He can imitate you.

You don't have to be perfect. Just be honest about your disrespect and seek forgiveness for failing since that models for him how to rebound from his disrespect. A mom wrote, "As far as our sons go, they are thirteen and ten. Old enough to understand the basics. When we took the class the first time, I had to seek their forgiveness for not respecting their dad. Well, that began the journey of passing this on to them. So now they will ask if they have done something unloving or disrespectful when communicating with us. With each other it is usually a 'Hey, dude, you're on my air hose.'"

Finally, a mother shared about the periodic conflicts between her husband and son:

> I have sometimes modeled for [my son] how to take his concerns and rephrase them respectfully. I have noticed that this then allows them to openly dialogue about issues. . . . I have been able to talk to my son about how to respectfully appeal to his father when he feels things are unfair or feels the need for more reconciliation or clarification on an issue. (This doesn't necessarily mean that dad changes his position, but it typically leads to better communication.)
>
> I have had great success at guiding my son in a conversation with his father using respectful language about difficult situations. To begin with, I have had the opportunity to teach him to apologize for not respecting his father in a given situation, if it is appropriate, and then to respectfully discuss issues with his father.

As you move forward, applying this glorious concept of respect, you inevitably will talk to other moms about your discoveries. When you do, the first question most mothers ask is, "What do you mean, respect my son?" This chapter provides the answer to that most common question.

The challenge for each mom is to realize that her default mode appears disrespectful when she corrects her son—albeit she is motivated by love.

Negative regard toward the spirit of her son will not motivate him to be positive—not with her. For this reason, respect should be her positive regard toward her son, no matter what he does. A mom should respectfully confront behaviors that are not respectable. Contempt toward the heart of a son never motivates a boy (or anyone) long term to be respectful and loving but only de-energizes him. The key is for a mom to demonstrate respect while demanding respect. When she understands and lives this way, so will her son.

3

A GAME PLAN

Mom G.U.I.D.E.S. with Respect

What does God expect of a mother? Does the Bible disclose His will to her in relationship to her son?

Yes, God calls you to do six things as a mother:

1. Give so a child's basic physical needs can be met.
2. Understand so a child is not provoked or exasperated.
3. Instruct so your child can know and apply God's wisdom.
4. Discipline so your child can correct poor choices.
5. Encourage so your child can courageously develop God-given gifts.
6. Supplicate in prayer so your child can experience God's touch and truth.

I put these in an acronym called G.U.I.D.E.S. When it comes to your son, you can be a mother who G.U.I.D.E.S. with respect. Each concept revolves around a foundational teaching in the Bible for moms and dads.

I based my book *Love & Respect in the Family* on what Scripture reveals to parents about parenting, not just random texts that might fit. I've taken the same approach with this book.

G.U.I.D.E.S. serves as a template to enable a mother to apply respect with wisdom and impact. This checklist excites me because it supplies her with the means to quickly and successfully assess her approach over the ages and stages in the life of her son (and daughter). It awakens her to the immediate opportunity to use Respect-Talk, whereas before she might innocently fail to spot vulnerable moments.

Please use this in the same way you might review information when your son falls ill. Mothers learn to review a list of the symptoms to determine what might be behind an ailment. Though mothers consult with a doctor when they cannot bring healing, most mothers do quite well at restoring their kids back to health.

G.U.I.D.E.S. reflects the heart of Abba Father, and it helps a mom determine the symptoms so she may get at the root issue quickly. What I found fascinating as I reviewed this biblical teaching to parents on parenting is that it captures the major dimensions of every child.

1. Giving the physical
   - Is your son negatively reacting due to a physical need, such as feeling hungry?
2. Understanding the emotional
   - Is he having an emotional meltdown because he feels exasperated and is losing heart and needs your understanding?
3. Instructing the mental
   - Is he feeling stupid because you forgot to instruct him on what to do?
4. Disciplining the volitional
   - Is he unruly and exerting his will against your will, which demands discipline so he can learn self-discipline?
5. Encouraging the social
   - Is he feeling rejected by friends on the soccer team and wants to

quit, and you need to encourage him to stay committed through this tough time?

6. **S**upplicating the spiritual
   • Is he in need of seeing you genuinely pray for him as he struggles emotionally and socially?

If you follow G.U.I.D.E.S., you can be assured that you will quickly discern what ails your precious son. As you enact these principles, you will touch the heart of God and the heart of your boy.

On the next several pages I will explain the scriptures behind each concept. Understand that this is just an overview. I will apply each one later in greater depth.

So what is the biblical teaching behind G.U.I.D.E.S.?

G for Giving

Give so a child's basic physical needs can be met.

What mother can neglect the physical needs of her son? If anything is nearly impossible, it is a mother's refusal to meet her son's need for food, clothing, and shelter. Isaiah 49:15 says, "Can a woman forget her nursing child and have no compassion on the son of her womb?" The answer is no. Even so, Isaiah makes the point that such a mother *could* forget her child: "Even these may forget, but I will not forget you." The rule is she would not forget, but there are exceptions to all rules. There are anomalies. Though not impossible for her to forget her child, it is nearly so, which is why Isaiah's deeper point about God's constant love for us penetrates our hearts more profoundly. His love never, ever fails.

So what is the rule about mothers? A mother has compassion on her child. She cannot forget meeting the needs of her nursing child. Next to impossible. What better picture of love is there than that of "a nursing mother [who] tenderly cares for her own children" (1 Thess. 2:7)? None.

Notice that Jesus assumes that a father will meet the physical needs of his child. The father represents both parents in Matthew 7:9–11:

Or what man is there among you who, when his son asks for a loaf, will give him a stone? Or if he asks for a fish, he will not give him a snake, will he? If you then, being evil, know how to give good gifts to your children, how much more will your Father who is in heaven give what is good to those who ask Him!

When your son asks you for breakfast or a snack because he is "starving," you feel compelled and compassionate to respond. Nurturing and nourishing is in your nature. Other than the pleasant breakfast in bed for mom on Mother's Day, you do not expect your son to feed you. Mom takes care of her son, not vice versa. Paul wrote in 2 Corinthians 12:14: "For children are not responsible to save up for their parents, but parents for their children."

Having said that, neglect is not absolutely impossible, as Isaiah 49:15 stated. Mothers do walk out on their families. For this reason we read Paul's warning against a refusal to provide for one's family. First Timothy 5:8 states, "But if anyone does not provide for his own, and especially for those of his household, he has denied the faith and is worse than an unbeliever." Rarely does any mom remotely come close to such neglect.

But here is a key question: "While meeting his physical needs, can she neglect his need for respect? Can a mom, though taking care of her boy because her love compels her, attitudinally convey disrespect while feeding, clothing, and bathing him?" Can she forget his deepest need?

Alas, yes. She can call him to breakfast, saying, "Your eggs, bacon, toast, and hash browns are ready, plus freshly squeezed orange juice. What? Who dressed you? A street person has more sense about what to wear than you do. Going to school looking like that would humiliate me. What would people think of me as your mother? If I were not here, I cannot imagine the horrible choices you'd make!" She loves him by feeding him. She disrespects him as she criticizes him. If not careful, she can speak out of both sides of her mouth: "I love you. I do not respect you."

U for Understanding

Understand so a child is not provoked or exasperated.

Mothers naturally nurture and empathize. Mothers actively listen and seek to understand. However, moms grow weary in doing good. Frankly, there are days when she does not want to be understanding but wishes he and everyone else understood her. Wiped out from a "terrible, horrible, no good, very bad day," she feels disrespected and has no interest in showing respect to a disrespectful boy. Her anger provokes his anger. Her exasperation exasperates him. Feeling misunderstood, she misunderstands. Though afterward she appeases him by trying to compensate, she finds herself in a pattern of provocation then reconciliation. But she wonders if she is closing off his heart to her.

We find in Ephesians 6:4 this admonition: "Fathers, do not provoke your children to anger." Why would a dad (or mom) provoke a son to anger? A dad's anger evokes anger.

We read in 1 Samuel 20:30 about King Saul, the father of Jonathan: "Then Saul's anger burned against Jonathan and he said to him, 'You son of a perverse, rebellious woman! Do I not know that you are choosing the son of Jesse to your own shame and to the shame of your mother's nakedness?'"

How did Jonathan respond to Saul's anger? We read in verse 34: "Then Jonathan arose from the table in fierce anger . . . because his father had dishonored him." This is seen by many to mean that Jonathan had been humiliated by his own father. A dad's over-the-line anger that dishonors and humiliates the child, provokes the child to anger. It riles the child. Saul should have understood and empathized with the heart of his son, but Saul's vexation and disrespect provoked Jonathan to fierce anger.

A contentious mother can ignite the same in her son. Many women have read the following scriptures:

- Proverbs 21:19: "It is better to live in a desert land than with a contentious and vexing woman."

- Proverbs 25:24: "It is better to live in a corner of the roof than in a house shared with a contentious woman."
- Proverbs 21:9: "It is better to live in a corner of a roof than in a house shared with a contentious woman."

The above is not a mistake. The warning against living with a contentious woman appears two different places in Proverbs 21.

A vexed mother vexes her son. A contentious mom provokes arguments. Like Jonathan, in those moments, a son feels misunderstood and disrespected. He feels dishonored and humiliated. Not every angry son can rightly claim his mother does not empathize and honor him. Boys manipulate and guilt-trip a mother. However, a habitually vexing and contentious mother must acknowledge that this is more her problem than her son's. As indignant as she feels and as much as she feels the need to contend with him about some matter, she must deliver her message respectfully and for the purpose of understanding his heart.

Some sons are not angry but exasperated to the point they lack confidence to move forward. We read in Colossians 3:21, "Fathers, do not exasperate your children, so that they will not lose heart." Irritated by a faultfinding parent, he gives up. He deflates in defeat. "What's the use? Mom and dad will never be happy with me. I cannot please them. I cannot be good enough."

Instead of understanding the age limits of the child, the parent expects him to perform at a level he cannot reach. They expect the four-year-old to swing a golf club when he dreams of butterflies. They expect him to do what he may not have the hand-eye coordination to do. This isn't about his unwillingness to swing a club but his inability at this stage of development. He throws himself down on the ground in exasperation and loss of heart due to an undeveloped little body. Even mom and dad shank the ball but expect him to be the prodigy.

We must understand the age and stage of a boy. I love 1 Corinthians 13:11: "When I was a child, I used to speak like a child, think like a child,

reason like a child; when I became a man, I did away with childish things."
Kids will be kids. God designed little people to be un-adult. A mother
must understand her son's childishness. He will talk to her in immature
ways, think without wisdom, and reason with her in ways that are not
reasonable. But she is the adult whom God calls to be the understanding
one and to be respectful to this little person. He was created in God's
image and designed to be the way he is at this stage. She must not take all
of this so personally. Yes, he sins and needs correction. But much of his
behavior is childish irresponsibility. Mom is wired too tight and expects
too much from him and too little of herself. Every mother must take this
challenge: "A woman's family is held together by her wisdom, but it can
be destroyed by her foolishness" (Prov. 14:1 CEV).

I can say this with certainty: when fear controls a mother, she seeks
to control. In controlling her son from that which could harm him physically or hurt her emotionally, she feels less fear. Control reduces her
anxiety and insecurity. Control, then, is a good thing in her way of
thinking. But something unhealthy happens on the way to his manhood
as she exercises her motherhood. For some mothers, domination enables
her to control. This is why vexation and contention become part and par-
cel of her personality. She seeks to "protect" her son. She seeks to "help"
him. His compliance is for the greater good of the two of them.

But it is here a boy loses heart. He turns passive. He loses confidence in himself, in his maleness. She does not see him as the con-
queror, protector, provider, authority, strong one, problem-solver, or
friend-maker. She pushes back against many of these qualities, even
suppressing them. He loses touch with who he is and should be. He
lacks self-understanding in the face of a mother who refuses to understand the desires God embedded in her son. He evolves into a soft male.
But that's okay to her as long as she can minimize her fears. Of course,
other boys, the alpha types, erupt in rebellion at such a mother. They
do not deflate in defeat but fight to the end. The soft male, though, loses
his way in life.

I for Instructing

Instruct so your child can know and apply God's wisdom.

We read the refrain in Proverbs 1:8 and 6:20: "Do not forsake your mother's teaching." God expects mothers to instruct their sons. Nevertheless, God does not expect a mother to lecture her son on being respectful while delivering her message with a spirit of contempt for him. She must be an instructor who possesses an attitude of respect in keeping with her dignity as a woman.

Did you know that Proverbs 31, which describes the noble wife and mother, was penned by King Lemuel? We read in 31:1, "The words of King Lemuel, the oracle which his mother taught him." Lemuel could have been Solomon himself by another name or another king that Solomon quotes because of the effect Lemuel's mother had on him. Regardless, the wisest man on the planet found himself profoundly inspired by this mother's wisdom! Her instruction was passed on to billions of people. The teaching of a mother matters.

We read in Ephesians 6:4 about kids: "Bring them up in the discipline and instruction of the Lord." Beyond the three Rs of education, reading, 'riting, and 'rithmetic, parents are to coach their kids in the ways and words of Jesus—the instruction of the Lord. Timothy was the recipient of this kind of instruction. Paul stated in 2 Timothy 3:15–16:

> From childhood you have known the sacred writings which are able to give you the wisdom that leads to salvation through faith which is in Christ Jesus. All Scripture is inspired by God and profitable for teaching, for reproof, for correction, for training in righteousness.

Timothy's mother and grandmother made sure he received this kind of instruction since his Greek father did not have this worldview (Acts 16:1). All Jews lived under this call: "You shall teach them diligently to your sons and shall talk of them when you sit in your house and when you walk by the way and when you lie down and when you rise up" (Deut. 6:7).

Though all of us feel inadequate to represent God's truth on any given day, bringing Jesus into your teaching moments is foundational. However, this needs to be honoring to your boy, not shaming. Some mothers inadvertently use Jesus to hammer their sons. Whatever it takes to get him to do what she wants is fair game. That's a colossal misstep. She needs to convey a positive message.

For instance, during a moment when her son doubts God's being there or that He cares or has the power to act, she can say,

> "I share with you that Jesus loves you and is for you because He taught that He loved us and came to serve and to die for us. I know you feel that God is against you right now or is ignoring you. You see no miracles. I have felt the same way. This is a good struggle. I wish I could make this doubt go away, but this is part of the struggle that an honorable man must go through.
>
> "Because I believe in you and am excited about your future, I want to challenge you to trust in God's love for you though He seems far away. Some of the more godly followers of Jesus have gone through what they call the dark night of the soul. Even Jesus on the cross cried out, 'My God, my God, why hast thou forsaken me?' [Mark 15:34 KJV]. But I am confident you have the strength as a man to get through this disappointment. Thanks for sharing your doubts. You honor me."

This is instruction with Respect-Talk. In this instance mom acts on verse 22 of Jude: "Be merciful to those who doubt" (NIV).

D for Disciplining

Discipline so your child can correct poor choices.

Proverbs 29:15 declares, "A child who gets his own way brings shame to his mother." How true! You have observed this with other mothers and their sons. For you, it will be different. You will not spoil your boy. You will not subject him to the indulgence that can ruin him or yourself to the shame he brings to you. However, for some moms, the technique used to ensure a boy's obedience is disrespect. She gets him to do what he is supposed to do by dishonoring him. For many mothers, it works, but it works because the pain is so great to him that he obeys in order to stop her words of contempt. She can be compared to the dad who uses hostility and unloving looks to get his daughter to obey. She obeys to stop the pain she feels from his unloving words.

Some moms conclude that her disrespect and outburst of anger cause the boy to obey. But a son responds not to the disrespect and anger per se but to what he thinks is about to come next: her action. Unfortunately, some moms think the disrespect makes him behave, but it is the fear that she is about to "kill" him that causes him to obey.

See the difference? It is her potential action, not her disrespect and anger that drives his action. He is uncertain about what will follow her contempt, which motivates him to pick up his toys and make his bed or quit bouncing on the couch or start studying or hand over the car keys. How sad that a mom fools herself into thinking that she needs to use disrespect sooner and more often with great anger to get her boy to do what she expects. But ill temper and contempt never cause heartfelt affection, connection, or transformation. Respectful confrontation with clear and fair consequences motivates a son to behave over the marathon of a mother's parenting.

The Bible says in Ephesians 6:4, "Bring them up in the discipline . . . of the Lord." As the Lord disciplines, so must a mother. Jesus does not dishonor those He disciplines with an outburst of anger. He loves those He disciplines (Heb. 12:6), and according to the Bible's love chapter, "[love] does not dishonor others . . . it is not easily angered" (1 Cor. 13:5 NIV). How much clearer can it be? Such dishonor and angry disgust is unloving.

Discipline entails a subjective element. None of us discipline perfectly. Only God disciplines perfectly. As parents, we must let Hebrews

12:10 comfort and guide us. About parents it says, "They disciplined us for a short time as seemed best to them." I savor this verse and the phrase "seemed best to them." This reveals the subjective aspect of discipline. A mother moves forward based on what seems the best discipline for the situation with her son. Though she will second-guess herself, she must not be overly bothered by the thought, *I have no absolute certainty here*. She must move forward doing what seems best.

It is highly unlikely you are wrong if you respectfully confront and correct your son and enact consequences. I discuss this in more depth in chapter 7, "Authority: Respecting His Desire to Be Strong and to Lead and Make Decisions." When it comes to Respect-Talk and discipline, the key is to say,

> "I discipline you because I love you. In fact, I discipline you
> because I believe in you and the man you are becoming. Truth is,
> I discipline you as a way of honoring you. This discipline helps
> you become more self-disciplined, and eventually my discipline
> will end. You will be a disciplined, honorable man. I am not
> disciplining you because I want to punish you. I discipline you to
> put you back on the path that men of honor walk."

When disciplining, will Respect-Talk always work? No. Throughout the Old Testament the sad truth is demonstrated, and twice the New Testament states that children will be "disobedient to parents" (Rom. 1:30; 2 Tim. 3:2).

A father and mother can discipline a child with respect and love, but the child, as a moral and spiritual being granted freedom by God, can choose to disobey. Even when a mother can control her preschooler, she can only control external behaviors. Though a mother demands her son to say, "Thank you," she cannot coerce him into possessing a grateful heart. Though she takes him to church and demands that he sing, she cannot force him to be a true worshipper from his soul. Though she prohibits him from driving the car for a month due to his recklessness, she cannot create in him a genuinely submissive heart in the face of discipline. Though she commands him to memorize the golden rule (Luke 6:31), she cannot engineer within him a teachable spirit.

A parent cannot control these internal and ultimate outcomes within the child. The child himself is the one who must finally choose a parent's faith and values. The parent, for example, cannot order the child to believe in Jesus. All that mom can do, particularly as the child ages, is control her actions and reactions to her child. That means she seeks to create a loving and respectful environment that best motivates her son to choose her faith and values.

I once wrote an article titled "Why Biblical Parenting Has Nothing to Do with the Kids," which was picked up by a national news network. I make the point that the father of the prodigal has two sons. As you recall, the prodigal is the secondborn who demands his inheritance, leaves home, and squanders his newfound wealth on sensual, indulgent living. The firstborn remains at home but displays a self-righteous, angry, and judgmental spirit, especially when the secondborn comes to his senses and humbly returns home to confess his wrongdoing. The firstborn wants nothing to do with his hedonistic-turned-humble brother.

My question is this: Would we invite this dad to our church for a two-day parenting conference to lecture us on parenting? No. Yet Jesus prizes this father as the replica of Abba, Father.

In other words, is God a bad heavenly Father because you and I disobey? No. Neither is the father of the prodigal a bad dad. He actually parented as God. He parented God's way even though his son wanted nothing to do with him for years. This dad demonstrated love and compassion, as the text says, and when he put a robe and ring on the son, he showed honor and respect. He possesses love and respect in his sons apart from their disobedience.

Jesus Christ intends to reward you as a mother for your love and respect toward your son, regardless of your son's disregard of you at seasons. As you Give, Understand, Instruct, Discipline, Encourage, and Supplicate, you touch the heart of Christ. Actually, your son affords you the opportunity to show your obedience to God in the face of your son's disobedience. Even if your son chooses disobedience, you have done what seems best and, in fact, may have done what was best in the eyes of God.

E for Encouraging

Encourage so your child can courageously develop God-given gifts.
The apostle Paul provided us a clear picture of how a father ought to approach his children. He reminded the Thessalonians that he had been "exhorting and encouraging and imploring each one of you as a father would his own children, so that you would walk in a manner worthy of the God who calls you into His own kingdom and glory" (1 Thess. 2:11–12). As a father figure, he encourages, implores, and even exhorts to invigorate this local group of believers to follow God's call.

Should not every father do this toward a child? Should not every mother do this toward her son? As Paul believed in God's call on their lives, so a mother must believe in God's design and purpose for her son. For example, God wired her son with gifts and desires to work and achieve, to protect and provide, to be strong and make decisions, to analyze and counsel, to stand side by side with a friend, and to understand human sexuality. With wisdom, a mother can encourage her son in each of these areas.

This is important since boys, like every human being, will lose courage and confidence at times. We read in Colossians 3:21, "Fathers, do not exasperate your children, so that they will not lose heart." When mom observes her son is losing heart around dad or from life in general, she needs to pray for wisdom to speak words that precipitate grit and valor. She can share,

> "I know you feel discouraged and want to quit. But I see you as a man of honor who does not quit. I know right now your heart isn't in this, but let's give it some time. Just as you need to recharge batteries, you need some time to recharge your heart's batteries. I believe you have what it takes to move forward. I respect you."

If your son is growing in his faith, you might let him know what the warrior King David said to his son in 1 Chronicles 28:20: "Then David said to his son Solomon, 'Be strong and courageous, and act; do not fear nor be dismayed, for the LORD God, my God, is with you. He will not fail you nor forsake you until all the work for the service of the house of the LORD is finished.'"

Though this historical setting is unique, as it pertains to the building of the temple, and though a mother cannot falsely promise God will do with her son whatever it is he longs to happen, in principle she can say,

> "I do not know what God's ultimate will is for you. However, I know He has given you the strength and courage to take the next step. I know you are a man of honor who will do the right thing, no matter the consequences to you."

On the negative side of encouragement, a mother must guard against encouraging her son to help her achieve her selfish ends. We read in 2 Chronicles 22:3 about a mother who "encouraged her son to sin against the LORD" (CEV).

Regrettably, a mom can counsel her son to do boldly what he ought not to do. One would think no mother would do this, but it happens. Some moms can spur a son on to act contrary to the honorable man he knows that he ought to be. Rebekah said to her son Jacob, in her plot to trick Isaac into blessing Jacob instead of his brother, Esau, "Your curse be on me, my son; only obey my voice" (Gen. 27:13). She emboldened him to act courageously to achieve what should have been entrusted to God. The words of Jesus ought to sober us: "He who loves son or daughter more than Me is not worthy of Me" (Matt. 10:37). "Anyone who comes to me but refuses to let go of . . . children . . . can't be my disciple" (Luke 14:26 THE MESSAGE).

A mother can encourage her son to do that which she selfishly wants above what the Lord purely desires for her son. I recall a young man responding to an invitation from the pulpit to follow Christ to the mission field. That week his mother undermined his willingness to obey God. In fear, she put her foot down against the idea of foreign missions and redirected him with every incentive she could offer. She succeeded.

S for Supplicating

Supplicate in prayer so your child can experience God's touch and truth.

When it comes to prayer, women pray. In every church I've ever known, the prayer chain links woman to woman. Something in godly women connects them in their dependency on Jesus. They find motivation and peace in casting their cares on Him who cares for them.

These mothers know that parents continually brought their offspring to Jesus to be prayed over. We read in Matthew 19:13, "Then some children were brought to Him so that He might lay His hands on them and pray." Mothers believe the Lord is the source of power and love for the deepest needs of the heart.

When parents are desperate they come to Christ. John 4:47 states, "When [a royal official] heard that Jesus had come out of Judea into Galilee, he went to Him and was imploring Him to come down and heal his son; for he was at the point of death." When nothing else works, most pray.

Even the mighty King David felt helpless in the face of his child's illness. Second Samuel 12:16 reveals, "David therefore inquired of God for the child; and David fasted and went and lay all night on the ground." But beyond his despair over his impotency, King David knew God calls every believer to ask in prayer. Thus he prays on behalf of his son, who is about to embark on a most significant venture: "Give to my son Solomon a perfect heart to keep Your commandments, Your testimonies and Your statutes, and to do them all" (1 Chron. 29:19).

James says that we have not because we ask not (James 4:2). Certainly King David determined never to be remiss about asking. If you are praying with your son, do not shame and dishonor him in prayer, saying, "Dear God, you know how bad Johnny has been. Please help him change. Please help him be a good boy."

That is mothering, not praying. That is using God to make your point to your son. A boy will see through that soon enough, or worse, he will feel that God intends to hammer him since by implication mom is tattling on him and God won't like him.

On the other hand, what a great thing to demonstrate respect to your son by saying,

"Son, I am praying for you. I am excited about all that God has for you and how God has put many nobles desires in you. I thank God for your desire to work and achieve, to protect and provide, to be strong and make good decisions, to analyze and solve, to be a shoulder-to-shoulder friend, and to understand and treat girls as a man of honor. I really respect you. There is a verse that I pray for you. 'To this end also we pray for you always, that our God will . . . fulfill every desire for goodness'" (2 Thess. 1:11).

Simply stated, G.U.I.D.E.S. is your road map for Respect-Talk. You are essentially telling your son, "I seek to Give, Understand, Instruct, Discipline, Encourage, and Supplicate *because I respect you.*" At first, this might sound strange since as a mother you want to say, "because I love you." The phrase "I respect you" feels counterintuitive. The respect language seems stilted. It seems contrived, labored, and awkward. But as a mom acts on this information, she energizes the spirit of her boy, and her boy must be the aim here. There are two sides to the coin. Her desire to love is on one side, but his need for respect is on the other.

To bring this need for respect home to you, let's think of the book *The Five Love Languages.* Nearly everyone has heard of this classic and life-changing book. When its author, Gary Chapman, interviewed me on his radio program (we had held the Love and Respect Conference at his church earlier), I said that we need to look beyond the five love languages to what I call the Five Respect Languages because it is the language men naturally speak. I shared that males respond to the respect side of the equation. We had a delightful radio interview.

Along with me, Gary believes Ephesians 5:33 is where God commands a husband to love and a wife to respect. As you recall, Gary practically and powerfully discusses: words of affirmation, quality time, meaningful touch, gift giving, and acts of service. I shared with Gary and his radio audience that when we add the Respect dimension to each, a whole new world opens up toward men. The good news is that we need only ask: "How can I apply this to the men and boys in my life in order to create the Respect Effect?"

The following helps every mother apply the five love languages, with which she is familiar, in a quick, new, and powerful way. For some a light-bulb comes on with this simple creation of the Five Respect Languages.

For words of affirmation, say, "I respect you" instead of always saying, "I love you." Simple enough.

For quality time, instead of spending this time talking face-to-face about feelings, do shoulder-to-shoulder activities with a son, or even just sit and watch him play catch with his brother. Mothers find it hard to imagine that this energizes the boy to respond affectionately to his mother. But I tell moms to do this and observe what happens in the spirit of the boy toward her. I remind her that quality time is what a *boy* feels is quality time.

Is there a meaningful touch that feels respectful to a boy? Yes. Place a hand on your son's shoulder when you say, "I am proud of you." That touch differs from the hugs and kisses most girls request. With Joy, my daughter, during her preschool years, almost every day I inquired, "Have you been to the Kiss Factory today?" She loved that question. When I asked the boys, Jonathan and David, they looked at me like I was from another planet. I stopped asking them.

As for gift giving, I have voiced that a woman can buy a man anything in leather, and he will love it. The same holds true for a boy. A leather glove. A leather strap on his watch. A neat leather belt. Attach a card to it that says, "I give this gift to you just because I wanted to give it to you but also because I love you and respect the honorable man you are becoming."

Apart from gifting leather, moms can figure out respectful gifts with a little thought. For example, giving a thirteen-year-old a sword to hang on his bedroom wall as a sign of him moving from boyhood into manhood differs by a million light-years from gifting new clothes to him. Sadly, many moms envision the sword as a symbol of violence rather than honor, so she gives what she likes.

Concerning acts of service, when a mother benefits her son by doing some kind deed for him, such as cleaning his bike, she needs to frame this under the umbrella of Respect-Talk. When he says, "Thanks," let mom reply, "I am proud that you have learned to ride your bike so well. I knew this would help you out." Refrain from saying, "I did this because I love you." Though the latter is true, love is about her side of the coin. Connect the act of service with respect. When she uses the *respect* word, this energizes most boys far more than mothers imagine.

See how the Five Respect Languages work? I encourage moms to let their brains go to work on these five elements. Again, I am not requesting the cessation of "I love you." You will not and must not stop "I love you." But take what you know about the five love languages and open your mind and heart to a whole new way of communicating via the Five Respect Languages. Add to your verbal repository.

But I have more to offer. From a biblical perspective, beyond a practical psychological approach, I wish to go deeper in helping you use G.U.I.D.E.S. to convey respect to your son. I will devote a whole chapter to each concept. I do this because, even with the usefulness of my Five Respect Languages, there is nothing in these five that addresses God's command to pray, discipline, and instruct our sons. Again, G.U.I.D.E.S. covers the major dimensions: physical, emotional, mental, volitional, social, and spiritual.

Here Is How to Apply Respect-Talk After You Apply G.U.I.D.E.S.

Much of the following would be in your own words, of course, but the spirit of the message is the same.

After you Give: "Do you know why I love giving to you as I do, whether it is making your breakfast or washing your clothes? I enjoy meeting your needs, but also I respect the man you are becoming, and each day I give to you helps you become that man more and more."

After you try to Understand: "Do you know why I sought to understand your heart when you expressed your anger? I felt bad for you. But also because I respect who you want to be, and this tough moment is testing your resolve to respond as a man of honor."

After you Instruct: "Do you know why I instructed you? I want to add to the wisdom I see increasing in your mind. I respect the man God calls you to be. I am not trying to lecture you but to serve you with information that helps you."

After you Discipline: "Do you know why I disciplined you when you misstepped? I respect the self-disciplined man you are becoming, and I needed to give you a boost to act as that honorable man I know you want to be."

After you Encourage: "Do you know why I encouraged you? I respect your abilities to do what you should do even though you feel discouraged. I believe in you and intend to cheer you on. At the same time, I respect that this is a decision you must make for yourself to have courage."

After you Supplicate: "Do you know why I prayed for you? I respect the man God created you to be, and I love to pray for His favor to come to you. I don't know if God will respond to what I ask since He knows what is best. But I know He listens to me when I talk to Him about you. He loves you beyond words."

What if your son pushes back, telling you in one way or another that he doesn't want any of these comments or actions? What if he mocks you? He is probably upset about something unrelated to you and takes it out on you. Most moms are safe, more so than even dad. Sadly, your boy bites the hand that feeds him. He has taken aim at you but knows you are not his enemy. Even so, this is unfair to you.

Dr. Howard Hendricks once said that at age thirteen we should bury our kids and dig them back up at age eighteen. By the way, do you know why Abraham was commanded to put twelve-year-old Isaac on the altar? At age thirteen it would have been no sacrifice!

Humor aside, counter your son's disrespectful reaction with proactive Respect-Talk. Men and boys possess an honor code. It is not honorable to dis someone who seeks to genuinely honor them. The male temperament eventually pulls back from the bad attitude and softens. As a mother, stay the course with Respect-Talk.

Below is a brief paragraph on each concept that shows how a mom can move forward in the face of her son's pushback. This language works best for school-age boys, but preschool sons can grasp some of this quite well.

When he resists your giving:

"I need to give to you and want to give to you. You're becoming a man of honor who needs resources. I give these things because I believe in you and in the honorable man you are becoming. If I give too little, I will not be respecting you but depriving you of basic needs. See me as your admiring investor."

When he resists your understanding:

"I need to understand and empathize. You're becoming a man of honor who needs someone to bounce his thoughts off of. Because I respect you, I welcome hearing your heart. You honor me by letting me honor you. Do know I am always ready to listen when you feel angry or at a loss to know what to do. But here's the deal. Don't feel pressure to talk. That's your choice. Just see me as your 'hearing aid.'"

When he resists your instruction:

"I need to instruct you. You're becoming a man of honor who needs to learn, especially from my mistakes and experiences. If I withhold necessary information, I would not be respecting you but limiting your ability to weigh all the factors. See me as your informant, a hipster tipster."

When he resists your discipline:

"I need to discipline you. You're becoming a man of honor who needs coaching, like the PGA player has a personal coach who confronts and corrects. This discipline is about your improving and excelling. This is not about punishment. I would not be respecting you if I did not enact consequences to help you win at life. See me as your coach."

When he resists your encouragement:

"I need to encourage you. I believe in your gifts and courage. I would not be respecting you if I did not voice my confidence in you to be brave and to use your talents. See me as your cheerleader."

When he resists your supplication:

"I need to pray for you. Did you know the strong and brave apostle Paul needed prayer? My prayers are based on my belief in you. I do not pray because you are bad but because I believe in the talents God has entrusted to you. I would not be respecting you if I did not ask for God's best for you. See me as a friend of the King, asking daily for His favor in your life."

Limit Respect-Talk

"But, Emerson, can I overdo G.U.I.D.E.S.? I mean, shouldn't I do less at times?" Yes.

There are moments when you must limit this approach. Here's how to use Respect-Talk with boundaries on G.U.I.D.E.S.

When you should give less:

"I need to give to you but not too much. You are becoming a man of honor who must not get everything he wants. If I give you too much, I would not be respecting you but spoiling you. Honorable men learn how to delay their gratification. I know that's tough to hear, but you are tough."

When you should be less of a bleeding heart:

"I need to empathize and understand but not too much. You're becoming a man of honor who must control his emotions, not expecting me to always agree with those emotions. If I feel too sorry for you, I would not be respecting you but letting you feel too sorry for yourself. I must not celebrate your pity party. Your anger and defeatist attitude can be excessive, and I must not rob you of the opportunity to be a man and stand strong."

When you should instruct less:

"I need to instruct you but not too much. You're becoming a man of honor who must learn on his own. If I provide you with all the answers, I would not be respecting you but letting you cheat. Wise and honorable men will tell you that they learned some of their best lessons sitting alone in the school of hard knocks. I believe you have what it takes to find the answers, as tough as this feels right now."

When you should discipline less:

"I need to discipline you but not too much. You're becoming a man of honor who must be self-disciplined. If I always discipline you, I would not be respecting you. I must not try to control you 24/7 but appeal to you as a man of honor to control yourself. This is not about my catching you in some misbehavior and disciplining you but about your doing what is right when no one is watching. This is a decision an honorable man must make for himself; a mother cannot discipline a son into that decision of the heart."

When you should encourage less:

"I need to encourage you but not too much. You're becoming a man of honor who must be brave and courageous on your own. I must not always be your cheerleader—which I love being— otherwise, I become too responsible for inspiring you to be confident and courageous. I would not be respecting you if I always create a cheer to make you brave. There are moments when you must be brave on your own. You must take courage on your own. You must stand alone."

When you should supplicate less:

"I need to pray for you, but you need to pray for yourself. You're becoming a man of honor who must pray. You must hear from God like Jesus did. If I alone pray for you, I'd not be respecting you but trying to be the one who hears from God on your behalf. As a soldier of Christ, you too must pray and trust. I will not prevent you from experiencing the power of God on your own."

The Checklist

Run through G.U.I.D.E.S. as a checklist in your mind. Use the language from the above scripts to energize your son and motivate him to better understand your motives and to connect with you.

Don't allow yourself to feel uncomfortable with the language of honor and respect. Think of it as a recipe book with six ways to serve chicken. Would you say, "Wow! They keep repeating the word *chicken* in every recipe"? Exactly! They are recipes for chicken. This book is a recipe for Respect-Talk. It must be part of every verbal meal you give to your son. You'd be thunderstruck at a father who said, "That book on fathers and daughters keeps telling me to express my love to my daughter. That's too repetitious." When you get to the point where the word *respect* is as free-flowing for you as the word *love*, you will be that much closer to the center of your young man's soul.

4

SEEING THE MAN IN THE BOY

His Six Desires: C.H.A.I.R.S.

Who is the man in the boy? The best way to see the man in the making is to recognize the six desires God seeded in your son. God designed him with the desires to . . .

1. work and achieve;
2. provide for, protect, and even die;
3. be strong, lead, and make decisions;
4. analyze, solve, and counsel;
5. do friendship shoulder-to-shoulder;
6. sexually understand and know.

These desires reside within his maleness. As he ages, mom will behold each of these. When a mother studies her son, she will see these inclinations and aspirations oozing from his masculine soul. This is the man in the boy.

In the movie *Finding Neverland*, Sir James Matthew Barrie says,

"Young boys should never be sent to bed . . . they always wake up a day older." That comment captures what many moms feel. She wants her little boy to remain so forever. She prefers her precious baby to stay the cuddly bundle of joy.

However, every mom knows that she cannot keep her boy a baby, nor can she keep the man out of the boy. A day arrives when he awakens more boy than baby, and another day later when he is more man than boy. Mom's Respect-Talk affirms the six desires God crafted and grafted in him.

An Acronym: C.H.A.I.R.S.

To help you remember these six desires, I created an acronym that describes each: C.H.A.I.R.S.

- **C**onquest
- **H**ierarchy
- **A**uthority
- **I**nsight
- **R**elationship
- **S**exuality

You will see that each reflects what God reveals about masculinity in the Bible.

I refer to it as C.H.A.I.R.S. because God expects men to be the "head" and "manager" in their families (Eph. 5:23; 1 Tim. 3:4–5). Your son will one day begin to see himself as one who chairs his circumstances. Right now, he is under mom and dad's authority, but the little lion cub manifests headship and managing tendencies. He is not narcissistic, nor does he try to control or treat others as doormats. Instead, something in him compels him to move forward responsibly. Yes, when he attempts to chair from such a young age, he does so immaturely but rarely from ill will.

Mom may inwardly laugh as her five-year-old boy dressed as Superman avows, "I will protect you, mommy!" But when she looks beneath his cuteness and listens to his message, she notices that he feels the responsibility to be the strong overseer who is called to act with wisdom in defending and rescuing. Granted, he is incapable of protecting her, but he nevertheless desires to do so. Why do so many little boys dream of one day being a fireman or a police officer? It is not the siren on the fire truck that ultimately attracts him but the mission to bravely save the endangered. It is not the blue lights on the police car that magnetize him but the pursuit of the bad guy who is hurting the innocent. He sees himself being the respected hero.

C.H.A.I.R.S.: A Template for Respect-Talk

C.H.A.I.R.S. is a template that serves as a checklist. For example, use C.H.A.I.R.S. to ask yourself the following questions.

Conquest: Can I express appreciation for some pursuit of his? For example, "Billy, I see your commitment to work hard at building that intricate LEGO jet. You amaze me at how you stick with it until you have it all made. I respect that about you."

Hierarchy: Can I affirm his desire to protect or provide? For example, "Josh, I appreciate your longing to be protective of your little sister. When a brother protects his sister, it means the world to a mother. I respect that about you."

Authority: Can I compliment a good decision he makes? For example, "Jackson, not only do I see you becoming stronger, but I also see your strength to persuade others to do the right thing. You convinced Bill to stop accusing Josh until Josh had a chance to explain his side. High-five it! I respect that about you."

Insight: Can I praise an insight that I hear from him? For example, "David, the way you resolved that argument among your buddies today was just short of brilliant. Because you think about treating others as you want to be treated, I see you offering great insight in resolving conflict. I respect that about you."

Relationship: Can I respect his desire for friendship, shoulder-to-shoulder? For example, "Brad, your friendships with others amaze me. You are there for your friends, and your friends are there for you. You have each other's backs. You know how to be a good friend. I respect that about you."

Sexuality: Can I support the honorable way he treats the opposite sex? For example, "Johnny, I appreciate your commitment to treat girls the way your dad treats me. I salute you. I respect that about you."

Okay, I hear you. "I don't talk this way." I know. Most mothers do not use the language of Respect-Talk. Many of the words are not endearing to women. This kind of dialogue sounds foreign, and it should. This is not her mother tongue. For this reason, she must push through the awkwardness and let me provide the script that this generation of mothers has lost. I believe mothers on the homestead in two centuries past used Respect-Talk far more than mothers do today. When her son shot the bear near their cabin where his sisters were playing, she sang his praises. When he gutted it and gave her the hides, she thanked him for all the hard work, expressing sincere appreciation.

I devote a chapter to each of these concepts of C.H.A.I.R.S. and will explain each in depth, showing the salient scriptures supporting each idea.

Some Moms "Get It"

Sarah and I unpack each concept of C.H.A.I.R.S. at our Love and Respect Marriage Conference; plus, I explain each in my marriage book, *Love & Respect*. After wives learn about C.H.A.I.R.S., as related to their husbands, they immediately comment that C.H.A.I.R.S. applies to their boys as well. One mother wrote, "I am generally mystified by male behavior, both adults and adolescents, and there is obviously a connection to your principles. For example, how could I use the C.H.A.I.R.S. acronym to spell respect to my sons (ages sixteen and a half and twenty-two)?" This mother tracks well!

Some mothers, upon learning about C.H.A.I.R.S., have immediately applied it to their sons. A mother e-mailed the following to me:

When my son gives me his insight I say, "I really respect what you have to say," or "I respect the way you handled that situation." Or "I really respect how you are taking initiative to get things done and follow through with . . ." These things have made my son smile like I have never seen. I talk more about respect with regard to sporting events and showing respect for other opponents. My son knows without a doubt that I love him . . . now I feel he knows that I value him and his ideas, which I may not have done so well in the past. . . . Thank you so much for sharing God's message.

On the other hand, some moms have not paid attention to the man in their little boy. A mom told me, "My son is eighteen, and even though it's hard sometimes to remember that he is a man, I've tried to give him respect in certain situations, and he seems to really respond to it . . . but after all, he is a male, and you all are made the same way, and age is not a factor. . . . I will try to remember that he is not my baby boy anymore, and he needs it as much as any other male."

Do her comments strike you as odd? The boy is eighteen. She should have started Respect-Talk when he was eight. This "baby boy" could join the Marines and die for his country. But it is never too late for a mother to learn that her son responds to respect.

But Wait! Don't Women Have the Same Six Desires as Men?

Aren't men and women the same, and, therefore, these six desires also reside in women?

This is a common question. In fact, whenever I focus on the male, a percentage of women ask, "What are you saying against women? Are you saying women do not need respect? Are you saying girls do not also have these six desires?"

My first response is, "Just because I am saying something wonderful about your sons does not mean I am saying something against your daughters." Inadvertently, some women hijack the conversation and shift the attention away from the male. They are not mean-spirited. They feel the need to defend females, believing that applauding a male virtue is the same as attacking women. They have been conditioned to counter. At some level that's commendable, but I have tracked this long enough to know that they push men and boys into the shadows. They change the topic from the son to the daughter. Every time. As a case in point, there will be a percentage of women who pick up this book, read the title, and say, "What about 'Father and Daughter: The Respect Effect'?" That's their first thought. Forget the boy. What about the girl?

Let me be clear. Women have desires related to C.H.A.I.R.S. Many mothers have chimed in, "My daughter is interested in working, achieving, and leading." Indeed, men and women have a common humanity, thus the crossover of desires. Think female medical doctors. Yet they do not have these desires in the same passion and preoccupation when married. God instilled different desires between a husband and wife. Compared to the man, she feels less intensity and interest, for instance, to be the bread-winner, protector, and rescuer for her husband. She wants these *from* her husband, which explains the many e-mails I receive from wives—seeking to mother several children—weighed down with having to fulfill the breadwinner role due to an unemployed husband. I have yet to receive an e-mail from a husband complaining that his wife is unemployed and failing to be his breadwinner.

Commonly, the wife prefers to be the princess, and he prefers to be the prince, with all that symbolizes. This is something innate and wholesome, not sinister. Author Dannah Gresh wrote, "As a little girl I was predis-posed to dressing up like a princess and dreaming that my prince would one day come. No one taught me to do that. It was a natural yearning as my heart began its search for my life partner."[1] God designed girls with a princess mind-set. Check out the costumes sold for kids. What do most little girls long to wear? This is not a belittling comment but endearing. She yearns to love the man who finds her and finds her captivating.

As we look more in-depth at C.H.A.I.R.S. in the following chapters, we will observe the salient Bible verses that describe masculinity. When a mother meditates on these various texts, she discovers God's design of her son. It is as though God highlights in yellow precious truths about the masculine soul. When a mom pays attention to these nuggets of gold, a whole new world opens up to her about her boy.

Scripture Differentiates Male and Female

Jesus asked, "Have you not read that He who created them from the beginning MADE THEM MALE AND FEMALE?" (Matt. 19:4). Jesus taught that males and females are not the same. Though God created us equal in value, He did not make us the same in function or desire. We are equal but not the same. God expects us to value His design and these differences. For example, a husband brings the sperm, and a wife brings the egg. It will never be any different.

Neither will men ever have babies. Jeremiah declared, "Ask now, and see if a male can give birth" (Jer. 30:6). Only women who have functioning ovaries and a uterus can become pregnant and give birth. Did you know that 100 percent of the tribes, 100 percent of the time, know this as 100 percent true? No husband will ever experience what Isaiah described: "As the pregnant woman approaches the time to give birth, she writhes and cries out in her labor pains" (Isa. 26:17).

Of course, the differences continue beyond the ability to give birth. The nurturing nature of a mother takes over in ways that affect every part of her mind, emotions, will, and spirit. Men do not always have this kind of nurturing nature. And the research that shows females are the primary caregivers is off the charts. Something in women gives care to the people in their world. They default to this. In the Bible the nurturing nature of a mother is recognized as special. For instance, as we quoted earlier, a "mother tenderly cares for her own children" (1 Thess. 2:7).

Is there anything more pure and precious than this image? To argue that a father feels, thinks, and acts the same as a mother ignores the descriptors in Scripture, and it ignores daily experience. Just because the father of the newborn cries at the hospital as he holds his new son in his arms, it does not mean he will engage that child over the next two decades with the same affection as the mother. When the boy goes to school at age six, the dad will not be standing in the boy's bedroom, sobbing. He will not be on the phone, bawling to his mother, "Just yesterday I brought him home from the hospital, and now he's in first grade, and tomorrow he will be getting married. I am losing him. My precious baby is gone. Mom, what am I going to do?" That conversation happens between daughter and mother, not son and mother. This doesn't make men coldhearted, just less sentimental. He will care by working to provide money for the boy's college. Bottom line, what this mother thinks, feels, and does differs from that of this father—by light-years. As I wrote in my PhD dissertation ("A Descriptive Analysis of Strong Evangelical Fathers") as part of my dedication to my wife, Sarah, "Though I am committed to fathering, she is consumed by mothering." I have not met many fathers who debate me on this analysis. The differences between men and women are not restricted to mere biology.

The apostle Peter certainly agreed. Precisely because of a woman's femininity, Peter instructed a husband to understand his wife "since she is a woman" (1 Peter 3:7). To Peter her emotional, spiritual, and interpersonal needs matter. To Peter, every husband must appreciate that "she is a woman." He must recognize the gender of his wife, her feminine thoughts and feelings.

Soberly, when a husband misunderstands his wife's womanliness and dishonors her female role and value, his prayers are hindered (1 Peter 3:7). Put it this way: when a husband does not respond to the cry of his wife's heart, God does not respond to the cry of the husband's heart. The wife matters to God, and He intends to protect her by providing an incentive to a husband to get it right.

Isaiah recognized the vulnerability of a wife when he wrote, "Like a wife forsaken and grieved in spirit . . . like a wife . . . when she is rejected" (Isa. 54:6). Taking what he observed as an all-too-real situation with which his readers could identify, Isaiah used the wife as a metaphor to make a spiritual point to Israel about God's relationship to them. But this real-life episode brings home a truth in and of itself. The metaphor is true in experience, nothing foreign about this to the reader. A wife feels susceptible and helpless when rejected and forsaken. Peter referred to her as the "weaker vessel" when she is misunderstood and dishonored (1 Peter 3:7 KJV). Typically in conflict, husbands lean toward fight or flight; whereas, women lean toward tend, mend, and befriend. Husbands need to understand this. Commonly, it is the husband's failing to love, which is why God commands the husband to *agape*, that is, to love unconditionally; whereas, there is no command for a wife to agape. By nature she seeks to do the loving thing, which is connect, reconcile, and reestablish rapport.

For any number of reasons, wives can feel more rejected or neglected at the level of emotional intimacy than husbands. Wives drive the connection, "We need to talk." How cruel, therefore, of a husband to judge his wife when she feels grieved in spirit over his dismissive and repudiating attitude. He stabs her heart when he shouts, "Grow up. Quit being so childish! You are overly sensitive. You personalize everything. You have issues." What grieves the spirit of a wife more than her husband's rejection of her as a woman and companion?

I say these things to emphasize the male and female difference. If this difference is denied, a mother will not serve her son well since she will ignore coaching her son on how to love his future wife when she feels rejected and grieved. If he views his wife as the same as he is (as if there are no real differences), he could see her as having emotional problems, instead of hearing the apostle Peter's sobering admonition to husbands to live with their wives in an understanding way since they are created by God as women.

Interestingly, whatever upsets husbands often finds roots in the wives' caring about them. This is a virtue. For instance, wives confront because they care; they do not confront to control. I challenge men to see the virtue underneath those things that bother them as men. Once they do, once they understand, they can see their wives in a whole new light.

As with the virtues in females, the Bible highlights male virtues. The protective nature of the male is observed. The prophet Nehemiah urged his men to "fight for your brothers, your sons, your daughters, your wives" (Neh. 4:14). In fact, Paul challenged all of us to imitate this male virtue: "act like men, be strong" (1 Cor. 16:13). There are no verses that tell women to fight for their husbands.

Men Can Nurture and Women Can Fight

None of these verses are suggesting that men cannot nurture or that women cannot be warriors. Common sense, though, tells us where the natural instincts and interests are. A husband never dreams about nursing a baby. But squeeze a husband's arm, and he'll flex. Something inside of him envisions himself to be strong and the protector. He feels compelled to display that to the woman who squeezes his arm. A wife doesn't flex when you squeeze her arm—not that she can't, but what's the point? She has no desire or reason to do so. It isn't in her psyche even if she has a black belt in karate.

Men and women differ greatly when it comes to their desires. This has nothing to do with competencies but everything to do with their interests. This is about passion, not aptitude. For example, a widower has the ability to nurture his children and must, but his nature does not have the same obsession to nurture as his wife did. Dad is fully capable of taking care of the kids while mom is away for the weekend on a retreat. He is talented enough to do everything mom does with those kids, but dad does not have the same compulsion to do with the kids what mom does. He could comb his daughter's hair far better, but it looks fine to him. He could put place mats down on top of a tablecloth along with a vase of flowers as the centerpiece, but that doesn't really interest him. Besides, he's hungry, so he yells, "Let's eat! Grab a paper plate and plastic fork. Let's pray."

A widow can put on a tool belt, climb the ladder to the roof, and repair the damage there, and she may need to do this, but she has no great interest in doing so. This illustration provides us with the recognition that we are familiar with the male and female differences. Familiarity breeds "indifference to the difference." We do not pay attention to these gender patterns until the widow is on the roof, wearing coveralls and a tool belt. Then we stop and stare in stunned silence. We call out, "Grandma, what in the world are you doing up there?" But we think nothing of a widower climbing a ladder to fix his leaky roof. Instead we yell, "Hey, Grandpa, later on are you watching the ball game?" Gender differences go unnoticed not because they do not exist but because in foundational areas the genders rarely cross over. We don't pay attention since we don't know anything different and, thus, do not see the difference.

With the widower and widow, it has little to do with lack of ability and much to do with differing desires that reside innately within men and women. A woman can go hunting with four other women on opening day of deer season. They can sit next to each other without talking for three days. They can kill four bucks and gut them. But which of these four women really wants to do that? A dad can stay home while his wife hunts. He can take care of the kids. He can put various outfits on his daughter to determine which is best for church. But what man wants to do that? If he is home, he grabs the first dress he sees and, if he's like me, ends up putting it on backward. I know now that buttons go on the back for a girl. Stop laughing.

Along a similar vein, a little girl wants to play with a doll because she feels love for a baby; whereas, a boy wants to play fort and protect the innocent from the evil invader. The boy could care for a baby doll and play house, but he does not want to do that. A little girl can defend a fort in the backyard with her make-believe sword, but she does not desire to do it. We must be honest about the default interest and passion. The toy industry is honest about this and makes a ton of money because they face the facts.

Research Shows Biological Differences

Even so, chemicals determine gender issues. According to research specialists, during the first three months of life, a baby girl's skills in eye contact and facial gazing increase by over 400 percent, but there is no such increase in boys.[2] As researchers found, this is rooted in physiology, not socialization. But does this make boys less caring because they make less eye contact? No, it just makes boys different, not less virtuous. God designed boys with the six desires behind C.H.A.I.R.S.

As Jesus said in Matthew 19, God did not design males to be females. He does not intend for boys to be girls. Just as we do not say to women or girls, "Get in tune with your masculine side," we must not say to men or boys, "Get in tune with your feminine side." Though we should imitate the virtue of the other gender where appropriate, as Paul encouraged the women at Corinth to be strong like men of courage, God never expects a male to be feminized. Consequently, when a boy acts like a boy, a mother must not negatively react and suppress this maleness related to these six wholesome desires depicted in C.H.A.I.R.S. Rather, she must see God's call on her to honor the virtues God lodged in her boy as a male, the male to whom Jesus refers.

The Central Question

Why the issue of respect? Ephesians 5:33 has the answer. There, God commands a husband to love and a wife to respect. In fact, Peter taught that a wife should put on respect to win her husband (1 Peter 3:1–2).

Why the command? God commands a husband to love not only because his wife needs love but because he does not love naturally—otherwise, the command is unnecessary. The same holds true with wives. God commands a wife to respect her husband not only because her husband needs respect but also because she does not do this naturally.

Though all men and women need love and respect equally, Shaunti Feldhahn found a male and female difference, as did I from my research referenced in chapter 1. When given a choice between feeling completely unloved in the world versus completely disrespected, men are significantly against feeling disrespected. Seventy-four percent choose to be unloved.[3]

God commands a wife to put on respect during conflict because a man is very vulnerable to the appearance that a wife has no respect for him, in the same way a wife is vulnerable to the appearance that a husband has no love for her.

King David from the Bible needed respect. We know that Saul's daughter Michal loved David, her husband (1 Sam. 18:20, 28); yet later, "Michal looked out of the window and saw King David leaping and dancing before the LORD; and she despised him in her heart" (2 Sam. 6:16). It appears she was embarrassed by her husband's display. When David returned home, Michal let him have it. She "came out to meet David and said, 'How the king of Israel distinguished himself today! He uncovered himself today in the eyes of his servants' maids as one of the foolish ones shamelessly uncovers himself!' So David said to Michal . . . 'I will be more lightly esteemed than this and will be humble in my own eyes, but with the maids of whom you have spoken, with them I will be distinguished" (2 Sam. 6:20–22). Then it says, "Michal the daughter of Saul had no child to the day of her death" (v. 23). Michal, not David, was out of line. Their marriage ended right there.

A Man in the Making

Respect is a need in the male soul, not only in your husband but also in your little boy. The man is in the boy. This means that he will be less loving by nature than you and any daughters you may have. This also means that when he fails to be as loving as he ought to be, you may have a natural tendency to react in ways that feel disrespectful to him. Though you may mean very little by your disrespectful reaction, your son will personalize your disrespectful venting. A daughter gets mom's venting. As a daughter she vents in the same way. However, as a male, a son will be more vulnerable to the appearance of disrespect. Over time, he withdraws and stonewalls. He becomes silent and unresponsive. But when mom sees that her boy—a man in the making—needs respect in the similar ways to her husband, she empowers herself and influences the heart of her son. He softens and opens himself to connect with her. But every mother I have met struggles with what this respect toward her son looks and sounds like, just as she struggles with applying respect to her husband. But she must not become anxious about this. God did not design her to do this naturally. In the same way, a father will not love his daughter as naturally as his wife does. That's okay. Even so, both this mother and father must still learn to love and respect because the daughter and son need this love and respect.

For this reason, I invite every mother to better represent herself during heated fellowship with her son. You can have the best of loving motives, but if you misrepresent yourself, he will misinterpret you. That's why I urge moms to reassure their sons during tense moments.

> "Look, I am hurt and mad. I am deeply disappointed in what has happened here. But let's make sure you understand that I am not trying to be disrespectful to you. I am not using this issue as an opportunity to send you a message that I don't have any respect for you. I am reacting because I believe in the honorable man God intends for you to be. I do not respect what you did, but that differs from my belief in you and the respect I feel for the man I envision you will become."

This acknowledges the man in the boy, and he will keep his heart open to you.

Are You Ready to Learn More?

Are you ready to discuss more ways to apply respect? The next six chapters go in depth on a boy's C.H.A.I.R.S.: Conquest, Hierarchy, Authority, Insight, Relationship, and Sexuality. In each chapter I explain how to apply Respect-Talk. Included in each chapter is how to apply G.U.I.D.E.S. to C.H.A.I.R.S. When you respectfully Give, Understand, Instruct, Discipline, Encourage, and Supplicate, miracles can happen in the soul of your son.

Stay relaxed as you read.

Over the years when mothers e-mail me, they often request more cases and illustrations. Each mother thinks in terms of her boy's age and stage and about yesterday's conflict. She wants to fix it so she can stay emotionally connected with her boy. I have written this book with the hope that you will find specific answers to your questions.

Here's the challenge. Do not let all of this information overwhelm you and make you feel as if you are a failure for not acting on all the suggestions. Instead, see this as a resource book to which you can turn when curious and concerned about engaging your son in a more effective way. See the book as a template for future interactions that will lead to a stronger relationship with your son.

5

CONQUEST

Respecting His Desire to Work and Achieve

His Field of Dreams

Bubbling inside the soul of your son is a desire to enter into an adventure in some field, conquer an obstacle, and fulfill an honorable duty—even at the early stages of life. Reflect on the three-year-old who gazes, enchanted, at a fireman and his fire truck or gawks at a policeman and his squad car. In his little brain he dreams of the exciting conquest. Though his early years entail play, even his play evidences defeating a foe, climbing a tree, or winning a game. As he matures, his focus and interests change, but the desire to conquer something in his field of dreams remains. Part of the joy of mothering your son is discovering along with him the talents and passions God has instilled in him to use as he fulfills his desire to work and achieve. Keep your eyes and ears open to the *fields* your son explores as he gets older. Watch those places in which he shows an intrigue.

Even if he has a wide range of interests and does not have his sights set on a specific field, listen carefully and you'll hear him asking, "Where should I land, and will I make a difference?" You can catch him wondering, *Will I be man enough? Will I work and achieve with distinction and honor? Who will I be?* At those moments, you can respectfully say, "Yes, you will be an honorable man. You have what it takes. God has given you the abilities and desires to make a difference in the field of your choosing."

A mother's disrespect can undermine a son's confidence to succeed in a field. A mother wrote, "I am struck how the issue of respect ties in so well to the man's question: 'Do I have what it takes?' Over and over I see this question asked . . . in my three boys. When we are not showing . . . respect, we are telling them over and over, 'No, you don't have what it takes.' It is devastating for them."

Look for moments when he is working hard, maybe on something he does not enjoy but which needs to be accomplished. Because God placed a seed in every boy to conquer in some field, Respect-Talk adds water, enabling that desire to sprout. As the years roll by, a mother will behold her son's desire to engage in activities that involve mental or physical effort to achieve a purpose or result. Her respectful statements play to that bent and energize and motivate him.

Recognize Self-Doubt After Failing to Achieve

A mom e-mailed:

> We have two boys, and our oldest is almost eleven. I know that he feels a lot of pressure on him to be a good example to his three younger siblings. I tell him I love him all the time, but I had never considered telling him I respect him. This last Tuesday, I was cleaning his room, and I found a note he had written. It said, "Failure=Benjamin." He is very hard on himself. . . . I was devastated. I knew something had to change, and that something was us, his parents. We need to show him that we respect him.
>
> Before he got home from school, I made twelve notes and taped them around his room and hid them in places such as drawers and under his pillow: I love you. I respect you. I respect your ideas. I am so proud of you. You are the most creative person I know. You are a great big brother.

As soon as he got home and saw the obvious ones I had posted, he ran to me and gave me a hug! His eyes were sparkling, and he was so excited. He immediately took the notes and made a board that said "compliment board" and taped them all to it. I have written him letters in the past to tell him I love him and how much he means to me (he is very sentimental and has kept every note and letter). But telling him I respect him went over the top. I have made a vow to respect my son and treat him like I want his future spouse to treat him.

Another mom wrote to me:

Our son has had a difficult year academically. When I got home, my husband told me [our son] had been very hesitant to take out his progress report until he knew dad wasn't going to jump on him, and they talked about it. After looking at it myself (it went from As to Fs), I went to his room, where he was studying, and told him the truth: I could see he'd put a lot of work into his studies and knew it had been a hard year. And I really admired his grit and persistence, sticking with it when it's difficult. He got the biggest smile and quietly said, "Thank you, mom." I felt he was closer to me than he had been in a long time.

On the heels of his failings, Respect-Talk shapes a boy's self-image and inculcates a greater sense of self-worth and self-confidence. As odd as this sounds, Love-Talk with a boy at such a time can fall short. When moms speak Love-Talk to a boy based on what she would want to hear as a girl his age, she assumes that he feels what she would feel. This, of course, misses God's design of the male and female as different.

Why Is This Desire to Work and Achieve in the Boy?

The answer is found in God's creation of the first man, Adam.

God created Adam to work in the garden of Eden. We read in Genesis 2:15, "Then the LORD God took the man and put him into the garden of

Eden to cultivate it and keep it." Before God created Eve, He designed Adam to prepare and use the land within Eden for gardening. He would break up the soil by plowing, sow seed, and grow plants. He would hoe, water, fertilize, and prune. He would harvest. God engineered a perfect world and made the first man to work in it. God did not bring Adam into being as a sightseeing vacationer.

Men identify themselves in terms of what they do in their respective fields. God put it in their DNA to work. They tell who they are by what they do. "I am a lawyer . . . doctor . . . coach . . . teacher . . . banker . . . architect . . . carpenter . . . entrepreneur . . . car salesman . . . pastor . . . scientist . . . administrator . . . office manager . . . cafe owner . . ."

What is typically the first question every man asks another man when they meet for the first time? "What do you do?" Everyone has observed this, and I want every mom to realize from this simple illustration that such a man is in your boy. In the future, innately your son will ask this question of other men. You won't need to coach your ten-year-old boy, saying, "Let's rehearse. In twelve years, when you turn twenty-two, I want you to ask the men that you meet, 'What do you do?'" No, no, your boy will do this automatically. It is in his DNA.

On this point, a mom wrote, "Jacob, my oldest, is almost thirteen and was telling me . . . on our way home from church . . . 'Mom, you know what's funny?' 'What, honey?' 'When us guys first meet each other, you know what we always ask each other first thing . . . "What kind of game system do you have?" First thing, mom, every time!' I about steered the car in a ditch! I couldn't believe it. It was the adolescent equivalent of 'What do you do for a living?'"

Back to Genesis. Later, after sin enters the world, God's curse on Adam relates to the field, and His curse on Eve relates to the family (Gen. 3:16–19). God cursed Adam in the field by the sweat of his brow and Eve in the realm of marriage and family with pain in childbirth. This points to men being field-oriented and women being family-oriented. As the consequences of sin, He cursed each where He created their deepest longings.

The husband works in the field, but he will never achieve perfect respect in the field. Perfect and lasting glory in the field is fleeting due to sin. We do not typically remember who won the MVP award in any sport after the moment has passed. Honor fades within days.

The wife treasures relationships within the family, but she will neither experience perfect love nor a perfect family. It is not that a woman is indifferent to the field since women—many of them with a child on their backs—have throughout history worked in fields. However, a woman identifies herself most deeply based on her relationships with her children and husband. And it is not that men are indifferent to the family, but they see themselves working on behalf of their wives and children.

Are there exceptions? Always, but the pattern is so pervasive around the world that the exception must never deny the rule. There are women on this planet who cannot stand caring for a baby. But would those unusual women negate the idea that women nurture by nature? The aberration does not disprove a time-honored truth about women.

Paradise has been lost. Infected with sin, the field and family fall short of everyone's expectations. The narrative in Genesis 3 provides us with a clue into the masculine and feminine soul: what matters most deeply to each. Men and women must now live on the edge of Eden, possessing the residual of Paradise but never tasting it as God originally planned.

Warning

May I provide a few words of warning? Just because your son has a desire to work and achieve does not mean he desires to do so wherever you choose for him. For instance, a mom loves her domestic domain—her nest. But her son does not have the same nesting instinct. In other words, do not hand your son a broom and dustpan, then say, "You like working and achieving, so sweep the garage! Conquer!" It doesn't pan out like that. This is not about *your* God-given desire but *his* God-given desire.

This is about the joy of helping him find God's field for him and feeding his desire to work and achieve in that field. Your son's lack of desire to work on your stage only means his stage differs.

Here is another warning. Have you noticed your goodwilled son negatively reacting to you? Do you find him deflating or getting provoked? Reflect for a moment. Decode!

Did you say or do something negative related to his work efforts and achievement? Even though you meant very little by your comments, did he interpret them as denigrating, as though you felt he did not have what it takes to exert the necessary effort? Did he feel belittled for failing to achieve in some situation? Did you even use disrespectful words to motivate him to act responsibly? Calling a son of any age an idiot, moron, loser, coward, mama's boy, jerk, creep, and so forth is never okay and never serves a healthy purpose. Such words discourage and defeat. As we have said elsewhere, that's comparable to a dad using harsh and hateful words toward his daughter to mold her into a fine woman.

Finally, guard against comparing his achievements with another's. Don't compare, but try to encourage him based on how he has improved. Why compare your son's violin playing with another boy's? Instead, compare his past efforts with present efforts. Honor him for personally improving, not because he replaced Joey as first chair. This is important particularly among siblings. A parent must guard against, "Why can't you achieve what your brother did?"

Apply G.U.I.D.E.S. to His Conquest

What can you do as a mom to feed this God-given desire in your son to work and achieve? As you recall the acronym G.U.I.D.E.S. (Give, Understand, Instruct, Discipline, Encourage, and Supplicate), remember I shared that you have a powerful role. Here's what you can do to apply G.U.I.D.E.S. to *Conquest*.

Give resources that help him work and achieve. Ask yourself, "What can I offer him to aid his work and achievement?"

Younger Boy:

Buy him his own little rake so he can help his daddy rake leaves. Refer to him as "Daddy's little worker man!" Say, "I really respect the way you work so hard and get those leaves in a big pile for daddy."

Older Boy:

So he can cut lawns in the neighborhood, invest in purchasing him a lawn mower at 1 percent interest, which he repays by the end of the summer. Communicate, "I believe in you. I respect your desire to work and achieve. I am impressed by the number of neighbors who want your service. This says a great deal about their admiration and confidence in you." If not a lawn-mowing business, is there another business idea that captures his interest? You can honor him by investing in this with him.

Guard against allowances. Giving must coincide with a son working. Don't give an allowance, but establish chores so he can earn money. The Bible reveals a principle: "If anyone is not willing to work, then he is not to eat, either" (2 Thess. 3:10). Though you show respect to your son, do not deprive him of the pleasure he gains from working and achieving. Set up a savings account in his name at a bank or credit union for him to deposit his money. Giving him too much can undermine the self-respect he gains from earning money.

At the same time, grace and benevolence are okay.

"Son, we are helping you to buy the bike you want for two reasons. One, you have demonstrated to us a great maturity in recent months, especially as you have been diligent in saving for this bike. Two, that bike ride to raise money for the church is coming up, and we believe you could raise some money for that orphanage in this bike-a-thon. So we are going to pay the final one-third of the cost for your bike."

Think of it like a company granting bonuses as a way of honoring the employees for their overall work ethic.

Let me add, it may not be only about giving money. A mom might volunteer to help coach his soccer team as a way of honoring him. She gives her time and talent. She enters his field, so to speak, to help him develop his skills in the conquests related to competition in sport.

Understand *his exasperation and anger as he works. Ask yourself, "Do I understand his struggle with working or achieving in a field?"*

Younger Boy:

As he works at his first real job as an eight-year-old painting a fence across a neighbor's field, he encounters the need to repaint due to a dust storm that left debris on the wet paint. This setback angers and exasperates him. Tell him that you understand and respect why he is upset. Share that you respect his work efforts and commitment to achieve even though things took a downward turn. Let him know that you respect his determination in the midst of this disappointment to start again.

Older Boy:

Since he worked hard to be the starting quarterback as a junior, understand the depth of his pain when hearing the coach's verdict of starting another player. Say to him,

> "I respect your heart's desire and dedication to be the starter. I can imagine that this feels like a kick in the gut. I appreciate how you have conducted yourself around the other players, even though inside you feel numb. You are a great example to me."

As you observe his work to achieve, he will fail sometimes. Those moments allow you to apply Respect-Talk. For example, if he cuts grass, which is not an uncommon job for boys, anticipate his lawn mower blade hitting a huge rock and his incurring an unexpected expense. As he subtracts the cost of doing business from his profits and throws himself in a pout on the couch, use Respect-Talk.

> "This is a setback. But you are an honorable boy now learning what other men experience when they run businesses. Remember, accidents happen. Mr. Smith runs a trucking company and his trucks break down. He has to plan on this as part of his overhead, as they call it. As painful as this is, I know you have what it takes to rebound."

Then exit the room. Don't see this as a moment to cuddle or attract his whining. Go busy yourself. Keep the Respect-Talk short, and do not spill over into Love-Talk. In general, boys talk less about their feelings yet need to hear words of respect—short and sweet. If he wants to cuddle, he'll come later to you. Right now, talk to him as a man, not as a baby. The beautiful thing is that when you talk to the man in the boy, the boy will probably be affectionate later on with mom.

Instruct him on how to better work and achieve. Ask yourself, "Can I instruct him on how to improve his work and achieve more?"

Younger boy:

Whatever it is that he does, whether building a LEGO car or trying to start a pet-walking business, when you provide input, how do you sound to him? Does it sound disrespectful, as if he is less than intelligent, or does he see you as a coach seeking to honor him with this information?

Older boy:

When he goes about to do chores in the home, in ways that really do not achieve what you have requested him to achieve, do you disrespectfully lecture him on how to do it the right way? Or do you ask, "How can I offer instruction without your feeling disrespected? Here's what I want you to do, but my intent is not to be disrespectful."

Remember, when instructing, convey the information honorably so your son remains teachable. A kindergarten teacher applied Respect-Talk to her boys and found this language created a new appetite in the boys to learn. She wrote:

> I have seen this work miracles in my kindergarten classroom (which is sort of a six-hours-a-day parenting situation . . .). Your principles have helped to turn respect-starved five-year-old boys into eager helpers and learners, and I have only begun to apply them. Perhaps as parents we forget that boys are males and girls are females from conception, and have the same love and respect needs we do as adults.

I love what this mom wrote:

> When our oldest son was three, it was repair time for the lawn mower. As he watched his dad work, there was a need for a screwdriver. After [my husband] explained to our son the differences in them, my son went off to the box and returned with the tool. My husband thanked him to which he replied, "Hey Dad, you need me!" I learned from my husband to always include the children in our activities. It takes time when they're younger, and it usually takes longer than normal at first and is usually much messier, too, but their self-esteem, sense of belonging, and being respected and loved is worth it all.

Providing instruction on the different tools enabled this boy to work, be needed, and feel respected.

You honor your son by feeding information to him in the area of his desire to succeed. For instance, thinking of his lawn-mowing business,

> "I came across information on how to sharpen a lawn mower blade with a file and a vice. And I pulled up a YouTube video that shows you how to do it step-by-step. Maybe later you can watch it. If you wish, I'll take you to the store to buy a file. I'll go in half with you.

As bad as that ding is, I have a hunch you'll have it sharpened in no time, knowing you."

Discipline him when he is inactive and neglectful. Ask yourself, *"Should I discipline him when he is too lazy or irresponsible?"*

Younger Boy:

"I respect the desire God placed in you to work and achieve. I backed your volunteering on Sunday mornings to greet people at church. But it was reported to me that you left early from greeting to go hang out with your friends in the church cafeteria. I know that can be more fun, but you made a commitment to the church staff to serve this way. You are becoming an honorable man at age nine, and doing what you said you'd do is part of that. Tell me that I don't have to give you extra chores next week because you exited early again, okay?"

Older Boy:

"It has come to our attention that you have been skipping classes, which appears to explain your poor grades from last semester. You are an honorable man. I need your counsel. Is it fair for me to work hard to earn money to pay your tuition while you neglect working hard? You know the answer. You need to go to class and bring up your grades by semester's end. If not, I would not be respecting you or myself if I let you neglect your duty. If there is no improvement, there will be some consequences. I say this because I feel as though I respect you and your abilities more than you do. Is this fair for me to say?"

All boys need challenges and exhortations. No boy will conquer every task with great success, and he will neglect some duties assigned to him.

With those missteps he definitely needs confrontation and correction. However, he does not need a look of disgust accompanied by rude words.

Let's think of his lawn-cutting business. He wants to play and not cut the grass. Mom's Respect-Talk kicks in.

"Son, I believe in you. Because I believe in you and the man you are becoming, my role is to help you to be a self-disciplined man of honor. Cutting grass is work. Playing is fun. But playing is so much more fun when our work is done. So here's the deal: you do not have to choose one desire against the other. You act on your desire to succeed as a businessman for the next forty-five minutes and cut Mr. Baylor's grass, and then you will still have two more hours to enjoy playing video games with Jerry. Presto! Both desires are fulfilled, and you will feel really good tonight when you lay your head on the pillow. On the other hand, if you refuse, then Jerry goes home, you still cut the grass, and you go to bed early. Of these two options, which is most honoring to you, Jerry, and Mr. Baylor?"

Encourage him to keep on working when feeling discouraged. Ask yourself, "Can I encourage him to keep on working and achieving when he feels like he does not have what it takes?"

Younger Boy:

"I know you are frustrated and angry over not doing as well as you want at soccer. The sadness comes when you do not improve as much as you like. But the thing I respect about you is your desire to keep getting better. Sometimes we just need to look at ourselves and get better rather than comparing ourselves with others. That is a lesson that will serve us well throughout life. But I asked Jerry, the high school soccer player that we know from church, if he'd

come over and kick a soccer ball with you. He was excited to do
that. He's actually bringing over some cones to run some drills
with you."

Older Boy:

"I know you wanted more hours as a car wash attendant this
summer. That the manager cut your hours is a bummer. But I
realized you can get another part-time job at the animal shelter.
They are hiring high schoolers part-time. This is right up your
alley since you love animals so much. Here's their number to call."

Back to our lawn-mowing business. Say a professional lawn service
came into the neighborhood, and of the six lawns your son mowed, they
took three of the homes. With his business cut in half, he feels punched
in the gut. He thinks he made a mistake in trying to run a business. With
your son's confidence and enthusiasm at an all-time low, your Respect-
Talk takes over:

"An honorable man thinks more about how he finishes than how
he starts. At a marathon, does everyone start together? Yes. Do
they all finish together? No. Many quit in the face of the better
competition and discouragement. You started your business with
six lawns. You lost three due to competition. Will you finish doing
these three as honorably as you can or conclude that because of
competition, you don't have what it takes? Right now, this isn't
about the competition; this is about your confidence as a finisher.
As a developing man of honor, how important is it for you to
taste of these setbacks? I would say this is a great privilege, not
a moment of defeat. This won't be the last time such a reversal
comes to you. How will you make it through this first one?"
(Mom, you can write this in a note or say it and then exit. If you
hang around for him to answer the question, he may whine. Don't

give him that opportunity. Let your wise words and questions linger in his heart, but you should not linger in his room.)

Here are some bonus expressions of encouragement:

Preschoolers (two to four years): "I respect you for the way you work so hard in picking up your toys, and you did it so fast, without stopping. Give me a high five!"

School-age children (five to eight years): "I respect you for how hard you worked to earn money to buy that twenty-dollar science kit. It will be fun to make fake blood and grow mold. You impressed me with having a goal and reaching that goal. High five!"

Tweens (nine to twelve years): "I respect you for reading ten books this summer. You amaze me with how well you read. I wish I had read as much as you read when I was your age."

Young teenagers (thirteen to fifteen years): "I respect you for how hard you have been working in basketball practice. The coach has been amazed by your improvement and what you are contributing to the team."

Older teenagers (sixteen to eighteen years): "I respect you for getting your driver's license and scoring so high on the exam. Perfect score! You are far more mature and capable than I was at age sixteen. Thanks for being such a great example of responsibility to your younger brother."

Young adults (nineteen and older): "I respect you for all that you do to achieve your goals. You are taking sixteen hours of credit, working at the cafeteria at school to help pay for your tuition, and volunteering with the youth group at church. God has exciting things for you. He honors such industry."

Supplicate *with him to receive opportunity and favor to work. Ask yourself, "Do I pray about his working or achieving?"*

Younger Boy:

Ben Carson, former brain surgeon at Johns Hopkins Hospital and a 2016 presidential candidate, said, "I was a terrible student. My brother was a terrible student. [My mom] did not know what to do. So she prayed. She asked God for wisdom. You know what? You don't have to have a PhD to talk to God. You just have to have faith."[1] After that, things began to turn around for Ben, and to this day he credits his praying mother with his change of course. James 5:16 states, "The prayer of a righteous person is powerful and effective" (NIV).

Older Boy:

A mother can have confidence before God about her son's opportunities to work. She can tell her son that God desires for him to work and earn money. She can explain that this does not mean God will give him a job where he sits around and does nothing, but that given he makes himself available to sweat at hard labor, the Lord will hear them when together they ask for employment. You can let him know that you respect his willingness to do whatever he must at this season of his life to earn money.

As for the lawn-mowing business, if your son welcomes your praying with him, ask God to give him more opportunity and favor in the immediate neighborhood to mow lawns. As in your life, do not hesitate to ask God for His help. You do not know if the answer will be yes, no, or wait; but in imitation of Jesus, you pray. Let your son know that praying is better than not praying. The apostle James said that we have not because we ask not (James 4:2 KJV). You can pray that God would give you resources, help you understand your son's exasperation and anger, help you provide instruction to be wiser, grant your son greater inner resolve to be disciplined, and help you believe in the abilities and talents that He has instilled in your son.

Sometimes you need to let your son experience setbacks and walk the journey on his own. Let him know that you are praying for him but that you see him becoming a man who must climb the mountain on his own. For example, the high school basketball coach informs your son that he will not be starting as before but will ride the bench during the remainder of the season. Younger players have arisen with better skills. As a mother, how do you respond to your son? As you observe your son enter a light depression, do you seek to affirm him with "I love you, and it will be okay. I am calling the coach to give him a piece of my mind"? Or do you say,

"This is a tough moment for you, but I respect why you feel down. You desire to excel. I admire that about you. I wish you did not have to go through this, but I also know you have it in you to accept the challenge. You do have what it takes. I admire your willingness to endure this on your own as a man of honor. Thanks for being an example to me."

6

HIERARCHY

Respecting His Desire to Provide, Protect, and Even Die

A mom shared a most delightful story of her six-year-old boy:

I took our five children outside to run off energy one evening after dinner. Thunder started rumbling. We agreed to stay out until the rain came. It began slowly but picked up momentum quickly, so the children were anxious to get back to the house. Our two-year-old was riding a push bike, and he wasn't bothered by the rain at all. So when the older children began to complain about how long it was taking, I gave them the house keys and told them to run ahead and get in the house. Three of them ran ahead, but six-year-old old Sam stayed with me and his little brother. I urged him to run ahead with the others and get in the house because by this time the thunder was loud and the rain was heavy. Sam replied, "No way, mom. I'd rather make myself die than leave you out here in this storm." Then after a short pause (he must have been feeling brave), he added, "And if a robber comes to the house, don't be afraid, 'cause I will be nearby." And although the cuteness of it made me want to giggle, I could see that he took it very seriously. Sam's daddy certainly models this sort of character, but I can't ever think of a time when Sam would have heard anyone talk like that.

Sam did not have to hear this kind of talk from his dad in order to be protective over his mother. God designed boys, including Sam, with a natural desire to provide, protect, and die for others.

The Protective Instinct

The man is in the boy. Early hints of this desire will appear in various ways. A mother needs to pay attention. When her boy is dressed up like a cowboy or a superhero and tells her that he will protect her, she often overlooks the significance of his comments and only notices how cute he is.

A mother should not dismiss these expressions any more than she would dismiss her daughter pretending to mother her baby doll. No mother turns a blind eye to her preschool-age daughter playing mommy. Instead, she affirms her maternalism with, "You are a wonderful mommy!" Mothers understand little girls because a few years ago they were little girls too. However, will she identify with her son's bold claims to insulate her from harm?

God put inside every boy something that stirs him to be brave and protective. There is no Scripture that announces, "Fight for your husbands," only for "your wives" (Neh. 4:14). God does not require a woman to be the primary protector of the man. Yes, she watches over the children, but he secures the family in other ways. This is a male phenomenon around the world. God put this chivalrous instinct inside men. To Christ-following men, safeguarding women and children is a divine duty.

When your boy moves into teen years, you will see his instinct to protect you when something arises that could threaten or harm you. Watch for his safeguarding penchant and sing his praises.

Early Signs in Boys

In studying male preschoolers, researchers have recognized their tendencies to defend their domain and property, to be competitive, and to combat without fear of conflict. Here's my question: Is defending property a good thing or a bad thing? Is this competitive nature without fear of conflict a vice or virtue? Sarah asked our four-year-old grandson, Jackson, what he did at preschool with his friends when outside playing. "We got to keep away the bad guys."

There is virtue here. A mom can see the early formation of an honorable man learning how to defend what he thinks is right. In pretend play he protects the fort against evil invaders. Or when his friend unfairly grabs his toy from him, he grabs it back, and they tussle with each other. This is less about getting the toy back and more about fighting for justice. That is a good thing. He should not be shamed for demanding justice. Fair is fair. Even so, he needs coaching on better ways to handle these moments. There is a front-sided strength in the face of his back-sided weakness.

Mom can take her son aside and say, "I respect your desire to be treated fairly. He was wrong for grabbing the toy. I know that troubled you, and I am glad that it did trouble you. But as an honorable man, what can you do next time?" Ask him for a solution. Give him the opportunity to figure it out. Kids are moral and spiritual beings who know right from wrong and need to be asked. When they come up with their own solution, they own it.

As for the boy who says, "Well, I don't know what to do. He keeps grabbing the toy from me," a mom can say, "Okay, the next time it happens, come to me, and I will talk to him." Every mom needs to see her young son's desire to defend against injustice and do combat on behalf of justice. Once she perceives this, her boy's play takes on a whole new meaning.

What about those moments in which he selfishly and foolishly grabs a toy or enters a fray with no thought of personal safety? When a boy selfishly defends what he wrongly thinks is his, a mom needs to instruct,

"Johnny, do you know what I see in you? You want to be a strong protector. I like the way that you defend what is yours. At the same time, I have a question: What do you feel when your friend takes what is yours? I know you don't like it when he takes what is yours. For this reason, you must not take what is his to play with, and it is not honorable to fight with someone who has a right to play with his toy."

Affirm his virtues; correct the vices. You must appeal to this honorable nature of your boy.

Remember, boys are not girls. Girls will naturally negotiate; whereas, boys can be much more aggressive in the early years. There is a bad side to this aggression, but as the boy ages, he will naturally and physically defend and protect the weak. For example, most boys will physically go after another boy who kicks his sister's cat. Evil is in the world, and evil does not negotiate. Most violent crimes come from a small percentage of men, and other men must go after these men. Yes, there are female cops who carry guns, but on a day in, day out basis with families around the world, the men are prepared to physically defend the family unit. My grandson Jackson gets it right. There are bad guys out there, and somebody needs to keep those bad guys away.

In my home I live with the thought that there is one deranged man out there, within a fifty-mile radius, ready to enter my home and do us harm if he can get away with it. Men know that man is out there. Women are a bit more naïve because they are not predators. It isn't that they do not know these things, but generally, they are preoccupied with love relationships and do not pay attention to the shadows. Sarah does not think about a deranged man showing up at the door. I do. Truth is, he may never show up; but I feel conscious of the possibility and responsible to do combat with this guy in the event he showed up in the middle of the night to do Sarah harm. It is not in my nature to scream and then cry out, "Sarah, do something!" That's laughable. God wired me to protect, and most every wife I have met rejoices over the feeling of being protected by men, not vice versa. For this reason, every mother must affirm this desire in her son.

What I find odd is that the same woman who wants her husband to defend her against a disrespectful clerk at the gas station and wants to know that her husband will do combat on her behalf when she hears an intruder in the middle of the night is the same woman will also pounce on her little boy's combative nature when he goes after a boy who pushed his sister. Voices in the culture declare, "He will be violent and abusive unless you rebuke him." But wait a minute here. We cannot have it both ways. If a woman wants her husband to defend her with no concern about his personal safety, she needs to give some leeway here to her boy who has no regard for his own safety when defending his sister. Yes, maybe he shouldn't get physical. But boys play tackle football, and such scuffles are not that damaging to their self-image. They do not interpret it as abuse but courage. The chaplain of Wheaton College, Jim Hutchens, the first clergyman wounded in the Vietnam War, told me, "You need to let boys react naturally before you demand that they learn how to react supernaturally." Boys learn through trial and error, and wrestling the boy to the ground who pushed his sister is not necessarily a bad thing. Mom may want to look the other way. He will learn soon enough if he wants to do that again or negotiate.

Headship of the Husband Equals Dying as the Savior Died

We read in Ephesians 5:23: "For the husband is the head of the wife, as Christ also is the head of the church, He Himself being the Savior of the body." God does not call a wife to fulfill the headship role. What woman wants to be the one with the primary responsibility to provide for and protect her husband, and even die for him?

Headship means serving and dying as the Savior died, and this is a male thing. Let me reiterate: headship (*hierarchy*) is felt in a boy as a responsibility, not a right. As Christ acted responsibly as the head of the body, being the Savior, so most men feel like the Christ figure, who must fulfill his duty to protect. A boy desires to be this umbrella of protection out of a sense of honorable duty. He envisions himself as the prince rescuing the damsel in distress. That desire is not a chauvinistic zeal to exercise dominance over a woman. He is light-years away from thinking, *I will treat her like a doormat under my feet.*

Jesus said in John 15:13, "Greater love has no one than this, that one lay down his life for his friends." This idea of laying down one's life runs deep in men.

We saw this God-given desire in our son David displayed during his college days. Sarah recounts:

When we did a Love and Respect Conference in California, near where my son went to college, Emerson and I brought along our daughter, Joy, a senior in high school, who was on spring break. It so happened on that first day, she stayed in the hotel room, catching up on the three hours difference in time. When my son David, Emerson, and I came to her hotel room, we knocked on the door for her to come with us. We could hear the television up very loud, but she did not come to the door. So Emerson knocked again, and she still didn't come to the door. Her room was on the ground floor and had a sliding door to the outside, a garden hotel room. Emerson decided to go around to the side. He saw the sliding door slightly open, but he could not push it open. When he returned, I saw a look of alarm on his face. He turned to David and commanded, "David, you stay here. I'm going to get the manager. If anybody comes through that door, you nail him." I thought, *Whoa! This is serious.* Emerson did not ask me to nail the guy coming out of the room. I wasn't a part of the solution here. I think they knew I'd be praying, but what I saw in my son was this: he put his shoulders back; he didn't say, "No, dad, no, don't make me do that." I mean, he rose to the occasion. And it hit me. This guy is going to take on anyone who runs out of that room. He's going to nail him. Now, if you had said to me when those two kids were little that he would die for his sister, I would not have believed you. But what I saw in him is something designed by God. Well, Emerson went to the manager, who returned to unlock the door to Joy's room. There she slept, dead to the world. She sat up, wondering what all the commotion was about. We were thankful she was alive, but oh what a lesson I learned that day about men being willing to die.

In Aurora, Colorado, a madman entered a theater during a movie and opened fire on the crowd. Three young men threw themselves over their girlfriends and took the bullets. Later the girls walked out of the theater; their boyfriends were carried out—dead. Some female commentators in the media expressed their perplexity over this disproportionate death toll of men to women. That perplexity showed the gradual dimming into darkness for some about the male virtue to protect. This is not to degrade females or argue they lack bravery. Had these girls been mothers with little children, they would have thrown themselves over their kids like mother hens. They would have died. But the pecking order remains: men protect women and children, women protect children, and older children protect younger children. I can tell you this: not one man on the planet found himself perplexed by those guys dying for their girlfriends.

At our conference, I ask, "A murderer enters the home of a father, mother, and three children. He enters to kill one person and then promises to let the others go in exchange for this death. Who dies?" The crowd answers in unison, "The man!"

Many women have confided in me that they pay little attention to this desire in men to protect and die, but when they do honor this desire, it is deeply touching. A female Texas professor who has received many accolades followed my teaching about men needing respect. She incorporated a man's need for respect in her lectures. She wrote:

Yesterday I spoke in Austin for the State Comptroller. After I spoke, one father hung around to visit. His heart is broken because of a wayward son. After discussing it, he said, "I wish women understood just that one word, *respect*." He mumbled something about his son's troubles being partly because of his divorce with the mother. I told him I knew he was an honorable man, and if a terrorist walked in, I knew he would stand between the terrorist and me. He said yes with much conviction and told me he would take the bullet for me. That is so precious to me. I said, "I think your son would too." I encouraged him to tell his son he was proud of him and how he respected him and to try to separate the son's performance from his respect for him.

This intellectual gets it.

Toys and Gun Violence

Step back and observe the types of toys marketed by toy manufacturers. For girls, why did figures like My Little Pony, Barbie, Care Bears, Strawberry Shortcake, and Cabbage Patch Kids keep selling for years? It isn't because moms and dads tell girls to want these endearing figures, but such toys appeal to the nurturing and loving hearts of girls. Boys, on the other hand, lean toward action figures. An object to respect. Toy manufacturers get it! G.I. Joe, Star Wars, and Transformers. An adventure to enter, danger to face bravely, and strength to overcome. Boys long to be the respected character who conquers the foe and saves the innocent. Such a gift appeals to that instinct.

Again I ask, in having a pretend gun, is the little boy combating a foe or manifesting the early signs of a violent and criminal nature?

In his little mind every boy manufactures weapons as he enters combative play. Try as she might to control him by removing all toy guns and swords, one mother I heard about relented. "I give up. At the table this noon he turned his toasted cheese sandwich into a gun and sat there shooting out the window." She could not stop him. It is innate. Then there's the mother at the store I heard about who avoided the aisle with the toy pistols and light sabers, only to have her four-year-old son dart off to that section. When she caught up to him and grabbed him to stop him, he said, "Mommy. You do not like guns. I do like guns. You do not like coming to the guns. I like coming to the guns. Do not come with me."

What is going on in these boys? Some declare this behavior proves a boy's violent nature. But ask the boy, "Do you see yourself as a bad man out to hurt people by shooting them, or do you see yourself as a good man only shooting people who want to hurt innocent people?" He will answer it honorably.

As a mother studies her son more closely, she will see things that heretofore she would have brushed aside as unpleasant male behavior. Now she can value the richness of God's design and honor the desire that drives her son.

Honor and guide your son. With the younger boy, say, "Johnny, I see you want to be strong and to protect the innocent against bad people. I respect that about you." Watch his countenance in response to your Respect-Talk. You will see the Respect Effect. He will stand taller and think more about what is honorable. With the older sixteen- or seventeen-year-old boy, say such things as, "Having you in the home with me while your dad is gone makes me feel secure. I appreciate you." Watch his response.

Honor the Little Things Your Boy Does

Here's how one mom applied Respect-Talk once she realized this truth about her son:

> I've seen the qualities of serving and protecting in my nine-year-old son toward me. When the [Love and Respect] seminar was over, I told my son (as we sat side by side) how honorable he was in coming to the stores with me at night and for waiting until I got into the car first, and I thanked him. He had a big goofy grin on his face, and not only did the same as he always does when I had to go to the store that night, but he opened and closed doors for me too!

Is this tough for you to say to your son? Some have completely missed the masculine soul's declaration, "I wish to take care of you." In the movies when the hero rescues the damsel and vows care of her for the rest of

his life, out come the tissues, but in the halls of academia some of us posture ourselves differently.

When the longing in a boy to be respected and honored for this desire
to provide and protect meets with scoffing in some quarters, it leaves him
feeling bewildered and doubtful about himself. Apart from actually being
pushed down, a boy will have normal doubts. He asks himself, *Will I have
what it takes to be able to provide, to protect, and even die?* As a mother who
loves her boy, you can respectfully answer, "Yes, you will have what it
takes."

Beyond doubt, he will have fears. For example, a preschooler fears
many things. He needs his mom's comfort and protection when he feels
fear. He will not always be the brave warrior. Thunder, animals, and new
people can create apprehension. In no way tease or taunt him by saying, "I
thought you were brave. Are you a scaredy-cat?" Your son needs to experience freedom from ridicule when he shows fear. You need to encourage
him to approach you during those moments without shame. Let him know
that the bravest of men feel fear at times, and that's okay.

Some miss the opportunity to verbally salute the teen boy dead-set on
protecting his aunt, sister, and neighbor during a sudden storm of tornado
potential. He herds them to a place of safety and stays on the lookout until
the threat passes. Some wish to suppress this respect, for fear the vulnerability of the female will undermine her equality with a man; so giving
praise to the son is silenced to prevent the conclusion that a female needs
a male.

Apply G.U.I.D.E.S. to His Hierarchy

Give*: Can I give something to help him provide and protect?*

Younger Boy:

Set aside a space in the utility room for him so he can get a puppy that he
has requested. Assuming he has verbally committed to feeding and caring
for the dog, communicate,

"I believe in you and respect your desire to provide for and protect this dog. You are ready for this. You have what it takes to be responsible."

Older Boy:

Let him know that you are proud of the way he babysits his younger brother and sister while you go on a date with dad. Tell him how blessed you are to know that at fifteen he is capable of protecting them and fixing dinner. Say,

> "You are incredible. Not only are you worth the ten dollars an hour, but also you are such a great influence on your brother and sister who look up to you. Thank you. I respect you."

Understand: *Do I understand his struggle with providing or protecting?*

Younger Boy:

As he becomes responsible for his first goldfish but ends up forgetting to feed it and it dies, what do you say to him? Tell him that you understand why he feels so bad and sad—because deep in his heart, which you respect, he had a desire to provide food for Ernie, his goldfish, and to protect it, but other things distracted him. Let him know that he will learn from this heartbreaking lesson. This loss will motivate him to make sure his next fish is fed every day.

Older Boy:

As he experiences getting laid off from a factory job midsummer when he needed to earn money for college in the fall, understand his feeling that he is unable to provide for himself. Empathize with the manly pressure he feels in the face of this unexpected and costly turn of events. As he deals with this setback, say, "I do not have a solution for you, but as a man you will figure out how to generate this income somehow." Note: men need to be respected for their independence and finding their way. An adult son doesn't need his mother to fix the situation for him.

To better understand what your son feels, recognize how men view each other. A great biblical story is that of David, the future king of Israel, taunting Abner, the soldier responsible for protecting King Saul. David had snuck into a cave as Saul slept and stolen his spear and water jug. He did so to prove he meant no harm to Saul since he could have killed him and become king. In 1 Samuel 26:15, David asks Abner, "Are you not a man?" Ouch! This hit Abner hard. A man guards that for which he is responsible. A man protects, which is a central component of the definition of the word *man*. David called Abner's manhood into question. In the case of your son, he feels compelled to prove himself a man when among men. This is part of his makeup, and as you watch him, you will see this clearly.

Instruct: *Can I instruct him on how to provide and protect?*

Younger Boy:

When he seeks to protect his dog but leaves the gate open for the dog to run away, let him know that you instruct him because you respect him. Make sure he knows that you instruct because you have confidence in who he is becoming as a responsible protector, and the dog's running away provides a great lesson and reminder.

Older Boy:

When he saves his money to buy an old clunker to drive to school, instruct him on his need to purchase insurance to protect himself and others— making sure to impart this information respectfully as one adult to another. Even though he may finagle to have you pay for the insurance, be sure to counter, "Look, you are a responsible and honorable person, and this is a teaching moment to learn about the way expenses add up.

I would not be honoring you by removing these frustrations from you. Responsible people learn about and pay hidden costs."

Discipline: Should I discipline him when he is too uncaring or fearful?

Younger Boy:

"I respect the desire God put in you to provide and protect. I supported your request to buy those gerbils. However, look at their cage. Two days have passed, and you have not cleaned it. Though you gave them food and water, the cage is a mess and smells. A man of honor cares for his animals. Here's the deal. Each time I clean the cage, I take two dollars from your savings. Those gerbils look to you for their survival. They need you."

Older Boy:

"We purchased that four-wheeler so you could ride the trails and back roads. But our deal was that you would service the machine, making sure it was clean, gassed, oiled, and responsibly handled. We saw your maturity and felt you'd protect this investment. Your dad and I went for a ride, only to run out of gas a half mile away from home. We had to walk back to get gas and then back to the four-wheeler. We also noted the right mirror had been shattered, and two of the tires were low. Can I be assured that you will take care of these matters because you wish to honor our agreement, or should we sell it on Craigslist?"

Guard against talking down to your son when disciplining him. A mom wrote:

Until recently, when I would discipline my oldest, I would talk down to him. You may ask yourself, *Did this work?* Obviously not. I was frustrated with the matter and had been praying for an answer on how to understand my son and his needs as a young man. Well, they are not very different from my husband's. He appreciates respect, and his response has been positive and less frustrating to me.

When a mom discerns how her negativity appears and makes an adjustment, her relationship with her boy changes for the better. You do not need to ram home the truth with rudeness. In fact, when he knows you seek to honor his spirit while confronting his misbehavior, he'll stay emotionally available. Soften your words. Truth will carry its own weight.

Encourage: Can I encourage him to keep on providing and protecting?

Younger Boy:

"I know that bully bothers you. Calling you a coward rips your heart apart. I am fully confident that you have the courage to ignore him. I respect your courage. But I also know this kind of thing lights a fire in a boy's belly to learn self-defense. Karate is great exercise, and it makes one strong in self-defense. Would you like to attend a few karate classes? It's a great way to learn how to protect yourself against a bully and to protect others against that bully if need be."

Older Boy:

"The project you created last year in high school to provide a shoe box of needed items to kids in poverty got off to a good start with over a thousand shoe boxes given away. You said last year that you would continue these efforts. But I noticed in the last two weeks when you should be planning to contact various people to donate items that you haven't done anything. I sense you are growing weary in doing good, which the Bible specifically addresses. I respect you and your vision. I know you must sacrifice personal interests for this outreach. But let me encourage you to roll up your sleeves. Here are some pictures and notes from a few of the kids as a reminder that the cause is worthy. This is so honorable."

A boy is a boy. He wants to play, not be the father and husband who provides and protects. However, there are moments when he manifests this masculine desire to provide and protect, and when he does, use Respect-Talk as I suggest with these ages and stages.

Preschoolers (two to four years): "I respect you. When you put on that Superman outfit, I see you protecting the good people from bad people."

School-age children (five to eight years): "I respect you. Today in the rainstorm I told you and your younger brother and sister to run to the house. But you said, 'No, mommy, I need to stay with you and the baby.' Thank you for wanting to protect me."

Tweens (nine to twelve years): "I respect you. I watched you just before you went on that bike ride with your buddies. You checked their tires, made sure the locknuts were tight, and handed everyone a helmet. Your precaution showed me thoughtful leadership."

Young teenagers (thirteen to fifteen years): "I respect you. I heard you defend your friend's sister against that boy's cruel comments about her. You are an honorable young man."

Older teenagers (sixteen to eighteen years): "I respect how you drive. Before you leave, you check the mirrors and gas, and you make sure everyone puts on their seat belts. While driving, you focus on the road rather than engaging in conversation. I feel safe with you."

Young adults (nineteen and older): "I respect your longing to serve in the military. That you wish to serve bravely to protect our freedoms touches me deeply. You are an honorable man. Thank you."

With boys, these kinds of statements do not need to be made every day but at significant moments. These words ring in a boy's ears for a long time. He remembers these comments. He feels energized and motivated by them.

Supplicate: *Do I pray about his providing or protecting?*

Younger Boy:
His kitten ran away. This is a good moment as a mother to pray with your son that God would help you both find the kitten. Though you cannot promise that God will bring the kitten back, you can say to your son,

> "Your sadness reveals to me how much you cared for this kitten and wanted to provide for and protect it. You are an honorable boy."

Older Boy:
As your son realizes he lacks the money for tuition for college, you can let him know that you are praying that God gives him the wisdom to know how to solve his need to provide for his education. Express this respectfully. Do not convey that he needs God because he is incapable of making ends meet.

See the big picture. Many years down the road this instinct in your son to provide and protect will kick in toward you, especially if you become a widow. During those years, your son will detect when others are trying to take advantage of your age. This ability and desire in your son works to your long-term advantage. Nurse it and praise it. Say, "I really respect your desire to protect me."

In earlier centuries women honored the protective and provisional nature of their men. As women in the open range, their survival directly depended on the courage of their men to protect and provide. Women valued this strength and bravery. Today, men still attempt to express this same sentiment, but many women pounce on it as an attempt to keep women pregnant and barefoot. As a mother, do not succumb to that false idea about your boy. He isn't thinking about suppressing women but about being respected as the protector and provider. Your son does not see himself as endowed with a divine right to lord over the family but as entrusted with the divine responsibility to protect the family. He feels called to serve and die as the Savior served and died, but in his younger years he wonders, *Do I have what it takes?* You can speak to that.

7

AUTHORITY

Respecting His Desire to Be Strong and
to Lead and Make Decisions

When we talk about a boy's desire related to authority, what do we mean? He desires to be strong and to lead and make decisions. This can be a good thing or a bad thing.

There is a virtuous component. Deep in his soul he desires to be unbeatable, in command, and resolute. Understandably, he reacts to the charge that he is weak, timid, and indecisive. This strikes at the core of his manhood. Few things stress him out like this.

A man at any age will react strongly to anything that challenges his authority. Authority is a big deal to a boy even if he doesn't know what the word means. Research reveals, "Girls begin to react more to relationship stresses and boys to challenges to their authority."[1]

Preschool Boys

As early as preschool a boy seeks to show his strength, assert rank, command others, defend his territory and possessions, and warn of unpleasant consequences (i.e., threatens). In and of themselves these are not bad things to seek. Parents display such qualities. They assert rank over the kids, command children to do their chores, and warn of unpleasant consequences if they fail to obey.

Regrettably, there is a less-than-virtuous side to a boy's authority. He can exercise authority immaturely toward a sibling or friend or try to flex his muscles against mom.

Anyone dealing with preschool boys and girls regularly recognizes the challenge boys bring to the preschool setting. Primarily, the boys cause the day care workers to pull out their hair. This is not to stereotype girls as "sugar and spice and everything nice" but to evaluate innate patterns between girls and boys.

A kindergarten teacher said,

One of the most common factors among "problem" boys is that they struggle academically. They often resort to bullying, sass, tantrums, power struggles, rebellion, and the like to compensate for this critical shortcoming in the classroom. Too often, we female teachers (and most of us are female at the primary grade levels) resort to loving techniques across the board (to boys and girls), and don't even think about respectful techniques. I found that the boys would respond to the unconditional love I would show but never with as much success as the girls, and it was a tenuous, precarious balance in the relationship. When I read your books, it was like a light went on! I started playing to the strengths of the boys who were particular management problems, using them as examples, and validating them as leaders in certain areas whenever possible. (The girls don't seem to care much about this, interestingly enough. They are content to know I think they did well.)

I love her comment about validating them as leaders. Some feel this validation inappropriately feeds the ego, but I contend that it calls out the honorable man in the boy.

What About His Authoritarianism?

Most everyone agrees that in the early years, boys evidence a greater aggressiveness than girls. A preschooler boy can appear twenty times more aggressive than a girl the same age. For example, a mother will over-hear her son taking a stand against a playmate that sounds like the early stages of a gestapo officer:

"I can beat you up!"
"It's my house, and I get to say what we're going to do!"
"You're not the boss of me!"
"This is mine. You can't have it!"
"I am warning you. Do that again, and I'll punch you!"

Within his tiny domain, he does not see himself as weak, without say, a mere follower, a pushover, or wishy-washy. He sees himself as right and with rights.

This kind of domineering frightens mom since she observes her daughter sweetly negotiating a conflict with her friend. "Why can't he be like my daughter?" Though girls are lippy and sassy, they are less threatening physically. Few declare, "I can beat you up."

In dealing with the overly aggressive boy, a mom must not disrespectfully repudiate or malign his inner sense of authority just because he immaturely applies it at this age. For a mother to deny and denounce this in her young bull is to wave a red flag in his face rather than herd him in the right direction.

In dealing with a boy's authoritarianism, a mother must respectfully keep her husband engaged in the parenting process. Deborah Tannen, in her classic work *Talking from 9 to 5*, has addressed what she calls markers of authority. Men are "taller, more heftily built, with a lower-pitched, more sonorous voice."[2] These markers obviously contrast with women, who are shorter, slighter, with a high-pitched voice.

A son picks up on these markers of authority. He knows. Nature, not political correctness, dictates a boy's belief about his mom and dad—generally speaking. Ask any mother of a teenage boy. This is not to foolishly proclaim that a mother or woman ought not to be respected. She must be. But neither must we unwisely default to the statement, "Women ought to be respected" as though that automatically equalizes the sexes on this matter and changes a teenage boy with hearing mere words. The point is simple: a woman has a greater challenge to appear authoritative, inside and outside the home. Because some women do not want this to be true—that they have less obvious markers of authority—does not make it untrue. It is what it is. That Deborah Tannen promotes the truth that women ought to be respected still differs from the reality of what she calls the markers of authority.

Our nature does not always submit to political correctness or to what people think ought to be. In the case of mom, she needs to be respected in spite of not having the markers of authority that her husband possesses. No one debates that idea. But dad still brings his markers of authority to the teen boy, and mom needs to enlist her husband to back her. Dad is a key factor to countering the authoritarianism in her teen boy and in supporting mom's instruction by using the authority that his teen son recognizes. It is okay to tell dad that his markers of authority are needed. Honor him.

His Sensitivity

As he ages, he is hypersensitive to any one of the following messages:

"You have no power and credibility to influence others."
"You are not strong but weak."
"You lack a commanding manner."
"You have no leadership ability."
"You do not have any special knowledge."
"You couldn't make up your mind if your life depended on it."
"You do not have any right to give directions and make decisions."
"You have no say."

A boy, generally speaking, takes these expressions as an affront to his manhood. These statements threaten him at his core and pain him like few things hurt him. He hears the message: "I find you inadequate and do not respect you." He feels he must defend himself so he fights back. Though he inwardly doubts himself because of the degrading words, he must prove the person got it wrong. He moves into combat mode, unless mom beats him down so far he turns passive and soft.

A girl, generally speaking, hears these comments and eventually turns inward. She might say, "You don't like me. You are rejecting me. You find me unacceptable. Why do you see me as so bad? What have I done so wrong that you would say these things to me?" She feels socially and emotionally disconnected by such statements. She fears where the relationship is headed. Will she be unloved and left alone?

Are there exceptions? Do some girls feel disrespected and fight back, and do some boys turn inward and feel unloved and all alone? Yes. Typically, though, a girl does not stiffen because she does not interpret others as challenging her womanhood but as rejecting her as a person. A boy, however, arches his back at challengers. For a guy, it is less about feeling rejected as a person and more about an attack on his manhood.

Strength and the Holy Word

Young men respond to the appeal to be strong and overcome evil, and mothers ought to use such language with their sons. The apostle of love said in 1 John 2:14, "I have written to you, young men, because you are strong, and the word of God abides in you, and you have overcome the evil one." Instead of saying, "Be nice, and don't do bad things," a mother can lift the language to the heights of John's vocabulary. John uses Respect-Talk. Mom can energize and inspire her son when she shares with him,

> "I see you as strong, not only physically but spiritually. I see you having the power to overcome the bad with your good. God's truth is in you. The Lord be with you."

Though every boy fails, the appeal to be strong calls out that desire God placed within him.

The Bible acknowledges male strength, and every mother needs to accentuate this dimension of her son's personhood. First Corinthians 16:13 says, "Act like men, be strong." This is a significant verse that underscores a male trademark. Suppose two hundred collegiate students, which consisted of one hundred nineteen-year-old women and one hundred nineteen-year-old men, were on a beach for a worship service. If a motorcycle gang of twenty men rode in to disrupt the service, the males would prove to be the perfect fighting specimens. Men are strong, and good men use that strength to protect women and children. Yes, several women may have their black belts and can join in the fray, but worldwide it goes down as I have described. Yet I know of one Bible scholar who wanted to change the translation of 1 Corinthians 16:13 from "act like men, be strong" to "act like people, be strong." In his opinion, women had most of the virtues, and where men had virtues, women needed to be positioned as equal, even if it meant changing the Word of God.

First Kings 2:2 states, "Be strong, therefore, and show yourself a man." The text does not say, "Be strong, therefore, and show yourself a person." First Samuel 4:9 says, "Take courage and be men." It does not read, "Take courage and be women." This was universally recognized and urged whether one lived in Israel or Philistia.

Most powerfully, Proverbs 20:29 states, "The glory of young men is their strength." God spotlights strength as a young man's glory. Can this be said any other way to get our attention? We are talking about a boy's glory when we are talking about his strength. Boys sense this about themselves. Yes, for some it moves into self-centeredness and the beating of the chest, just as a woman with beauty can turn vain. But on the whole, men use their strength to serve others, and we need to admire them for this and honor them.

Though we read of a wife's and mother's strength in Proverbs 31, this is not a reference to her glory. When comparing her strong arms to that of her teen son, there is no comparison.

Research confirms the uniqueness of male strength. For instance, in 2006 research done on hand grip strength found that 90 percent of women produced less force than 95 percent of men.[3] The physiological differences are so drastic it blows the mind. The sample included highly trained female athletes compared to the men, and the strongest female athletes were scarcely above the median grip strength of men.

On a practical level, in a fire, when firefighters must lift and rescue a 280-pound person, few firefighting women can bring that individual to safety. This isn't to put women down but to point out the obvious. Most women are smaller than men, so it takes a stronger man to carry a larger person out of harm's way. Making this personal, when this guy saves your father from a fire, you won't be complaining he is sexist when he said to the female firefighter, "You can't save this guy. I can. I can carry him out over my shoulder. Besides, I know his daughter. She's my friend. I care too much to let him die. I have to go."

The wisest man who ever lived, King Solomon, said it: "The glory of young men is their strength" (Prov. 20:29). We must not disparage but honor this truth.

A mother said, "Just the other day Benji (age six) came to show me his biceps. Funny, none of the girls have ever shown me their biceps." When a son does this, a mom need only say, "I respect you for being so strong." That statement doesn't feed his ego but answers his question at that moment: "Am I strong enough?"

A grandmother shared that she and her husband used Respect-Talk with wonderful results:

After viewing the Love and Respect video, we employed these principles [of respect] on our eight-year-old grandson when he came to visit us for a month last summer. We, and others, saw such changes in him. One thing he said that said it all was the following: "When I came here I wasn't even as strong as my little brother but now look!" He then pulled up his sleeve to reveal his skinny little arm. Even though we could tell no difference, it was his belief in himself to accomplish, to be a worker man, a bull that showed. He was a new person.

The Bible on His Management: Leading and Deciding

Ecclesiastes tells us that "wisdom is better than strength" (9:16). Beyond his physical prowess, a boy has leadership and decision-making desires.

For some in this culture, any mention of headship and management meets with disparagement, but a wise mom knows we are talking about her flesh and blood. We are not sitting in a gender class at a secular university making this point among people obsessed with attacking "headship" as the male's intention to exercise "divine" rights and dominate women. As she reads this book in the quietness of her home with her son doing his homework nearby, mom knows the spirit of her son. He doesn't think about demanding rights but aspires to be an honorable man who acts responsibly. She detects that he feels this as his obligation and call. She knows that he is asking, "Do I have what it takes?" He is not asking, "What can I take?"

Each mother must decide what she believes. Does God call men to manage and chair the household in a way that He does not reveal to women? This does not mean women lack gifts of leadership and administration; God's Word reveals that these gifts are given to various members of the body of Christ (Rom. 12:8; 1 Cor. 12:28). However, do Paul's comments to Timothy capture what every man feels is his duty? We read in 1 Timothy 3:4–5, "He must be one who manages his own household well . . . (but if a man does not know how to manage his own household, how will he take care of the church of God?)" The same is said in 1 Timothy 3:12: deacons of the church "must be . . . good managers of their children and their own households." From the pool of worthy men, elders and deacons are to be selected. A mom must resolve in her own mind, "Did God place this desire in men, for lack of a better way to express it, to be the head manager of the family unit?"

In the Western culture, boys struggle with how to give voice to their desire to lead and make decisions in the family. The pushback from goodwilled feminist voices silences these boys, who instinctively feel a responsibility to oversee their families with their male virtues and strengths. What these boys feel as honorable some castigate as unfair to women. Such chiding cuts him to the core of his being. As he gets older, he silently wonders, *Why do they not recognize who I am? I feel like I should be the leader. Why do they make me feel like I am bad? I see myself responsible to provide, protect, and rescue, and maybe die.* Men struggle with putting a voice and vocabulary to their desires. Most go quiet. Many have self-doubt. But mom's Respect-Talk can motivate and mold him.

Apply G.U.I.D.E.S. to His Authority

Give: Can I give something to help him to be strong, to lead, and to make decisions?

Younger Boy:

Do not be afraid of giving him gifts that can serve as an opportunity to use Respect-Talk. For example, when buying him a light saber, see the advantage of that moment. Comment on Luke's strength of character in *Star Wars.* Say,

> "I really respect Luke's decision to remain a man of honor and not go to the dark side. I present this light saber to you as a sign of your strength to defend the innocent against the dark side. Use this light saber to lead and make decisions that serve the universe."

What a beautiful occasion to capitalize on his honorable imagination instead of flatly interjecting, "Don't hit anybody!" Sadly, some moms miss the moment. She buys her son a light saber for Halloween and hopes her liberal friend does not verbally blast her for turning her son violent.

Older Boy:

Because he mentioned his desire to get stronger, buy him a twenty-five-pound dumbbell to keep in his bedroom. With repetition, a dumbbell will build up his muscles and strength. Help him with healthier eating. Squeeze his muscle and say, "I find it fascinating how God has made men to be strong. You are becoming a man of strength. I respect this about you." But as much as possible, focus on the deeper character quality, not the outer appearance. Say things like,

> "Son, I respect your commitment and discipline to become a man of strength. Women feel secure around a man strong enough to protect her. Though she does not care as much about his raw muscles, she respects his determination to be strong enough to guard her if needed."

Understand: *Do I understand his struggle with being strong, leading, and making decisions?*

Younger Boy:

When he makes a bad decision, such as using the money he saved to buy a cheaper remote control helicopter that crashes and breaks the first day he flies it, tell him that you understand why he is angry and sad. Convey that you respect his desire to make good decisions when buying things he wants. Say,

> "The cheaper helicopter was not your best decision; even so, I respect you because I know this lesson will cause you to become a better decision-maker."

Older Boy:

After signing up for an advanced English class for summer school, he struggles with all that he must do for the course. How do you respond when he calls into question the wisdom of his decision to take the class when he could be hanging out with his friends? Say,

> "I respect your willingness to get ahead academically, to take a hard class, and to worry about your grades as a sign of how conscientious you are. I believe you made an excellent decision, though the easier way out could have been to play video games with your buddies and shoot hoops."

You and your son will have strong disagreements. For instance, he may disagree with curfew. Respectfully listening to his objections is a good thing. Acknowledging his right to have a different opinion is okay and respectful. You can empathize with him, saying, "I understand that you want to stay out later, that you're having fun. If I were in your position, I'd feel the same way." However, respectfully state the reasons you won't change your mind.

> "You need your rest, I do not need to stay up worrying, and nothing good happens after ten p.m. For now, the curfew stays the same time. Of course, if you want to fight me on this, I will gladly change it to nine p.m."

Understanding does not mean acquiescing.

Though he's imperfect, let him know that you value his desire to make good decisions. This is a moment to see his deeper spirit even when he has made a poor choice. Reassure him that your aim is not to be rude or condescending. Many conflicts evaporate when mom understands why her son reacts.

Instruct: *Can I instruct him on how to be strong, to lead, or to make good decisions?*

Younger Boy:

When he makes a decision about immediately spending the money he earned from doing chores to buy candy rather than saving some of it for a future purchase of a skateboard, share with him that you instruct him on decision-making because you respect him. Help him to recognize your instruction as an honorable desire to see him manage his money better so he can gain what he wants.

Older Boy:

Recognize his tendency to overeat, which is leading him to put on extra pounds. Say,

> "A small reminder is in order. Part of being the man of honor means disciplining yourself by controlling the calories. If you are to be strong and fit, which I know you desire to be, you need to exercise harder and eat less sugar and carbs."

When a boy leads poorly, a mother can appeal to her son's sense of honor. She might instruct,

> "Son, you are developing into a man of honor. Permit me to give you input on how to develop more quickly. In this conflict with your brother, I know you believe you are right about this issue, and much of what you said to him is true. But here's the deal. How you said it came across as iron-fisted, as though everyone must stand at attention and salute you as the new dictator on the block. Let me share a couple of insights with you. One, 'Wisdom carries its own weight.' In other words, you don't need a bossy delivery to get your point across. Instead, learn how to be wise in what you say and let the wisdom touch your brother's heart. Two, 'You can be right in what you say but wrong at the top of your voice.' Loudness and screaming undermine your wisdom and being right. I believe God has instilled strength and leadership in you. I believe He has created authority in you. However, when you get really loud with people, they won't hear what you are saying."

When teaching him about his physical strength, you might say,

"I respect you for trying to get your younger brother to do what is right. However, God intends for you to use your power and strength to serve your brother, not threaten him. You don't need to prove that you are big and in control by threatening. Use your strength to help, not hurt people. Might does not make right. When he doesn't respond, come to me. I will help. That's partly why God gave you a mother."

When instructing him concerning leadership, you could remark,

"I appreciate your desire to be a good leader, but barking commands at others doesn't mean you are a good leader. There is a difference between leading and lording. Think about it. What do you feel when they boss you around, especially when you don't want to do what they want?"

As you impart wisdom to him on decision-making, you could convey,

"Use your mental strength to come up with a solution that both of you like. We call it a win-win. It takes some thought, but you have the ability to figure this out. Make decisions democratically—not as a dictator."

Talk to him about his future spiritual leadership and that his wife will long for it. Talk to your son about what it means to be a spiritual leader in the family and what that means to you as a woman. Talk to him about how a wife comes under the umbrella of a husband's authority when she believes he genuinely has placed himself under the umbrella of Christ's authority. Let him know how honorable he is before God when he leads as Christ leads. Talk to him about the power of inviting a wife to pray for a few minutes about the things burdening her heart.

Discipline: Should I discipline him when he is too unruly or bossy?

Younger Boy:

"I respect the man in you. I respect the desire God planted in you to be strong and to lead and to make decisions. However, an eleven-year-old boy should not boss his nine-year-old sister. That's being a dictator. When you ask her to do something, ask her kindly as a gentleman of honor would ask. If she says no, stay cool and drop the matter. You will need to do it yourself, or ask me to help negotiate. If you insist on being in charge, I will put you in charge of cleaning out the garage. When I discipline you, I do not want you to feel bad or embarrassed. I want to help you become the strong and brave man who knows how to deal with people like your sister."

Older Boy:

"Look, you are becoming a man's man, so much so that soon you could join the Marines and fight for your country. However, as a man of honor, you also know that you live under this roof with curfew rules. One reason for curfew is that I cannot stand worrying about you when you are not home when you agreed to be home. Do you intend to dishonor me by violating the family rule on curfew? I don't believe that's your intent, but that's the second time you've violated the rule. So give me the car keys. I am driving you to school this week and bringing you home Monday through Thursday. If you abide by this discipline respectfully, you get the keys back for the weekend."

One mother wrote, unsure about her authority:

I wonder how to balance the authority I need to have as a homeschool mom and the need he has for respect from me. I see that my older son (now twelve) reacts poorly when he is undermined by some comments I make in frustration. I feel as if God is showing me this now so I can raise my son in a loving, respectful environment. . . . It seems as though it is more complicated for mothers raising sons because, eventually, a son will be the head of his own household and will have godly headship over a woman. At this age my son still needs authority, and he clearly needs correction, which creates a small stumbling block for me on occasion, as there is a fine line between authority, correction, and speaking to him respectfully.

This mother must never compromise her authority by coming under his authoritative manner. She is the parent. She must not let her strong-willed boy continually rebel, move from leading into lording, or make self-serving decisions.

Some believe disrespect must accompany discipline, and that's a huge mistake. A mom wrote:

We had four daughters, but a friend, a single mom, has four teenage sons. I see her trying to love, guide, and nurture them, but they are pulling away. I think she is too controlling and not willing to give them the respect they are beginning to crave. When I opened this topic with my friend, she didn't see how she could show respect and maintain discipline as a single mom.

The answer is: she must. Disrespect is not the key to motivating a son to obey. Strong-willed boys will buck a mother when she disciplines them out of contempt for who they are. Males do not submit to disrespectful treatment. This explains why they pull away.

A mom should not be afraid of telling her son that she wishes to speak respectfully when disciplining him.

"Son, I want to say this respectfully to you, and please stop me if I appear disrespectful. But we have rules in this home, such as

putting your dirty clothes in the clothes basket, making your
bed, cleaning the bathroom sink, brushing your teeth before
bed, and getting up for school when your alarm clock goes off.
As you become a man of honor, I need you to obey these rules.
Yes, I know you feel we created some unfair rules. But for now,
you need to follow them. One day you will be out on your own,
but to be a good leader, you need to first learn to be a good
follower."

Being stern is not disrespectful. It's okay to use a tone of voice that lets
your son know you're not okay with his behavior. It isn't okay to yell and
scream to exercise final authority.

As a mother disciplines, she must not say, "I don't respect you."
Instead say, "I don't respect what you just did." She needs to maintain
respect toward the spirit of her son though she feels no respect for what
he did. Remember, a major reason boys react is their perception that
their person and authority are being belittled. The boys know they were
disobedient, but they recoil at the way in which mom delivers her confrontation. A mother will be less effective when she flippantly degrades
what God engendered in her boy. Condemn the behavior, not the boy.
Disrespectful words attack his self-image. And never go over-the-top in
some kind of tirade: "Women are better and smarter than men. Men only
think about themselves. Men only want to get their own way and control
others. Men want to treat women like doormats. Men are power hungry."
This creates havoc in a goodwilled boy's mind.

I loved what a friend of mine, a professional consultant to teachers
of preschool to second grade kids, tells teachers. "You cannot love a boy
into changing his behavior, but you can respect him into it." Obviously,
that is too dogmatic, but the nugget of truth here is a ten-pound piece
of gold.

Boys don't like the phrase "be nice" when it sounds like they are being
asked to act like girls. This won't calm him. A mother and preschool direc-
tor wrote:

We have four children, two boys and two girls. Our boys are in the middle and sixteen months apart. Our boys were arguing, bickering, and annoying each other on purpose around ages nine and ten. (Some might say it was developmental and part of growing up, but it was not consistent with our family's biblical worldview: we are made in His image.) I would remind them to "be nice" or "show kindness," and their actions would change for the moment, but it didn't reach their hearts. As I applied the respect principle to them and said things such as "You aren't showing your brother respect when you _____." Or "You show your friends respect, so you need to extend that same respect to your brother." It was life-changing; it spoke to their hearts. Don't get me wrong, they still have disagreements at thirteen and fourteen, but they are quick to resolve them, and they are best friends.

Don't get discouraged; your strong-willed son has all the qualities of changing the world for good and God. Right now, you are in the process of molding him.

Encourage: Can I encourage him to keep on being strong, leading, and making good decisions?

Younger Boy:

At the fifth percentile in height, he appears so small that people think he is several years younger than he actually is. This discourages him. However, you can begin the message that encourages him to realize that strength is more than just physical size.

"Many great men have been small in stature but compensated by learning to make good decisions and to lead others. As hard as it was to accept what they could not change, they worked on what they could change: their strength of character, mind, and decision-making. The thing I respect about you is that you know this. As painful as this is, the gift that God has given to you is the opportunity to develop abilities that many of your friends will not think about for another twenty years. This sadness can fuel something great in you. Later in life people won't follow someone seven feet tall who does not have leadership ability. People follow leaders, and you can be a leader."

Older Boy:

After deciding to work at a Christian summer camp, he is losing confidence in the decision since he learned of a raise in his tuition for college. Worried about lacking the necessary funds, he has grown discouraged. Typically, a mom tries to soothe him to make him feel better by saying, "Oh, I feel so bad for you, but everything will work out. It always does." I recommend she say,

"In a sense, I am excited for you. You committed to serving others not knowing of these unexpected expenses. This has put your back up against the wall. You did what was right and noble based on the information you had. My experience tells me that God honors a person who asks Him for wisdom on what to do in these circumstances. I am confident God will help you, but I am also confident in your ability to figure out what to do."

With an older boy, mom must let him be independent as a sign of her respect for his maturity and manliness. This can be a precious episode that allows him to feel that you see him as a man. Letting him deal with this on his own does not make you a neglectful and uncaring mother. This frees him to overcome his discouragement with courage. It enables him to discover that he has the ability to overcome this setback.

When verbal encouragement is given, it comes best on the heels of his deflating and losing heart. But those are delicate situations. Before she speaks, she needs to ask herself, *Is what I am about to say going to sound respectful or disrespectful? Is it going to sound to my son as though I am declaring him inadequate and disrespected as a human being, or will it sound honoring to him?*

My friend who is a consultant to early childhood teachers advocates that "it is respectful to believe a boy can be better than he is. So if a boy is acting inappropriately, it is reasonable to say to him, 'That behavior just isn't the real you that is inside you; I expect better things from you' (or words to that effect)."

Affirm his good leadership and decision-making as a way of shaping him. For example:

> Toward a *tween*, say, "I respect your thought process and decision. I heard you say to your younger brother, 'I know there are drugs and smoking and stuff like that, but I am not going to do that kind of stuff. It just leads to trouble.' Wow! That shows your leadership and strength of character."
>
> Toward a *teen*, say, "I respect your ability to make good decisions when you drive and to resist when your friends tell you to 'floor it.' I want to thank you for being your own man. That is not easy when friends want you to prove yourself to be gutsy."
>
> Toward a *young adult*, express, "I respect your decision to go to the community college for two years and then transfer into that Christian liberal arts college. I loved your insight when you said, 'The first two years of college consist of getting your general education classes out of the way, and I can do that for a fraction of the cost at a community college.'"

Supplicate*: Do I pray about his being strong, leading, or making good decisions?*

Younger Boy:

Praying with him, say,

> "Lord, you know Bobby's desire to be strong, physically, and to be a strong, positive influence on his friends. Lord, I respect this and know you will honor this desire in the years ahead."

Older Boy:

Let him know you are praying about his decision as to which university he should attend. Ask him if there is anything he needs insight on or confirmation about, and would he like you to pray for these matters? You can humor him by saying, "Sometimes God answers my requests in the way I've prayed He would, and sometimes He doesn't. But He knows best, and I certainly believe in your future."

When in conflict with older boys, say the following:

"Look, things have heated up here. I am not trying to be disrespectful toward you, and I know you are not trying to be disrespectful toward me. So let's take a five-minute time-out to calm down and pray about this situation, asking God for wisdom. I know He has given you discernment and the ability to figure out what is best. We don't have to agree, but let's discuss this respectfully. You need my respect, and I need your respect. Is that fair? Maybe the Lord will give us wisdom on how to proceed."

Be in the Spirit of God. One mother wrote:

I have been focusing on a few of his strengths and trying not to get wrapped up in a negative cycle of thoughts and anger. He of course feels some comfort from this cycle even if it is negative. He tries to pull me back in with disrespect or disobedience. When I am in the Spirit of God, I can resist or turn away from the tug-of-war. I keep my voice calm and focus on the correction to guide him. There have even been times when the Spirit has prompted me to just give him a big hug. I have seen some major changes within our relationship. I am always thinking about my boys' need for respect, value, and esteem.

Pray for yourself. Ask God to help you be a woman of dignity. Proverbs 31:25 states, "Strength and dignity are her clothing, and she smiles at the future." We read in 1 Timothy 3:11, "Women must likewise be dignified."

⇜

To conclude this chapter, a mother's experience is most fitting. She shared with me the dialogue she had with her seven-year-old son:

> Mom: I respect you.
> Son: (half of a charitable grin)
> Mom: Do you know what that means?
> Son: (quick side-to-side shake of head, meaning no)
> Mom: Well, it means I'm proud of you, and I think you're honorable, and I think you are a strong man.
> Son: (sitting up straighter with a sheepish grin) Thanks, mom.
> Mom: Which do you like to hear more? That I'm proud of you and think you are a strong man, or that I love you?
> Son: Proud and strong.

This mother closed her letter by observing: "This teaching on mothers respecting their sons has been lost. I pray that as I begin to focus on it, my sons will be raised without any confusion regarding who they were designed to be."

8

INSIGHT

Respecting His Desire to Analyze, Solve, and Counsel

What Is the Issue Related to a Boy's Insight?

I love this mother's shrewdness about soliciting her sons' insights, counsel, and solutions:

> When my sons were teens, they loved being asked their opinions—especially when I listened to them and affirmed their insights about things, like:
>
> "What do you think about what the pastor had to say today?"
>
> "I need a new cell phone. Would you have time to do some research and then make some recommendations?"
>
> "I can't decide which of these vacation pictures to keep. Would you help me?"
>
> "I'd like some new music for my MP3 player. Can you recommend something you think I would like?"
>
> "Did you read the article in the paper about the new bridge? What do you think about the city's plan?"

I see another mother's astuteness when she asks for her son's advice on how she should paint. "While painting a wall in the den, our eleven-year-old told me how to get smooth brushstrokes using a special technique. Well, since I've been painting for years, this was not news to me, but again this was an opportunity for me to respect his input and thank him for his help."

A boy desires to offer his insight. Insight refers to his inclination (not always his ability) to analyze, solve, and counsel. When was the last time you honored your son's insights? I ask this because sometimes when a boy offers his insight, he does so in a pushy manner and thereby does not receive an open-armed reception to his ideas. He may be rejected and disrespected for his input. The tension that swirls around the conversation causes a frustrated mom to miss an opportunity to use Respect-Talk. Because she feels compelled to correct him for how he spoke, she puts on the back burner the answers he put forward. She brushes aside his analysis. A mom ends up obsessing over the poor interpersonal traits she sees in her son while failing to notice the positive perspective he advances.

His Solution-Orientation

A mom wrote to me about an incident that occurred just after she had attended a Love and Respect Conference. Her daughter, age ten, and son, age twelve, had gotten into an argument in the car after the son, with a helpful demeanor, attempted to answer a question the daughter had directed at her mother. The daughter flat out rejected his offer. She blurted out, "I asked mom!" The mother commented, "I had never noticed such disrespect coming from my daughter." The boy, huffy at not being heard, shut down and moved to the back of the van. The mother wrote that, normally, she would have told her son to get himself together, but that this time she gave him a few minutes of silence and then asked her daughter to apologize for snapping at her brother. A few minutes later the mom asked him if he could answer his sister's question, and he happily did so.

This kind of episode can be tough for a mom. Sometimes when a boy offers his insights to a family member, such as a younger sister, tempers flare because no one has asked for his commentary. Mom centers her attention on how the boy acts rather than on what the boy says. The boy feels hurt, frustrated, and angry when his ideas meet with disrespect, and the mother pays more attention to his reaction than to what triggered his reaction.

However, if mom can keep in mind that boys lean toward the analytical side and help by offering answers, it makes it easier for her to better understand her son. It helps her see why he speaks the way he does—because he is solution-oriented. It aids her in discerning why he negatively reacts when his helpfulness is not valued.

Not Wrong, Just Different

Women are more empathy-oriented than their husbands and sons. A woman may empathize with a sad person who has a problem in order to ease the sadness. Her son and husband, on the other hand, try to solve the sad person's problem in order to ease the sadness. The virtue in all of this is that he thinks about remedies when it comes to the concerns of other people.

My friend Shaunti Feldhahn reported to me personally that though wives yearn for emotional support during hurtful situations, her research shows that 80 percent of them readily acknowledged that the advice their husbands offered was good. Men have good solutions. I share with women, "Why not say at that moment, 'That's a great insight and a solution, but right now, I just need a listening ear. I will feel better after I share what burdens me. In many cases I know what I should do.'" Unfortunately, some wives yell, "Quit trying to fix me!"

Your son will offer advice to others in the same fashion. He seeks to help. At such a moment, thank him and then share respectfully, "Right now, your sister just needs a listening ear." No need to show contempt. He is doing what God designed boys to do.

Are Boys Always Sensible?

In effect, mothers have said to me,

> Emerson, I just want my boy to think! He needs to think smarter about his tasks, think wiser about his choices, think kinder about people, and think cleaner about jokes. He needs to think before talking, before jumping, before throwing the ball at the ceiling fan, before coming down to breakfast with a plaid shirt and plaid pants on, before putting play dough in the microwave, before using a garbage bag as a parachute, before speeding the car down the neighborhood street, before listening to his friends dare him to drink . . .

I concur. The Bible states in Proverbs 7:7, "I saw among the naive, and discerned among the youths a young man lacking sense." For this reason, a mom must act on Titus 2:6, which says, "Urge the young men to be sensible." Young men are not always sensible. A mom needs to implore her boy to be practical, realistic, reasonable, logical, balanced, levelheaded, thoughtful, and wise.

From the folklore of the word *sophomore*, many see a compound word that means "wise fool." A boy goes in a nanosecond from wise to brain-dead. The *sophy* part means "wise," from which we get *sophisticated*. Others contend that *moros* means "stupid," or "foolish," the root for the word *moron*.[1] This captures the sixteen-year-old. On Monday a sixteen-year-old boy demonstrates a sophisticated wisdom beyond his years, but on Tuesday he borders on moronic behavior that a five-year-old would not entertain. Boys frustrate us, as does the drama of a teen daughter.

Certainly mom must never respect foolishness. Proverbs 26:8 remarks, "Like one who binds a stone in a sling, so is he who gives honor to a fool." And Proverbs 26:1: "Like snow in summer and like rain in harvest, so honor is not fitting for a fool."

But mom must keep looking for the *sophy* amid the *moros*. Honoring him for *sophy* can limit his *moros*. When he is wise and insightful, she must verbally honor him. Proverbs 12:8 says, "A man will be praised according to his insight." Mom needs to praise what she can.

Can Mom Overreact?

A boy's foolishness can cause mom to become too negative. If she becomes too critical and complains about her son's inadequacies, she can fail to see his good thinking. If she gives way to a contentious and vexed manner that feels disrespectful to him, she could shut him down and lose his heart. A mom shared:

> If my son does something that is not worthy of respect, I can quickly fall into this trap of disappointment and even the disdain that you talk about. It then gives me a feeling of, *Oh, he might never change*. Then I feel like a bad mom because I feel indirectly that his behavior is somehow my fault or reflects on me. . . . After this, I probably give off this attitude of disappointment, and I know only too well that my son can tell. The very hardest thing then is to see your son defeated and down. . . . As you have pointed out, we practice and look for ways to love, but maybe more importantly we should be looking for opportunities/ways to respect our sons.

Proverbs 21:19, which we quoted earlier, in chapter 3, says, "It is better to live in a desert land than with a contentious and vexing woman." This verse refers to a woman in the home. Some restrict it to the wife, but it can include the mother. That God calls women to refrain from contention and vexing suggests that some women habitually take issue with what they see as wrong—that's their bent. Instead of exercising a more disciplined quietness, refraining from negative and emotional comments, she moves aggressively to complain and criticize. The word *vexing* refers to how she makes others feel—annoyed, frustrated, and angry. The word *contentious* means given to arguing or provoking arguments. In the case of a mother and son, a mom can provoke her son to anger by blasting him as insensitive and uncaring when truthfully he attempted to be wise in his input.

A mom may feel he is insensitive in the way he treats his sister, but it does not mean he is uncaring. It also does not mean that he is wrong. Some moms severely judge the boy as uncaring when quite often he offers answers with solutions because he cares. He merely does not approach it in the way mom would approach it.

Controlling Negativity and Unfriendliness

Mothers readily confess the intense negativity that overcomes them within the home, particularly toward a boy. Mothers tell me that they are more upset over what their son does wrong than happy over what he does right. After all, he is *supposed to* do what is right, so why celebrate that? However, he is not supposed to do wrong, and that needs confronting—right now, and with sadness.

I invite every mother to consider her initial reactions to her son when he is wise and when he is foolish. Does she fixate more on her son's missteps than on his good insights? Does she come at him negatively when he lacks sense but says very little positively when he makes perfect sense? Does she need to pull back from her gloom-and-doom attitude? Because a mother nurtures, she cares about her son's mistakes. If not watchful about her care, she can focus on his shortfalls and overlook opportunities to show respect for his insight. Maybe this is why she needs older women to encourage her to be friendlier in the home (Titus 2:4). The Greek word for love in this scripture is *phileo*, not *agape*. In other words, like the city of brotherly love, Philadelphia, a mother needs to be more brotherly or friendly. Firm but friendly.

As a boy ages, a mother must not remain the helicopter mom she probably was when her son was younger. When he was a tot, she needed to hover over him and control him so he'd not run into a busy street. But as the boy ages, she must transition from controlling, to counseling, to casting off.

I received an e-mail from a helicopter mom of an older son. She continued to hover over him in fear, swooping in to try to change whatever she saw as substandard in him. She had her expectations of what she wanted her boy to look like and focused on what she'd like to change in him. Unfortunately, she ignored all the amazingly good things. Predictably, as she kept up her hovering, her boy spent less and less time at home when given the chance to stay away. Home reminded him of all the ways he was not measuring up in his mother's eyes. Though the helicopter mom's motives were good, they were counterproductive in getting the results she wanted—a happy, close family.

I had a female counselor evaluate a helicopter mom who had a seventeen-year-old and a nineteen-year-old. The situation was filled with incredible goodness, but mom didn't see it. Both sons were dating strong Christian girls, but mom said one girlfriend was too quiet, and she worried that they didn't spend much time socializing with others. The other son had chosen to work in the family business, was baptized, and had given his testimony publicly a few months earlier, but mom focused in on the fact that he didn't go to college, was too transparent about his anxiety, and complained about his audacity to move out on his own at the age of nineteen.

What did this counselor recommend? "I would encourage her to make a list of all of their good qualities and decisions and thank the Lord each day for them. She needs to reframe these incidents as a compliment to how she (and her husband) raised them. Her son, who admits to being anxious, had the courage to move out to be on his own, despite his anxiety. (Could his mother's own anxiety be affecting him? Perhaps he knew he needed to get out of that environment.) They are right on target, doing the things that are age-appropriate for them to do. Does she really want her sons to remain living at home as adults? Dependent on their parents?"

Okay, mom, let's shift our sights to the positive, if you have not done so. Here are some suggestions on positive Respect-Talk. Ready?

Apply G.U.I.D.E.S. to His Insight

Give: *Can I give something to help him analyze, solve, and counsel?*

Younger Boy:

Invest in Dave Ramsey's materials for kids on how to manage money well. Let him know that you respect his ability to think about money—how to save it, spend it, and share it.

Older Boy:

Buy the DVD gift set called *The Graduate's Survival Guide* by Dave Ramsey, which prepares him for his experiences at college. Say,

> "I respect how you analyze information and use your findings to solve problems. I want to give you these resources to broaden that ability along financial lines."

Honoring your son by investing financially in those things that sharpen his thinking skills is well worth it. Our grandson Jackson, four years old, enjoys doing mazes, so Jonathan and Sarah purchase books with mazes. This develops his ability to navigate. He thinks in terms of beginning and end.

What a great thing for mom to think about using her resources to develop his problem-solving ability. A plethora of materials exist that shape the thinking skills and problem-solving abilities in a boy. Go on the internet and look for items based on the age of your boy. Purchasing these things can prove exciting and worthwhile.

Understand: *Do I understand his struggle with analyzing, solving, or counseling?*

Younger Boy:

When he gets his math problems wrong after much effort to solve them, do you tell him you understand and respect why he is angry and exasperated? Do you respond with,

> "I respect your desire to analyze and solve the math problems.
> I respect your desire to do well and figure things out. I can only imagine how frustrating this is"?

Older Boy:

Do you understand his struggle in knowing what to say to his girlfriend who just lost her grandfather to cancer? Do you say,

> "Sometimes there is nothing we can say, and the most loving and honorable thing to do is just listen and let them know you'll be praying. You did that, and I respect this"?

Maybe the concept of understanding his insight means just listening. God calls women to exercise the discipline of quietness in a way that He does not call men (1 Tim. 2:11–12). We read in 1 Peter 3:4, "But let it be the hidden person of the heart, with the imperishable quality of a gentle and quiet spirit, which is precious in the sight of God." This is not a sexist comment but a word of caution to protect mom in the home from speaking too quickly, too much, or too one-sidedly. A mother's impulsive love prompts her to speak to a situation that troubles her. That can be a good thing, but sometimes she speaks solely on what she sees as a woman rather than seeking to understand her son. Proverbs 18:13 says, "He who gives an answer before he hears, it is folly and shame to him."

Because a mother nurtures, she can make a mistake of mothering a son in such a way that when she corrects the son to be more insightful and loving, the son hears disrespect. A mother wrote, "He was voicing some prejudices against certain people groups. I responded by trying to show him a better way, a way of love, which I have now learned was a lack of respect toward him and his ideas. He shut me out for a long time." Instead of impulsive love that corrects the boy, why not refrain from making statements and ask questions such as, "Tell me your observations on these folks. Why do you feel the way you do? How have they hurt and dishonored you?" When mom does express her concerns, she must ask herself, before she speaks, *Is that which I am about to say going to be truthful, necessary, and/or respectful?*

Seeking to understand his opinion does not mean you agree or change what you say or do. It just means that you acknowledge his right to have an opinion of his own. Say,

> "I respect that you are seriously thinking about this problem and feel strongly about the remedy."

Though the busyness of life distracts you, listen to your son's opinions as best as you can. When you hear his thoughts, he feels esteemed. When you echo what he mouthed, many times he relaxes, especially if he was too intense about his opinion. Or perhaps he can even correct you if what you understood isn't what he meant.

Instruct: *Can I instruct him on how to analyze, solve, or counsel?*

Younger Boy:

When he insensitively blurts out solutions to his sister who has asked you a question, respond with respect. Instruct him to ask his sister if she wants to hear his answer since she asked you, not him. At the same time make sure you acknowledge and honor his goodwilled efforts to help his sister.

Older Boy:

When his friends invite him over to their home on the weekend and you know their parents are gone, say to him,

> "You and I both know this isn't just a social time. It will entail enticements. As a man of honor, I cannot control you 24/7. At a certain level God calls me to trust and respect your choices. But

a good rule of thumb is to decline those invitations and have the courage to take their mocking on the chin. Also, in these situations, I recommend coming up with a more enjoyable activity for yourself. What if I gave you some extra cash to take your brother to the baseball game this weekend?"

You can help your son see himself as a problem solver by asking questions. Why give your son the answer when you can give him the opportunity to figure it out? "What idea do you have? What do you think?" Affirm his thought process. Ask him for several ideas, not just one. Don't put him down if he is wrong, but ask, "Why do you think that?" You can always ask, "Is there some place else that we can get more information on this?" You can help your son think ahead. "If we do such and such, what do you think will take place? Can you predict what might happen?"

A consultant to schoolteachers said to me, "When I talk to teachers who seem to be successful with boys they (1) expect a lot of the boys; (2) communicate the belief that the boy has it within him to figure it out." He continued, "One of the things I have learned about problem solving with boys and girls (and probably men and women) is this: if you don't address the feelings of the girl before offering a solution to a problem, your solution won't have validity with her. If you don't ask a boy for a solution before offering a solution, your solution won't have validity. The reverse doesn't seem to work (boy with feeling, girl with solution)."

What if he blurts out, "Mom, that's wrong"? Will you receive his truthful insight or feel offended? What if he exclaims, "Mom, you need to chill out"? Will you take offense? Will you listen to him when he says, "Mom, you expect us to jump through too many hoops. You want everything and everyone to be perfect"? Will you receive his assessment as valid if it is valid?

Sarah tells of the time that Jonathan said, "Face it, mom. You wanted a perfect family and didn't get it." That spoke to her heart. She did not expect perfection but realized how she appeared to Jonathan. As tough as this is, as a mother models teachability, it returns a huge favor to her. She can appeal to her son to follow her example:

> "Just as you pointed out things about me that I needed to face, as a man of honor do you have the inner toughness to hear about a few things I see you doing that do not represent the real you?"

Recognize that he can counsel everyone in the family but fail to heed his own counsel. That's true for most of us. All of us know more than we do. It is a piece of cake to tell others we know what they ought to do. So a mom needs to give her son some grace when she finds herself miffed at his critical comments about others while conveniently looking past his gaffes.

Boys need instruction even though they claim to know everything. Mom must still instruct. She can say,

> "I respect that you feel you know what to do. I respect that you want to do things on your own. That's a good thing. But let me tell you a secret. No one knows everything. We are a team and need to listen to the suggestions we offer each other. In the long run, this makes us smarter, happier, and better."

Discipline: Should I discipline him when he is too unteachable or foolish?

Younger Boy:

> "I respect the desire God instilled in you to see our shortcomings as a family. Yes, your older sister had a meltdown that she should not have had, and I left the hamburgers unattended, and they burned to a crisp. I appreciate your critique. But need I remind you that you failed to do the dishes last night, you let the bathroom sink overflow, and you did not pick up your wet towels? As an

honorable man, you need to learn a proverb: 'he who lives in a glass house must not throw stones.' I think it would be respectful of you to be more teachable before you offer us counsel. So tonight you will do the dishes even though it is your night off, and do not instruct me on how unfair I am, or I will find more for you to do."

Older Boy:

"We all have moments of anger. Anger can be a good thing. I respect that you get angry over injustice and dishonor. But sometimes you get bent out of shape over not getting your way. This is not a matter of injustice or dishonor. That your basketball uniform had not been washed does not justify a senior in high school driving off foolishly and in a fit of rage. If you hit a child, you could be sitting in a jail cell for manslaughter. So you will lose a week of driving privileges, and this weekend you are grounded to do nothing but work. You are an honorable young man, but this was conduct unbecoming of the wisdom I see in you."

When a boy is foolish and unteachable, mom's tone and look must not be contemptuous. It is ineffective. A mother told me,

It was this suggestion to relate respect to our love for our sons that first turned my heart in this area. I was able to see how my little boys would hear contempt instead of correction when I would reprimand them firmly. When I was harsh with them in my voice and facial expressions, they became immediately focused on whether or not mommy still loved them rather than the issue I wanted addressed. When I eliminated the harshness in my voice and was careful to communicate my concern about their behavior, with respect in my eyes and kindness in my voice, there were no more tears and meltdowns in response. They simply corrected their behavior. Miraculous!

Start with a respectful statement when disciplining. A teacher wrote:

For years I knew I was not giving the boys I was teaching what they needed. But now, suddenly, I have a new tool to use in the classroom: respect. I get very positive responses from my teenage male students now, even when I have to discipline them. I always try to start with a respect statement like, "I want you to know that I really respect your competitive nature and the confidence you have in your own abilities." Then when I have to correct a behavior, they are so much more responsive.

In disciplining your son for being foolish or unteachable, listen to this school consultant. He told me,

I do have one theory that seems to bear up in practice. . . . For discipline, it is better to give boys a job than to take away a privilege. My theory is that giving a boy a job (think five-year-old boy in this case) is a statement of respect. "I believe in your ability to do something valuable." I also encourage teachers to give the boy a job that he can do with the teacher. Most of the boys who seem to drive teachers nuts will get an ADD or ADHD diagnosis sooner or later and, consequently, have probably not bonded well with adults. So the do-the-job-with-me assignment in effect says, "I respect you enough to trust you with responsibility, and I like you enough to invite you to work with me (shoulder-to-shoulder friendship)."

I recommend doing a job that demands that you solve a problem. "We have these logs in the backyard that we need to get to the garage. What is the best way to do this?" He is being disciplined by also solving a problem.

Are you reacting disrespectfully to what appears as open defiance when it is nothing more than his inability to solve a problem and fulfill your expectation to think like an adult? You may need to consider carefully what reasonable expectations are—if it's within reason for a child to figure out some problem or to have the attention span to do so. Mom's negative and disrespectful reaction won't remedy the child's immaturity.

Encourage: *Can I encourage him to keep on analyzing, solving, or counseling?*

Younger Boy:

Noticing your son's perfectionist tendencies, you observe how this leads to intense frustration when he tries to figure out complicated puzzle mazes. Earlier you'd say, "Get a grip, this is no big deal!" Now you voice,

> "I respect your desire to solve problems. You work hard at analyzing these mazes. Though I want you to control your temper, I applaud your determination to take the correct path and find the proper end. Men of honor work hard at taking the right path."

Older Boy:

He calls home in the early summer from the Christian camp where he serves as a counselor. He tells you that he feels inadequate to know how to lead someone to Christ. He wants to be a good counselor who rightly divides the Word but feels discouraged. A couple of teens said they were not ready to receive Christ. Encourage him with,

> "Honey, my read is that they fully grasped the gospel message you presented, which is why they want to wait. They clearly understand that they must ask Christ to forgive them personally and then surrender themselves to Him. Many times over the years women have said to me, 'I am not ready.' I did not conclude I was unclear. Let me encourage you to ask them how they are doing, and what they heard you say to them. Tell them this would help you grow as a counselor."

Mom must thoughtfully balance her comments:

"Son, what you said was quite true. I respect your honesty, insights, and desire to help. Thank you. But earlier, when you got angry at your sister, you almost shut us down so that we did not value your insight. At such moments, I recommend saying to your sister, 'I think I know the answer. If you are interested, I could share what I think.' This allows her to invite your insights and will probably meet with a calmer heart. Yes, she should have welcomed your input, and did apologize, but this could make it easier next time. Let me encourage you to act this way toward your sister. Thanks for listening to me. I respect that about you."

God has enabled mothers with the ability to pepper their soft rebukes with language that honors their boys. A mom has the verbal aptitude to applaud her boy's insight and truth-telling while helping him to calm down and to be more patient, kind, and loving. But she must recognize the level of disrespect that comes hurling at him when she does not filter the exchange as he does. She sees pink while he sees blue. He desires respect for his ideas and gets angry when rejected. His whole desire to help by contributing eye-opening information flies out the van window.

Consider ways to affirm and encourage a boy with Respect-Talk:

Preschoolers (two to four years): "I respect the many things you know in that brain of yours. You know your colors and when something is the same or different, you can count, you know your shapes, you can do puzzles, and so much more. You also know how to cooperate with other people and take turns."

School-age children (five to eight years): "I respect something about you that I see changing. You used to say, 'I never get anything right.' I hear that less. You realize that lacking insight in one area on a board game, for instance, doesn't mean you lack all knowledge about the board game. You have a lot of insight and knowledge. None of us knows everything about everything. The key is to keep learning as best we can, and I see you trying to do that and I respect that about you."

Tweens (nine to twelve years): "I respect the way you are thinking. For instance, the other day as I listened to you talk about what you might do this summer while mom and dad are traveling the last two weeks in June, you offered several options about what you could do. What I respected was the way you looked at the pros and cons of each before making your decision. Any of them would have been good, but I liked how you decided what would be best for you and others."

Young teenagers (thirteen to fifteen years): "Wow, what you said is a great solution to the problem. I really respect what you stated. But I think the first solution for your younger sister is to hear from her brother that he cares about her sad heart. She needs his support right now. But, yes, what you said is very insightful. Thanks."

Older teenagers (sixteen to eighteen years): "I respect you for pointing out information to me that I did not know when driving. Foolish me. I did not know about getting in the far lane when passing a police officer who has pulled someone over. Thanks! You just saved me from getting a ticket."

Young adults (nineteen and older): "I respect your insight that you have about relationships. You said something very profound that I never thought about. 'All of us are focused on trying to find the right person, instead of focusing on trying to be the right person.' Wow! Brilliant."

A lady from Michigan shared how she'd been at a coffee shop with her sixteen-year-old niece and eighteen-year-old nephew. The niece was going on about something, and the nephew spoke up and said, "Is this something you want me to fix, or are you just talking?" She said, "Oh, I am just talking." So he sat back in his chair and listened but didn't say anything. The aunt said she was so impressed with how they had picked up on the Love and Respect message from their parents. As much as this aunt found refreshment in this episode, what I find curious is that this aunt said nothing to her nephew. There was no Respect-Talk to him. No one praised him for his insightful response to his sister.

Supplicate*: Do I pray about his analyzing, solving, or counseling?*

Younger Boy:

Pray with him about figuring out if he should play peewee football or join the community soccer league. Let him know that God wants us to pray about everything. Let him know, though, he is free to choose either sport but that you respect his wish to ask God. Tell him that is honorable.

Older Boy:

Your young adult son says he doesn't know if he loves Jesus. Having joined the army, he candidly tells you about his doubts in trying to resolve his faith. That kind of comment hurts a mother. You need to respond with,

> "As much as that comment weighs on me and makes me very sad,
> I applaud your honesty with me. Honesty about what one believes
> about Jesus has to come first. As you know, there are many who
> pretend to believe, but they are not honest like you. You refuse
> to be a hypocrite as you analyze what is true. As you know, I will
> pray for God's favor to come to you."

As you pray for your son and apply G.U.I.D.E.S., I want you to consider Eve. First Timothy 2:14 says, "And it was not Adam who was deceived, but the woman being deceived, fell into transgression."

Why was Eve deceived? Eve had Paradise but wanted more. Some refer to this as the insatiability of the female. The female is never satisfied.

Though God created Eve perfectly in His image, she craved to be more "like God" (Gen. 3:5).

Eve longed for more goodness than the goodness of Paradise and yearned for more wisdom beyond the wisdom of Paradise. We read in Genesis 3:6, "When the woman saw that the fruit of the tree was good for food and pleasing to the eye, and also desirable for gaining wisdom, she took some and ate it. She also gave some to her husband, who was with her, and he ate it" (NIV).

Ironically, the deception revolves around what is good, what is wise, and what is godlike. In her thinking, what's wrong with wanting to be like God and enjoy more goodness and wisdom? Because these things mattered to her, she became aggressive and intentional to gain them. No one interprets Eve as a doormat or a milquetoast.

How in the world does this apply to mothers? Most Christian women want to be godlike—good and wise. They intend the same for their husbands and children. This attitude surfaces when we hear women confess, "When I am honest with myself, I want a perfect marriage and a perfect family. Truth be told, I want everyone to be like me. If everyone was like me, we'd all be happy."

Such a mother knows perfection is not possible, but she refuses to believe imperfection should be allowed, and she won't allow it. Her husband must stop his imperfections. Her children must cease their imperfections. They are wrong.

In her favor, I believe God allowed the residual of Paradise to remain within a woman's heart. Something within her as a woman feels an idealism about what is good, wise, pleasing, and godlike. When the family does not align with this ideal, she aggressively mothers each person until each changes into someone who is good, wise, pleasing to the eyes, and godlike—as compared to her.

Unfortunately, for example, sons do not adjust as they ought or as quickly as they should. Therefore, to help achieve her idealism, she complains, criticizes, controls, and even coerces her boy. As loving and nurturing as she is, she gives way to another side of her femininity that uses ineffective methods. When her son does not change to her ideal, she becomes unfriendly and contemptuous. She uses the Disrespect Effect, referenced earlier in this book.

Though she does not expect perfection beyond the perfection of Paradise, as Eve did, this mother wants perfection in an imperfect world, and therein lies the problem. At that juncture she is slightly deceived. Though Jesus died on the cross to save the world from this sinful predicament, some mothers do not accept this biblical worldview that all are fallen and will never be perfect (Rom. 3:23). For instance, such a mother subscribes to the idea that her son is a clean slate for her to write upon. She says, "Be like me. Do it my way. Now!" When he fails her standard of perfection, she complains, contends, and shows contempt.

Is this how all mothers are? No. Many mothers recognize this propensity of insatiability. She is learning to balance the ideals she has for her boy to be godlike against sin with the ideals she has for herself to be godlike in extending grace and forgiveness when he gives in to sin.

How can a mother know if she has achieved this balance? She never uses disrespect toward her son. When jarred by her son's shortcomings and sin, she refuses to up the ante by denouncing him with contempt for not being perfect. She has no right to do that. When he fails to live according to the virtues of C.H.A.I.R.S. by failing to analyze correctly, solve problems prudently, and counsel wisely, she holds back from adopting the Disrespect Effect. The good news is that when she displays a respectful demeanor when correcting his imperfections, she'll best achieve balance.

9

RELATIONSHIP

Respecting His Desire for a Shoulder-to-Shoulder Friendship

"Can We Please Stop Talking Now?"

Many mothers write me when their boys turn four. They share stories like the following and wonder what is happening to their precious baby:

> After attending the conference and having a sitter come and stay with our two kids (a twelve-year-old girl and a four-year-old terrorist), I was asking Johnny what he did with the sitter. Did you play games? Yes, mom. What were they? Hiding games. What did you hide? Toys. What kind of toys? My toys. Did Sissy play too? Yes, mom. Did you find all of the toys? Yes, mom . . . can we please stop talking now?

More than a few mothers have heard from their sons, "Can we please stop talking now?" What gives with these boys? As males, boys talk less about the topics moms wish to discuss. Interestingly, because a mother needs to envision what happened, she needs information. To gain the particulars, she must ask questions. But replaying the events for her isn't a felt need in the boy, only in her. He is ready to move on to the next activity. Why talk about the past?

Though some boys talk all the time, as with some husbands, the pattern from research on males in the family reveals a different tale. Most remain quieter when peppered with questions from moms. Whereas moms themselves readily engage such questions—appreciatively and energetically—they find themselves discombobulated in the face of their sons' cantankerousness when feeling barraged by her questions.

When our son David was in the fifth grade, both Sarah and I struggled to understand his disinterest in talking to us and sharing his heart so we could give him all kinds of wonderful advice and wisdom. Sarah recalls picking him up from the first day of school and asking, "How was your day?"

"Good."

"What did you do?"

"Nothing."

"Anything exciting happen?"

"No."

On the second day of school it was more of the same.

"David, how was your day?"

"Good."

"What did you do?"

"Nothing."

"Anything exciting happen?"

"Nah."

Third day: "David, how was your day? Anything exciting?"

"No . . ."

On the fourth day David looked at his mother and said gently but firmly, "Mom, I am going to say something. It's the same every day. If anything changes, I'll let you know." So she decided to cut down the twenty questions routine but would still try, from time to time, to draw out our son and get him to talk—to little avail.

She would say to me now and then, "I just don't understand David.

He won't talk to me the way I want him to talk." At that time we had not clearly zeroed in on how male and female children talk with parents. For example, females generally talk about their feelings more frequently than most males, including such topics as how they felt about their day. From my observations this behavior starts very young. Sons typically do not remember play-by-play conversations and experiences and therefore do not eagerly share them as often as daughters do. It was perfectly normal for Sarah to ask, "How was your day?" and it was perfectly normal for David not to want to talk about it. As Sarah often says, she wishes she had learned this in the fifth grade—David's fifth grade, of course.

Later, as David reached his teens and we were teaching Love and Respect principles in marriage conferences, Sarah found that a key to bonding with your son is not to confront him with direct questions but just to be with him doing some activity he enjoys, shoulder-to-shoulder.

Just be with them . . . and talk less!

Shoulder-to-Shoulder, Without Talking

When mom aggressively pursues her son to talk about his feelings face-to-face, she is like the north end of a magnet moving toward the north end of her son's magnet. Even though she is positive (+) and he is positive (+), she ends up repelling him. This is a law of interpersonal physics between mother and son. However, when she approaches him in a way that feels less than positive to her, she attracts him.

The answer is shoulder-to-shoulder time without talking. Of course, that comment mystifies some moms, leaving them staring at you, like deer in the headlights. She feels clueless and uncomfortable. Even when she applies shoulder-to-shoulder time without talking, it still feels counterintuitive and countercultural.

An essential belief in a woman is that heart-to-heart connection comes from talking about what happened during the week related to the relational stresses. The giving of the report creates rapport. The dictionary defines *rapport* as "a close and harmonious relationship in which the people or groups concerned understand each other's feelings or ideas and communicate well."[1] This is what mothers wish to do with their sons. To mothers, not communicating prevents understanding and closeness. Mom feels distant and isolated from her son. The lack of connection distresses her. This is why she wants to say to her son, "We need to talk." But she knows that is too direct, so she asks questions. Sarah refers to this as "mother's twenty questions." To mom's credit, she sees her questions as sensitive. In her mind, she is not commanding him by saying, "Talk to me."

Yet her questions too often meet with her son's resistance to answer. This leaves her bewildered and powerless. A mother wrote, "My thirteen-year-old son, Anthony, tells me he feels like I am always interrogating him. Pray for me that I would respect him and not bug him so much. I am just trying to connect!" There it is. Mom wants to connect. She asks honest questions because she cares to know and cares to connect. But to some boys a mother's questions can feel like she is calling *him* into question. It does not feel like honest inquiry but a form of interrogation.

"But Emerson, my daughter readily answers my questions." Yes, because she's female. A daughter does not interpret questions as calling her into question. She sees it as loving—not disrespectful. When mom asks questions, a daughter has a sixth sense as to why mom inquires. "Mom cares and knows I will feel better after talking." For example, when stressed over her misgivings about being liked and accepted at school, which is a daily experience, a daughter instinctively knows that mom seeks to discover what she feels in order to alleviate her stress. Talking releases her pent-up anxieties, and she feels better afterward.

Boys develop rapport differently. Boys bond by doing an activity shoulder-to-shoulder, as part of a mission. For example, the best male friends were in combat together; they won a state basketball championship; they created the winning science project; they ranked third among cello quartets in New England; they served on the police force together as partners; they built houses together; they did surgery together as ER doctors; and the list goes on. Fathers and sons who are the closest do purposeful activities together. It can be hunting, working in the workshop on a lathe, or cheering for the Detroit Lions. The emotional connection comes from mutual activities, not the talking per se. The talking stems from the sense of connection, and that connection comes from the shoulder-to-shoulder activity.

Shoulder-to-Shoulder Leads to Talking

So do men never talk? As good friends who trust and respect each other, men talk, but they talk less and in ways women do not prefer.

In one study from linguist Deborah Tannen, a series of tests were run on males and females from four age groups, each pair of which were best of friends: second graders, sixth graders, tenth graders, and twentysomethings. The format was the same: each pair, alone, entered a room, and were told to sit down on two chairs, and wait there until they received further instructions. The researchers videotaped each pair in that room—unknown to the pair—to see what they'd do in that room. As the test proceeded, every pair of females, no matter what their ages, responded the same way. They turned toward each other so they could be face-to-face, leaned forward and talked. The males responded differently. They did not turn toward each other in any way, but sat side by side, shoulder-to-shoulder, looking straight ahead except for an occasional glance at each other. Because the females turned toward each other or literally turned their chairs to face one another for direct face-to-face contact, the researchers assumed they would have the most intimate conversations. Actually, the most open and transparent of all the pairs, male or female, were the tenth-grade boys.[2]

This did not surprise me. Men open up with a side-by-side friend.

When men sit shoulder-to-shoulder, they talk transparently. Men do not fear transparency; they fear shame, disapproval, or a lecture. They fear disrespect. When they withhold what they want to say, it is because they lack confidence in the listener.

How does this apply to mom? To get her son to talk, she must come at him sideways. A mom wrote:

I figured out why my son and I have difficulty communicating. He has often said to me that I just don't get him and that we can't communicate. So I began to sit on the couch next to him (shoulder-to-shoulder) to watch him play video games without my saying a word. (Yes, there are miracles!) He was so blessed. As I've made this major adjustment, it has changed our relationship. We went out to lunch the other day, and he couldn't stop talking; whereas before, conversations would have been strained. Wow! What an improvement!

Did you catch her words? "He couldn't stop talking." Boys will open up, but only after they feel mom's friendly shoulder-to-shoulder interest. And mom must accept the side-to-side interaction more than the face-to-face.

Here's another mom's discovery:

I quit trying to ask him questions on the drive home from school. I just greet him with a big smile and say, 'I'm so happy to see you,' then I leave it up to him whether we talk or not. Sometimes it's a quiet ride; other times he chats the whole way home. I have also been trying to take time each day to stop what I am doing and look at him and really listen to him, giving him my undivided attention when he wants to tell me something, rather than multitasking so much.

A mom shared:

The most recent major event happening in my boy's life is puberty. It has been one of my toughest things, emotionally, as a mom since I left him at his desk on his first day of first grade. There is a sense of loss along with this change of life in him. The lullabies stopped abruptly, the needing me to comfort him when he was hurt physically, and the sense of belonging to me has faded away. As I was pondering this over the last few months, I realized I needed to relate to him in a different way. I read once in a Dobson book that talking to boys while doing some task was more effective than talking like girls do while sitting on the couch. Tackling this was harder than I expected—as the things I am interested in are so opposite from my son. I decided to bake cookies. Of course, boys love to eat them, but it's a different story when you are actually mixing flour, sugar, and all the other ingredients. So instead of inviting him to bake, I just started by myself. He noticed, watched, and eventually joined in. We talked about our family, what my mother did when I was growing up, school, dreams, and so many other subjects. As my son rolled each ball of cookie dough into the cinnamon sugar, I learned more about what was on his mind. After putting ten dozen cookies in the oven and taking them out, we finally enjoyed some. It was a rewarding afternoon and a great time to reconnect. This was the same evening my soon-to-be twelve-year-old asked to be tucked in. He must have felt the same things I was feeling too. All because I took the time to slow down and let him just be.

Tucked in? Yes, side-by-side activities that a boy enjoys create fond feelings of affection. Boys want to connect.

Shoulder-to-Shoulder Motivates a Son to Respond to Mom

When mom commits to a shoulder-to-shoulder approach to her son, good things soon follow. What do I mean? Suppose a mom has two boys, a nine-year-old and an eleven-year-old. Both head to the backyard to play catch. I recommend that mom slip out there for fifteen minutes to watch them throw the baseball. Let her pull up a chair and sit silently. She must not read or do anything to distract her from watching. She is to focus solely on them. Then, after fifteen minutes, she can leave to fix dinner. Soon enough she will notice something. In calling the boys to come in for dinner and telling them to wash their hands and to hang up the towels, I predict the boys will immediately respond. There will be no lollygagging, and the towels will be hung up (sort of; I promise no miracles here). Why? Watching the boys without saying anything to them energized them and endeared mom to them. This softens their hearts and makes them more responsive to mom's wishes. As she honors her boys, she reaps the Respect Effect. This discovery overwhelms many moms with unspeakable joy.

A mom told me:

> My husband wrestles with our sons several evenings a week, and they worship the ground he walks on and always try to please him. Trying to emulate my husband's example, when it is necessary to discuss my sons' behavior, I find that the fewer words I use, the better. The more I talk, the less respected they feel. But they are generally more at peace and willing to obey after I do thumb wars with them, play video games with them, or sit next to them on the couch, shoulder-to-shoulder, without saying a single word. It's been a fun challenge to learn to be nonverbal with my sons.

Hear a Boy's Request for Shoulder-to-Shoulder Time

When mothers reflect, they can recall the invitation of the boy to come watch him. A mother wrote:

> Another thing I've struggled with in relating to Josiah is what to do when he wants me to play with him. I tried zooming his matchbox cars around with him, driving his tractors through the dirt, and filling his dump truck up with gravel, but he kept saying, "No, mommy. Don't do that." I was left feeling really frustrated. I wanted to respond to his sweet "Come play with me, mommy," but he clearly didn't appreciate how I played. Again, it was my husband who explained another concept from your book. Boys like shoulder-to-shoulder time together. I was flabbergasted. You mean he just wants me to sit there beside him, not do anything, and he calls that "playing" with him? This concept truly blew my mind. . . . And yet that's precisely what he wants! I know; I've tried it.

Another mom shared:

I found especially interesting the need that men have for a shoulder-to-shoulder relationship with their wives, and after reading about that, I saw it in one of my sons. He's twelve years old and was heading outside to go to the swing set. My husband and I have observed that he's getting too old for a swing set, but he goes out there when he seems to need time alone. One day my son and I were both headed out the back door at the same time, and he said to me, "I'm going to swing! Want to come?" I knew right away what he was really saying.

Shoulder-to-Shoulder Energizes a Boy

When Sarah began to consciously apply the shoulder-to-shoulder concept to our sons, they were older. Jonathan, for instance, was in his twenties and owned a truck. One summer we took a vacation, and Sarah and Jonathan drove together to our destination in his Toyota while the rest of us traveled in my car. Sarah decided not to talk unless Jonathan talked. He said nothing except should we turn here, should we get gas, and should we turn on the air conditioner? That's it! But she believes that was the best family vacation we ever had. She set the tone by simply being with Jonathan shoulder-to-shoulder without talking. She energized Jonathan, and he conducted himself in more caring and loving ways.

Moms, as freakish as this sounds to you, envision your silence this way. The recipe for boys to converse and connect requires shoulder-to-shoulder marinating. The relationship needs to be soaked for a longer period of time, side by side, without talking. The good news is that mom's quiet presence softens the son, and the process alters, enhances, and flavors the relationship more to her satisfaction.

Jonathan is now a clinical psychologist and works with me as my executive manager at Love and Respect Ministries. He clearly describes himself growing up as melancholy and introverted. So when Sarah, a farm girl from Indiana, helped Jonathan refurbish his starter home, she once again applied the silent approach. An electrician who attended our church said, "Jonathan, you have your mom here. How much does she cost?" Jonathan shot back, "She's priceless." Those words still ring in Sarah's ears. As a mother those words proved to be priceless for her.

Shoulder-to-Shoulder Feels Friendly to Sons

Within the nature of every woman is a nurturing capacity that ensures the world is a better place. When lost in an amusement park, children are told to look for a mommy with three children hanging on her and go tell her that they've lost their mommy and daddy. This mother is the only island of virtue, the only safe haven that remains in our secular culture. The world would be a horrible place if we did not have mother-love. But to a mother, a relationship is all about agape, or unconditional, godly love. She feels this kind of love, dreams of this love, responds to needs with this love, thinks of ways to express this love, sees such love, speaks this love, demands of her children to show this type of love, wants this love from her husband, and gives this love daily.

However, in Titus, Paul urged older women to "encourage the young women to love their husbands, to love their children" (2:4). Knowing these women live, breathe, dream, and feel agape 24/7 already, why would these younger mothers need encouragement from older women to love their kids? Don't they clearly do so already? The difference is that when Paul spoke of love in this passage, he did not use the Greek word *agape*. Instead he used *phileo*, which refers to a human, brotherly kind of love. I do not believe that this was just a slip of Paul's Greek pen but that he had a very specific message to send to the women under Titus's ministry and all Christian women from that day forward. I believe Paul understood that Christian mothers do not need reminders to agape their families because it's their nature to love husband and children unconditionally no matter what. But moms do need reminders to be a little friendlier toward their sons, especially when someone is severely testing her patience, which most often is her boy.

Ask a son, "Does your mommy love you?" He'll say, "Yes." Then ask, "Does your mommy like you?" He might say, "No, not today. I've been bad." Countless mothers testify, "There are days when I love my son but, frankly, do not like him."

However, when she is habitually unfriendly, mom needs to ask if she is motivating her son to act as she hopes.

One mother wrote:

Our son (age seven) is very different from me, and I have tremendous difficulty understanding him. . . . I read myself in the pages of your book when I read about mothers unconditionally loving their children but being impatient and unfriendly and sighing way too much. This is far too true of me. . . . While I love him dearly and know that he has a bright future ahead of him, I stay in some degree of frustration nearly all the time. . . . (Why does the answer to a yes or no question always begin without that simple yes or no?!)

Another mother wrote:

I want to like my kids (of course I LOVE them more than anything), and I want to love being with them. I feel so bad that I just don't. But I don't know how to change the situation. . . . Now I'm crying, and I guess I'm feeling sorry for everything. I just want to like family time. I just don't most of the time. It's just too stressful. And I feel outrageously guilty for thinking that, much less saying it. . . . I just don't know what to do.

Is your goodwilled son pulling away because he sees you as unfriendly? You can correct his image of you. You need not seek popularity but do shoulder-to-shoulder activities. When he invites you to come watch him, do not reply, "I don't have time, sorry." Instead, esteem his desire for a shoulder-to-shoulder friendship. Respond to his invitation and watch his fond feelings of love and affection for you grow before your eyes. Be friendly. It works.

When He Opens Up, Maintain Confidentiality

Do you share private and sensitive information about your son with other family members? Does this shame him? If those with whom you share have no right or responsibility to help solve the matter, then what business do they have in knowing? Does your need for catharsis justify exposing others to information about your son that is personal to him and would cause him to feel disrespected? Before you share, do you ask his permission?

Women talk about problems in relationships. Mothers talk about their sons. Mothers seek emotional support. However, a boy is not a robot without feelings and fears. Exposing him can humiliate him. He can feel deeply disrespected. He does not discern mom's need to get insight into how to deal with his situation. Instead, he feels ashamed and undefended. If he overhears such conversations, he thinks you have gone behind his back. And that from his own mom!

Just because a mom feels love for her son and seeks input from others does not stop a boy from feeling mortified. Her love does not justify such sharing with other women. This can undermine the trust between mother and son. Some moms wonder why their boys pull away from them. One reason could be that he overheard what she said about him to other women, and he made a decision to keep his inner thoughts to himself.

Boys lose vitality when moms bad-mouth them in front of others. A kindergarten teacher told me, "It always makes me wither inside when I praise one of these young men in front of their mothers, and the moms respond with something like, 'What? You're kidding! You can't be talking about Marshall. He's never that way at home.' I can only imagine how it makes the boys feel."

Saying, "I Am Sorry"

When one alpha male wolf passes through the territory of another alpha wolf, we observe something spellbinding. The traveling wolf cowers when meeting the alpha male of that terrain. He shows deference and homage by looking away and getting lower. Periodically, eye contact will be made but only for split seconds. The message is clear. "I am traveling through. I do not want to fight. I do not want to control you or take over this territory."

If, though, the traveling wolf gazes into the eyes of the resident alpha wolf, he sends the message, "I am not deferential or respectful." The expression "face-off" captures the meaning at this moment. The traveling wolf displays an attitude of confrontation, not conciliation. His facial and bodily posture provokes a fight, possibly to the death.

Imagine a six-year-old boy accidently knocking down a little girl. The adult says, "Tell her you're sorry. Go to her. Look her in the face and ask her to forgive you. Look at her!" For a woman it is all about face-to-face, and to her, one should look into the other's eyes when apologizing. However, let a little boy respond according to his male nature, and he'll approach the vicinity of the little girl; but as he nears, he stops, looks down, and says softly, "I am sorry."

He won't make eye contact other than a quick glance. Why? He possesses alpha in him. Instinctively he wishes to avoid eye contact that might convey, "I am not deferential or respectful." To decrease the odds of a fight, he intends to steer clear of provoking her, or feeling provoked, by making sure he does not stare her in the face. To avoid the risk of a flare-up face-to-face, he acts honorably. Unfortunately, many women label him unloving and find this behavior appalling. Typically, women are not physically aggressive during provocations, but men are. At a certain point, men stop talking and turn to force. To prevent that, men do what the traveling alpha wolf does. This behavior is wise, honorable, and loving.

My sister Ann wrote to me about her friend who teaches school. "Today Lauren said at school, on the playground, when she had to step in with boys who were fighting and had them to apologize, they kicked the dirt and kept their heads down but did say, 'Sorry.' She said if she had not watched your video, she probably would have said 'Now look at each other and say sorry.' She knows differently now."

A mother begins to see the light: "My sister-in-law told her son to apologize to my son for something, and he dropped his eyes and ducked his head to apologize. You know what she said, of course—'Ben, look him in the eyes when you apologize.' I immediately told her about what you had shared . . . about eye contact being provocative for boys."

At such moments it is less about the boy's feeling provoked and more about feeling embarrassed. The boy looks down and away to avoid the feeling of self-consciousness and personal shame. They're not trying to be unloving. When women look eye to eye, they don't feel the same self-consciousness and sense of shame—generally speaking. Instinctively they know they are reconnecting.

A mother must weigh the seriousness of her son's infraction. If he is responsible for being unloving and dishonorable, then he needs to look face-to-face and apologize. In really serious situations, looking face-to-face is honorable. However, most conflicts are of a smaller magnitude. It's best to say, "You are a man of honor, so please apologize." Let him then do it as he sees fit. Typically, he will glance at the person, look down, and say, "I'm sorry."

Apply G.U.I.D.E.S. to His Relationship

Give: Can I give something to help him develop shoulder-to-shoulder friendships?

Younger Boy:

Let him know that you respect how he and his buddy play for long periods of time in building a fort, doing so shoulder-to-shoulder, as best of friends. Tell him that many men stand back-to-back against enemy attacks, and ask him if he knows what *back-to-back* means. Gift him with children's binoculars so he and his friend can scout out the enemy from their fort.

Older Boy:

Respond to him making the high school football team as a freshman and as a lineman. Express in front of the family how much you respect him, not only for making the team but also for being such a great shoulder-to-shoulder player on the line defending the quarterback. Bring out a new set of football cleats, which he had hoped to buy one day, in appreciation for his hard work to make the team and be a team player. Honor him at dinner with the shoes.

Understand: *Do I understand his struggle with developing friendships?*

Younger Boy:

In recognizing that your son is shy as well as a boy who prefers shoulder-to-shoulder play, do you empathize with his tendency to be less social? Do you respect the way God formed him instead of shaming him for not talking? When you sense that he feels bad over his struggle to interact with others, do you reassure him that it is okay? Do you give him ideas on doing things for other people, such as acts of service instead of words of affirmation? This can be a great way to bless him with the idea that he is okay and that where he feels uncomfortable in one area, God provides other ways for him to deepen friendships. Some people use words to draw close to people, and others do acts of service.

Older Boy:

When rejected by the "in group" on the football team, do you tell him that you understand why he feels hurt and even anger? Do you disclose that you respect his recognition of people who influence and lead others and also respect that he is discovering what makes for true friendship? Do you tell him that this moment of rejection enables him to figure out the ingredients that make for a good friendship among men of honor? Let him know that we cannot be best of friends with everyone who is cool, but that does not mean friendships with others are less significant. In fact, let him know that not infrequently the "in group" guys end up working for the geeks ten years later.

Concerning your relationship with him, here are some approaches that create meaningful touch for him and can improve your friendship with him:

"Let me feel your muscles today."
"Give me a bear hug!"
"Come here and let me see you not laugh when I tickle you."
"Get on my back and let me carry you to bed."
"Scoot over, and I will lie down next to you in bed."

Instruct: *Can I instruct him on how to learn to develop friendships?*

Younger Boy:

When he pushes and hits, do you ask him,

"Did you know that honorable men only push and hit and fight to defend the weak? Honorable men do not hit and push to get their own way. If you have an ice cream cone that I want, I don't hit you to get it. That's selfish. But if daddy saw someone hitting you and taking your ice cream cone, daddy would use his strength to stop that person from hitting you."

Older Boy:

Do you say to him, "I believe in you and your ability to win friends and influence people"? For instance, if he is a high school student struggling with relationships, offer to help him gain instruction on improving his friendships and influence. As an example, in the Dale Carnegie course there are principles, such as "Be a Leader—How to Change People Without Giving Offense or Arousing Resentment." I would purchase Carnegie's book and find key sections that immediately apply to some of the interpersonal challenges your son encounters at school. When a boy has a felt need for information and mom supplies that content, it is the perfect fit, especially when the boy sees the solution as a significant remedy to the very problem he faces. I recall taking a course in college on interpersonal dynamics. That course changed the way I did relationships. I had no idea there was insight that guided me in practical ways. Your son may not know the science behind friendship, but once he learns this information, a whole new world opens up to him. It did for me.

Discipline: *Should I discipline him when he is too unfriendly or isolated?*

Younger Boy:

"A man of honor does not call his friend bad names. That's wrong. It is not respectful when your friends do this toward you. The golden rule says treat others as you want them to treat you. You will call your friend and apologize."

Older Boy:

"I respect your independence. Jesus said that a son shall leave his father and mother. God created you to be a respected man who lives on his own. You clearly have what it takes. However, you still live at home and we still have friends who visit us. That you ignored our dinner guests while we ate and just now exited our discussion in the living room without asking to be excused runs counter to the social skills I see in you. People enjoy you, especially when you take an interest in what they are doing and allow them to ask you questions about what you are doing. In a few moments I want you to return and engage our friends in conversation. Show them the respect you wish people to show to you."

Encourage: *Can I encourage him to keep on developing friendships?*

Younger Boy:

Joey, his best friend in the neighborhood with whom he has played for three years, just moved away. The boy is feeling overwhelmed by melancholy feelings, so mom shares,

> "This is what I really respect about you. You are a man of honor who really values his friends. This sadness is due to how good of friends you were. If you didn't care, you'd not be unhappy right now. That doesn't ease the pain, but I want you to know what a great example you are to me."

Older Boy:

As a starting sophomore on the basketball team, he hung out with the seniors on the team. They took him under their wings and included him in their social activities. But as their graduation approaches, it hits him like a ton of bricks that they will be gone next year. *What am I going to do?* he wonders. As a mother you can say,

> "This is a crossroad for you. As those seniors reached out to you and were friendly toward you, do you have what it takes to imitate them and reach out as a friend to those under you over the next two years? I know you can. As they were men of honor, they recognized you as a man of honor, and honorable men imitate honorable men."

Supplicate*: Do I pray about his developing friendships?*

Younger Boy:

Offer to pray with him about having a friend. He may react, "God doesn't hear my prayers." You can honor him by saying,

> "I believe in you, and I believe you know how to be a good friend. I know God knows this. So let's see what happens. Praying can't hurt, can it? Do you think we shouldn't pray? Jesus prayed, the

wisest man on the planet, as did Solomon and King David and as did Paul. We are in good company."

Older Boy:

Let him know you are praying for his buddies and list all the things you give thanks to God for concerning his friends:

> "You are loyal to each other. You have each other's backs. You show up when the other is feeling kicked in the gut. You make each other laugh. You don't tolerate bullies. You influence the younger guys on your football and basketball teams. And you are committed to being honorable men."

He Does Relationships Differently

A mom told me:

> I wish I'd known all this when my boys were young. I thought they were aliens! One thing in particular stood out to me. My older son, Robert, was telling me all about his friend at school. . . . He and Robert had several classes together, so they were fairly close. Being the typical female, I asked all the pertinent questions. What's "Bruce's" last name? I don't know. Does he have any brothers or sisters? I don't know. Where does he live? Mom, I don't know, are you writing a book? Right then and there, I thought, *here's a kid that doesn't even care enough to find out his friend's last name!* I thought there was something missing from him.

This mother sees her son as uncaring. But wait a second. Young boys engage each other differently. This doesn't mean her son is uncaring. His not knowing information she deems important does not mean he has a loose screw in his brain. Boys differ from girls, but that does not mean the quality of the relationship is shallow.

As men get older, they can do similar things. A wife asks about her husband's time with Harry. He replies that it was good. She asks, "What did you talk about?" He says, "Nothing." What he means is, "Nothing important to you." He talked about a technical issue at work, a concern about a political issue, the pastor's concept of predestination and free will, and how to gut a deer and use the leather. Besides, telling his wife these things means repeating information he has already addressed. There is a fatigue factor with men in going over things again. They do not receive as much energy as do women from repeating the report.

As for the boy, he is building a friendship with his buddy that is meaningful to him as a boy, but it doesn't revolve around his friend's relationships at home. In due time that information will be learned but not right now.

But mothers struggle with the way their boys relate to people. A mom wrote:

My fourteen-year-old son called his friend Peter. They spoke for thirty seconds, just stating the facts. "Pick you up, two p.m. We'll do this. Be ready." Click. Women could *never* do that. I told my son this. He said, "What do you want me to say?" He pretended to call Peter back and say, "Oh, Peter . . . how are you doing? Would you like to go to the movies? Which movie would you like? How do you feel about that?" I was laughing very hard. However, there are times when men don't know they are being very cold, and that sends the wrong message to the woman. . . . Men have a way of being short, to the point, just the facts, and then it becomes dry or cold . . . then moves into rude.

Yes, he needs to learn social graces. Mom is correct at one level. I preach the importance of interpersonal dynamics. However, in this instance, was mom expecting her boy to talk to his male friend in the way she converses with females? Was she assuming her son would talk to women the way he talked to his buddy? Though her son needs to apply what she says when talking on the phone to his aunt from New York, I can say to such a mom that men among men see verbal interaction as an exchange of information. Once the information is exchanged, they are good to go. Men see communication as functional, not always relational.

In this exchange between Peter and her son, neither boy was in the least bit bothered by the short, to-the-point interaction. Women, on the other hand, due to their nurturing nature, find themselves compelled to ask about how the other is doing and feeling. Because they want this for themselves, they assume boys should want this for themselves. Interestingly, I know of wives who, because they are running late to pick up a girlfriend for a retreat, have their husbands make a telephone call: "Please call her. I do not have time to talk." At that moment the man's approach is virtuous.

There is a saying: "To a hammer, everything is a nail." A surgeon sees the problem solved surgically. A dietician sees the problem solved via diet. A mother sees her son's problem solved by his becoming more like her. From her female view of life, a normal conversation on the phone with another human being does not last thirty seconds. But where in the Bible is this stated as a sin between two boys? Yes, rebuke him if he hangs up on his aunt, but leave him alone with his buddy. No doubt they'll join the Marines and save each other's lives but not talk much about it afterward—or the rest of their lives. Men are not wrong, just different.

10

SEXUALITY

Respecting His Desire for Sexual

Understanding and "Knowing"

A boy is a sexual being who is naturally interested in sexual matters. God instilled in him a curiosity to understand the realm of sexuality and to eventually "know" his wife, as "Adam knew Eve his wife" (Gen. 4:1 KJV).

Thus, there is an appropriate desire to understand and know.

God Designed Sex

The appropriate sexual interest is rooted in God's design of sex for marriage, in which there is pleasure and from which there is procreation.

For example, wonderfully, God commands your husband: "Let her breasts satisfy you at all times" (Prov. 5:19). Every wife is cognizant of the fact that her husband is visually oriented.

From eternity past, God, in His holiness and wisdom, created the blueprint. In Song of Solomon the king describes his attraction to the physical attributes of the woman he loves (7:1–9). There he expresses,

"Your two breasts are like two fawns, twins of a gazelle" (7:3). Before that he penned, "How beautiful are your feet in sandals, O prince's daughter! The curves of your hips are like jewels, the work of the hands of an artist" (7:1). He conveys with emotion, "How beautiful and how delightful you are, my love, with all your charms!" (7:6). In response she declares, "I am my beloved's, and his desire is for me" (7:10). Every wife longs for her husband to desire her—body, soul, and mind.

At our Love and Respect Marriage Conference, I describe the scene where a wife gets out of the shower while her husband brushes his teeth. He looks at her and quotes Proverbs 5:19: "Let her breasts satisfy you at all times." As he stares, he announces that he is making that his life verse. In realizing how easy it was to memorize this verse, he informs her that he should start memorizing more of the Bible because that recall came so easy.

We see a different scene the next day in the bathroom when he steps out of the shower. As she looks at him stepping out, she says loudly, "Get back in the shower. You are getting water all over the floor. I can't believe the mess you are making. Put a towel down on the floor before getting out. And put a towel around you. That's sick!"

The crowd goes crazy with laughter. Everyone knows this male and female difference.

I am not saying women have no interest in a man's body. Wives clearly enjoy the physical dimensions of their husbands. Nor am I saying that a man is only interested in a woman's body. He loves her heart and mind apart from how she looks, and this is clearly observed among the aged couples, like the ninety-seven-year-old man who adores his ninety-four-year-old wife.

I am saying that men find themselves attracted to the female body more than women are lured by the male physique. This concerns both of them. Wives write to me about the ways their husbands look at other women. Men do not write to me about their wives staring at men lustfully. Both know he must guard his eyes when going to the public beach, and she expects him not to stare at women in bikinis.

Yes, the visual orientation of some females has grown over the decades in America, and this can be a problem for some women (Ezek. 23:14–16). But most agree that a strolling male wearing a thong on a beach solicits a response in a wife that differs from her husband's response to a coed strolling by in a skimpy bikini. It should go without saying, a husband never needs to sit his wife down and ask, "Now, when we go to the beach today, will the men in thongs entice you?" Truth is, when this mommy sees a guy walk by in a thong, she wants to throw up.

Inappropriate Sexual Interest

If there is a suitable side to a boy's sexuality, there is an unbecoming side. The inappropriate sexual interest of the male, according to the Bible, can give way to lust (internally), fornication (premarital sex with another person), and adultery (a married man with another woman).

As for lust, Jesus said in Matthew 5:28, "But I say to you that everyone who looks at a woman with lust for her has already committed adultery with her in his heart." Jesus not only teaches the reality of lust, which we all know exists; He stresses the visual orientation of the male. This is a man. This man "looks at a woman." Jesus recognized the man's leering look can lead to lust. What a male sees can affect him sexually.

Because God hardwired a boy to be visually oriented, God reveals in His Holy Word for men to guard their eyes. For example, Job said, "I have made a covenant with my eyes; how then could I gaze at a virgin?" (Job 31:1). Proverbs 6:25 says in *The Message* paraphrase, "Don't lustfully fantasize on her beauty, nor be taken in by her bedroom eyes."

Fornication is premarital sex. Though it can include adultery, we hear Jesus saying, "out of the heart" come "adulteries, fornications" (Matt. 15:19, and similarly in Mark 7:21). Paul also separated fornication from adultery (1 Cor. 6:9). The writer of Hebrews stressed this distinction when he wrote, "Marriage is to be held in honor among all, and the marriage bed is to be undefiled; for fornicators and adulterers God will judge" (Heb. 13:4). Two unmarried people who have sex do not honor marriage. In this "hookup" generation our sons will be faced with the pressure of premarital sex, despite the damage that research repeatedly reveals it brings.[1]

Adultery is when someone married has sex with someone other than his or her spouse. In 2 Samuel 11:2, we read about King David, who was married; but "from the roof he saw a woman bathing; and the woman was very beautiful in appearance." We know the story: He sees Bathsheba, the wife of Uriah, and her body ignites a chemical reaction. Lust. He does not know who the woman is at first. He has no romantic relationship with her. David yields to the lustful desire that he ignited within himself while gazing at her unclothed body and then calls for her and commits adultery with her. James 1:14 states, "Each one is tempted when he is carried away and enticed by his own lust."

A Mother's Fears and Anger

Obviously, every godly mother fears that her son will give way to lust and sin sexually. The thought acutely discourages her.

For some mothers, their heavyheartedness drives them to do what they can to help their boy, which is why some moms turned first to this chapter. Worried, they want to know what to do now. I applaud these women.

Other mothers find this topic too daunting, and they prefer to believe their boys are different, and none of this lust stuff will be true of their sons. These mothers busy themselves with other matters and suppress this information. Out of sight, out of mind. They choose to see their precious boys as eunuchs in their thinking, believing they will have no sexual interests or intensity until the day they marry.

Still other mothers come uncorked with anger over this presentation. Author Juli Slattery wrote, "From the female perspective, male sexuality is often viewed as a sordid desire. It seems to represent the worst of masculinity—passion without love, drive without self-control, sensuality without sensitivity."[2]

These mothers react viscerally. They feel all of this talk leads to the sanctioning of their lack of love, lack of self-control, and lack of sensitivity. In their opinion, it is an attempt to justify the sexual sin of men and boys.

What we are up against is the difficulty some moms have in believing that a boy would struggle as much as he does with his imagination in response to images of female body parts. Some moms argue that boys ought to stop being so aggressive in this area of looking at the female form. To these moms an interest in body parts borders on deviant. They cannot imagine how the female curve, an accidentally unbuttoned blouse, or short shorts can be sexually provocative.

Some women seek to be sexually attractive but not for sex. They have no intention of being sexy for the purpose of sexually arousing men. To them a lustful response is rooted in the man's twisted mind. In the opinion of many gals, men are unhealthy for being aroused by women in this fashion. They believe boys, and men, are intentionally on the hunt to see what they want to see and are bringing all of this on themselves because they want to actively lust. These women believe boys are too animalistic and need to be like girls, who do not stare at boys for the purpose of undressing the boys with their eyes. They don't understand dreaming about the male image but rather dreaming about the relationship and love.

What drives this perspective among some women? Fear and anger. For this reason, I want you to pause and commit this topic into God's hands in prayer. At this moment, ask God to guide and guard your heart related to your fears and anger. This chapter is written to encourage you, not frighten or provoke you to anger. You need to think the thoughts of God on this subject of sex and the single boy. You need to be reminded that God designed sex. He works from the blueprint He designed from eternity past. Since you yearn for sexual purity in your boy, I recommend approaching this as a godly wise woman who is hearing things she does not want to hear but needs to hear as answers to her prayers to be the best mommy she can be for her boy. Her son has challenges that she does not have; therefore, her fear and anger won't serve her boy.

The role of your husband in discussing this topic should be addressed.

I recommend talking with your husband about the matter if he is receptive, and hopefully he is since he understands male sexuality. I would respectfully ask him to help you address these matters with your son or take the lead on this topic. The content of this chapter can serve him as he broaches the subject and gives guidance. If your husband refuses, you still can apply this chapter as you have with C.H.A.I.R.S. The same is true if you are a single parent, as was my mom for many years, as well as Sarah's mother. Though you feel fearful and angry for any number of reasons, please set aside these emotions and confidently and matter-of-factly aid your son with these insights.

The Challenges Encountered by Your Boy

You need to understand three challenges before your boy that he did not ask for: One, the challenge of his nucleus accumbens. Two, the challenge of his temptations. And three, the challenge to trust and obey God.

1. He will be challenged by his nucleus accumbens.

From a brain structure perspective, the nucleus accumbens appears to be an area in the brain that activates in men an involuntary, biological response to the female image. Something happens in his brain in response to the female form. From what researchers seem to be finding, the nucleus accumbens triggers a response in the male to an attractive female. In the initial encounter, it is not her person that attracts him but how she appears to him. The man may not even know the female. Presumably, King David did not have a prior relationship with Bathsheba. He only saw her from a distance. That, though, was ample to activate his nucleus accumbens.

It begins with the eyes. This is why we read in Job, "Let God know my integrity. If . . . my heart followed my eyes. . . . If my heart has been enticed by a woman" (Job 31:6–7, 9). In other words, Job knew the heart connects with the eyes, meaning a man could look at a woman inappropriately, which entices him and then ignites lust. Solomon penned that it will not go well with young men who "follow the impulses of your heart and the desires of your eyes" (Eccl. 11:9). He does not urge following the eyes since the verse continues by showing the devastating consequences later in life for following the desires of the eyes. For young men, the challenge begins with the look, and habitual looking over the years leads to a sad end.

But hear this point: the first look is not lustful. This is paramount for a mother to apprehend. At the outset of observing the beautiful female form, there is an involuntary, biological response that causes a boy to be keenly aware of what he is seeing, to the extent that other things can go unnoticed. In the movie *Catch Me If You Can*, the lead character needed to get through an airport, knowing the police were searching for him. He surrounded himself with a half dozen beautiful stewardesses and walked through the terminal. The male cops never saw him as they eyed the passing females.

Seeing the female form can be likened to coming around a bend and seeing the snow-capped mountain in the distance—the blue, sparkling lake in the foreground, and the rolling green hills surrounding the lake, all of which appear in HD due to the brightness of the noonday sun. One gasps at the sudden and stunning beauty flooding one's soul. We might say a man's first sightings of the beautiful curves and movements of the female body touch off an awareness within him of her inviting presence. I tell women to watch the eyes of a dozen men in a room when a gorgeous woman enters the room unexpectedly. All will look at her. The nucleus accumbens is operating. A man might declare under his breath to a buddy, "She's stunning . . . breathtaking." Yet he doesn't even know her.

The nucleus accumbens impacts females as well but not in the same way. For instance, when a woman sees a cute baby, she fixates on the baby and emotionally declares, "Oh, how precious." However, a few minutes later she is not still howling, "How adorable!" given the child is wailing. So, too, men do not stay fixed on the beautiful image. After a while on the beach, he reads a book and doesn't notice every female walking by. We must not conclude that guys are forever captivated by the female form, and that is all they think about. They have other things to do.

However, there is a line over which he has the ability to cross. Once aware, he might take a second look that lingers for ten seconds and then turns into a leer. At the point he ogles in a lecherous manner, he crosses the line. The old adage applies: you cannot prevent the bird from landing in your hair, but you can prevent the bird from nesting there. Sexual gazing is his choice. When he consciously and willfully undresses the female in his mind and envisions a sexual encounter with her, he has entered lust.

"But, Emerson, this is why women are better than men. Women find this disgusting, and you are disgusting for comparing the delight women have for babies with a male's feeling about the female body." I am simply stating what I understand goes on in the male and female nucleus accumbens. But let's add, what about an unmarried woman who sees a cute baby and three minutes later, envies the mother, a happily married woman? What about the bitterness that comes over her because of her unmarried state and the ire she feels for the man who just broke off their relationship? What about her anger toward God, whom she claims is against her for not hearing her prayers to have a baby? The first look at the cute baby lights up her nucleus accumbens, but she chooses to take the next steps into the sins of envy, bitterness, and unfaithfulness. This is no small struggle among many women. Both men and women have their struggles concerning the nucleus accumbens.

Not all looking is lusting. We are only pointing out that all lusting commences with the looking or imagining. In most cases, the male cannot stop the first look or thought of an image, but he can stop the second, third, and fourth. He cannot stop the attraction any more than he can ignore the beauty of a sunset (or a woman can ignore a darling baby), but he can take steps to prevent arousal from the attraction to the female figure. The female image unquestionably affects the male imagination, but what the man does with the involuntary response is now under his control. He has power. He is not a hopeless, helpless victim.

The initial sighting of a beautiful woman sparks something in the brain that also affects the male's physiology. Shaunti Feldhahn wrote in her book *Through a Man's Eyes* about a three-year-old boy at a fabric store with his mother. As the mother studied various fabrics, she thought her son was reading the children's book he brought along, but instead he was flipping through a book of sewing-patterns that showed women in underwear. He yelled across the store to his mother, "Mom! Every time I look at these girls my pee-pee stands up."[3]

On the one hand, such an episode proves disconcerting. None of us wants a boy's innocence robbed so early. On the other hand, this three-year-old had no idea about sex. The boy is not a pervert before he can tie his own shoes. What we see here is a boy's transparency and ongoing innocence (he was not robbed of it) about an involuntary, biological response. As amazing as this is, he recognized something in his groin area being responsive. This was not lust per se but a biological reaction to the female body.

The good news is that an older boy is teachable and can learn about this section of the brain. When we notice his noticing, we can provide information at a level he understands. A cool, calm, and collected communication about this information helps him understand himself. He can learn that all men have this involuntary, biological response to the first look at the female form. He can be reassured that he is not alone in noticing and that God made him this way. God made him to enjoy the female image. He can also be coached to look elsewhere after the first look out of a desire to be honorable and to honor the woman.

Here is a good place to include dad as your ally. Let your husband pick up this topic and proceed along with you to serve your son. You will be light-years ahead. But be careful to not use this as an opportunity to drill your husband. If you interrogate him with, "This is disgusting. Is this how you feel? Are you undressing women in your mind?" you will shut down your ally. This is not the time or place to seek reassurance from your husband that all is okay between the two of you. If anything, you need to reassure your husband that you are for him and your son. God has given your husband to you to serve your boy. Assume the best. If your husband struggles here and there in his imagination, this can prove the very impetus for him to change course in order to be a godly example to your son. If you shame them both, you will accomplish nothing. Proverbs 12:4 says, "An excellent wife is the crown of her husband, but she who shames him is like rottenness in his bones."

2. He will be challenged by temptations.

Should a visually oriented husband never, ever be tempted sexually outside of the marriage? That's a trick question.

Temptation in and of itself is not sin. Jesus was tempted: "Jesus was led up by the Spirit into the wilderness to be tempted by the devil" (Matt. 4:1). But he did not give in to the temptation. Being tempted differs from yielding to temptation. As with Jesus, your husband will be tempted, but that does not mean he has sinned. He sins when he gives in to the temptation.

Temptation arises in areas where each can be tempted. No human will be tempted to turn a stone into bread. In the wilderness Jesus was tempted this way because he could turn the stone into bread. As the Son of God, famished by fasting, he had the temptation because He had the capability. To the rest of us, we cannot turn stone into bread, so it will never be a temptation. By way of analogy, many women are not tempted by the bare body parts of a male. How easy then for a wife to tell her husband that he ought not to be tempted by the body parts of a female. Since she is not tempted, he ought not to be tempted. Since she is repulsed, he ought to be repulsed. But God designed the male nature to be attracted and aroused by a beautiful female body in a way that women are not designed. Male and female differ by God's creation.

To the married, the Bible says "Stop depriving one another . . . so that Satan will not tempt you because of your lack of self-control" (1 Cor. 7:5). The temptation is not the problem. Yielding to the temptation due to no self-control is the problem. For this reason all of us must know what tempts us and what does not tempt us. On the one hand, because I do not play the piano, I will not be tempted to be jealous of someone who does. However, if someone conducts marriage seminars and ten thousand people attend his live conferences each week, I will be tempted to be jealous. Why? I conduct marriage seminars. Because women are not tempted with the male form in the way men are tempted with the female form, it is all too easy for women to contend that men ought not be tempted by bodily forms.

Even the porn industry knows boys differ from girls. Intuitively the pornographers know about C.H.A.I.R.S. As a mother, you may be naïve about the appeal of pornography to your boy, but the image of the seductive woman as she poses is communicating a message that screams loud and clear to your precious son:

C: Conquer me sexually!

H: Be over me sexually!

A: I want to submit to you sexually!

I: Solve my sexual need!

R: Let's just be together for sex without talking!

S: Let me satisfy you sexually!

Though as a woman such statements disgust you, Satan uses the carnal female to send this message. And your son's weak flesh responds to the nucleus accumbens lighting up. Every boy wants to feel like a man, and porn deceives him into thinking this is what it feels like to be a man. However, your Respect-Talk counters that false source of honor.

Always, and I mean always, remember that your son is not the enemy but the victim of the enemy. Satan tempts (1 Thess. 3:5). The carnal world tempts (1 John 2:16). And your son's carnal, fallen nature tempts his inner man, who can get pulled into a world of lust. James 1:14 states, "Each one is tempted when he is carried away and enticed by his own lust."

Our hearts must go out to these boys. We must not be verbally blasting them as excuse-makers because of our own insecurities and resentments. The porn industry knows your boy's vulnerability and takes great advantage of it. When they go after your boy with these images, he must fight against the temptation in a way that girls do not need to fight. Girls have other battles.

The world, the flesh, and the devil will tempt your son with the female image, and he must decide whether he will resist the temptation or let it flood his imagination and sexually arouse him.

If your son were perfect, he'd never yield to these struggles with temptation. But he will lose various battles in his mind. The key as a parent is to help him fight against a pattern of giving in to these temptations. The good news is that God intends to help him. The challenge he faces is a simple one: Do I want to trust God to help me and to obey His leading when He extends help?

3. He will be challenged by trusting and obeying God.

Temptation is not a good thing long-term. You can let him know that trying to stare down temptation is like staring down a hungry lion. The Lord knows Satan roams about like a roaring lion seeking someone to devour. A boy must exit the presence of the lion. And God promises to aid us and provide a way of escape from temptation.

Every boy can be encouraged to anticipate and allow God's promised help. However, a boy may not know the promises, so mom and dad need to share the following truths with their boy. He will have to decide to enter the spiritual journey to trust and obey them.

What a comfort to read 1 Corinthians 10:13: "No temptation has overtaken you but such as is common to man; and God is faithful, who will not allow you to be tempted beyond what you are able, but with the temptation will provide the way of escape also, so that you will be able to endure it."

What a joy to read Hebrews 2:18: "For since He Himself was tempted in that which He has suffered, He is able to come to the aid of those who are tempted."

Why do we need aid when tempted? Each of us has weaknesses and vulnerabilities. We don't want to be weak, but the fact remains: we are not strong enough to face down certain temptations. We need a way of escape. We need to flee the hungry lion.

Each boy must meet God halfway. He must flee by running through the escape hatch that God provides. The Bible says, "Now flee from youthful lusts" (2 Tim. 2:22).

It won't always be easy. Joseph knew he had to flee Potiphar's wife, who came after him sexually (Gen. 39:12); otherwise, the temptation would have led to sex outside of God's boundaries. And by the way, Potiphar's wife knew she had the power to seduce Joseph. Women do not need to rape men when they can lure men, a huge difference between male and female. Ezekiel 16:36 compares Jerusalem to a prostitute, saying: "You chased after lovers, then took off your clothes and had sex" (CEV). Men become aroused by a woman disrobing in a sexual manner. We can argue that it ought not to be this way, but it is. Every woman on her honeymoon night knows the seductive power God has given to her. But apart from these scriptures, a boy needs to be told that it can be tough if one decides to flee. Joseph knew the way of escape was to run out the front door, but it led to a prison door. A boy's friends may entice him to do sexual things, and the Lord will whisper, "Say no and leave." His friends may say, "You are no longer our friend." There is a price to pay, but it is worth it. Ask Joseph.

How Can a Mom Respond to Her Son's Sexuality?

One, she must sympathize, not shame. Two, be poised and not panicked. And, three, depend on God—do not doubt Him.

1. She must sympathize with her son's challenges rather than shame him.

Giving a boy the benefit of the doubt is a good thing. Looking beyond his weak flesh to his willing spirit, as Jesus did with His disciples, is the best approach. Sympathizing with his willing spirit is the goal.

A mom can let her son know that she does not see him as the enemy, but as someone in a battle with periodic temptations in the world. The devil will try to entice his flesh. Sympathizing with his challenge can give him confidence in overcoming the temptation.

Does the call to sympathize sound like a call to endorse the male's weakness and to grant him license to indulge since "boys will be boys"?

To some, as we mentioned, this whole topic of a male's struggle frightens some women and infuriates others. The frightened are afraid their son will give in to sexual temptations leading to who knows what. The infuriated are angry at the pass they believe men receive to be sexually tempted. They are enraged over what they feel is excuse-making. In learning of the book *Every Man's Battle*, they interpret the whole sordid topic as a justification on the part of the man to indulge his lust. They think they are to go along with every man's lust.

But these godly women also intend to be like Jesus, and we learn our Lord does not show cold indifference toward us for our weaknesses but sympathizes. We read in Hebrews 4:15: "For we do not have a high priest who cannot sympathize with our weaknesses, but One who has been tempted in all things as we are, yet without sin." Because Jesus encountered temptations, He understands those of your son. Like Jesus, you can sympathize with your son's temptations without sanctioning his yielding to those temptations. Jesus confronted lust, fornication, and adultery. Sexual sin is serious to our Lord. The answer is to show a spirit of sympathy while confronting and correcting a son who crosses the line.

Sympathizing entails letting a son know the temptation evidences his normal sexual desires that God designed to be in him for marriage. Reassuring him that these desires are of God and to be enjoyed in marriage with pleasure can lift a tremendous weight from his shoulders. A mother's sympathy allows him to feel okay about his sexual desires while calling him to reject yielding to the temptations. The desires are not bad, but giving in to the temptation is the sin. At the same time, each mother must accept the reality that her son is not the Son of God. Her son, like her, is a sinner. As a fellow human being, she can sympathize with his fallen nature without ratifying the sin. A mother of ten shared with me, "After having ten kids, I can tell you this: they will sin." She did not endorse the sin but empathized while confronting the wrongdoing.

Shaunti Feldhahn provided an illustration in her book *Through a Man's Eyes*.[4] She created an analogy that she summarized for me in an e-mail message:

How creepy and frustrating would it be for a girl if every guy who walked by was able to touch her face, neck, back, etc. and essentially stimulate her without her consent? Her physiology is designed to be stimulated by the touch, but she DOESN'T want to be stimulated by these strangers—and that is what it feels like for a guy when he walks around and sees this stuff that stimulates him visually—it is coming AT him.

Adding to this, I thought, *What if every day at school or work a young man she liked and who liked her was permitted to come by every few minutes and gently, in humility and tenderness, touch her face, neck, shoulders, and arms? What eventually will happen to her? She will say to herself,* "Here he comes. He cares. He wants me!" At some moment her mind and body will go nuts with sexual desire. Imagine, then, the girl at school who comes on to your son by dressing provocatively and flattering him.

What about the everyday images of girls all around him? Let me be clear that your boy doesn't want to engage these images, and most often his eyes are focused elsewhere; but the mere images do affect him, and he must do battle with this in his mind when he sees something he should not see. He can win with support and affirmation of mom and dad, but not if he is told, "We do not respect you for this struggle. Stop it. Be like women." To say he ought not feel this way is comparable to telling a girl, "We do not love you. Stop being affected by the caresses of that caring young man."

Disapprove of the sinful behavior, but do not disapprove of him as a human being. When he feels you alone are the righteous one and he alone is the unrighteous one, you'll lose his heart.

My wife, Sarah, put me onto a truth when she shared that because most women do not struggle with sexual temptation as do men, some women can feel they are better human beings. Over time these women commit the number-one sin that Jesus had to combat in others: a self-righteous, religious, angry judgment like that of the Pharisees. Jesus could not get through to them, though he tried. We read in Luke 18:9, "And He also told this parable to some people who trusted in themselves that they were righteous, and viewed others with contempt."

You must guard against shaming your son as a worse sinner than you. One way to do that is to remind yourself that the ground at the cross of Christ is flat. By that I mean you need what Jesus did on the cross every bit as much as your son. Inherently, you are not better than your boy; you just sin differently.

2. A mother must be poised and not panicked.

When mom enters hysteria over her son's lustful actions, she stamps on the brain of her young boy the thought that sex and his attraction to it is a really, really bad thing. He won't know the why behind her terror since he is clueless about the goodness of sex, so he receives the impression that sex is dirty. Instead of freaking out, she needs to be cool, calm, and collected as she addresses what happened. Yes, easier said than done.

Toward the three-year-old boy in the fabric store, a mother can say,

> "Thank you for telling me that. I really respect how you tell me things. That is honorable. We can talk about all of this later. This book is to help mommies decide about fabric. I will put it back. I brought this book for you to read. In fact, what is Mr. Rabbit doing on this page?"

She must not panic.

As the boy nears puberty, mom will inadvertently catch her son looking at pictures on his iPad or will learn that his friend showed him such images on his iPhone. At that moment she must guard against screaming that which some mothers have been known to shout. "I can't believe you'd look at that filth. This is sick. What kind of person are you?"

As threatened as mom feels at such a discovery, she must work on a dignified and poised response—the one her Lord gives to her on the heels of her confession of sin to Him.

The trouble for some mothers is that, in their mind, this sex sin of their son's exceeds any sin she would ever commit. But is that the sin of the Pharisees? This is not to minimize your son's sin but to make your own as serious. Sarah has said that she takes sin very seriously, wherever it is found, and that includes self-righteous, angry, judgmental mothers.

Staying cool is vital. He needs to hear in your voice and see in your demeanor that you believe sex is a good thing and that boys have pressures that many girls do not understand.

In a dignified manner she must say,

"God designed you to be interested in the female body. He made you to desire and enjoy sexual intimacy with your wife. On the one hand, you will notice the female form; but on the other hand, when you look at these beautiful figures, your looking can arouse in you desires that need to be contained and controlled. You are not a bad person for these desires. God created you to have these desires. But we need to come up with a solution. What plan of action do you think will serve you best? What do you recommend?"

As we have said elsewhere, give the boy a problem to solve. That honors him, creates ownership, and may be more conservative than your proposal. Here is where dad plays a huge role in coming up with that game plan. Honor him for teaming up with you on this.

3. Depend on God; do not doubt Him.

Along with you I wish we still lived in Paradise, before sin ever came into existence. If we lived in a perfect world, we would not have to deal with our children's prurient curiosities. But we live in a fallen world and, therefore, must make ourselves available to Almighty God to guide our sons.

I am grateful that God understands all the emotions we feel about this topic. My heart aches along with yours as we face the reality of a boy's nucleus accumbens, the carnal and demonic temptations that knock at his door, and the option for him to distrust and disobey God's promises to escape these temptations. I, too, ache with you for having to sympathize, remain poised, and be dependent on God. For this reason, may I offer this prayer for you to pray?

> Jesus, You prayed. You prayed because You knew of these realities facing those You loved. "I do not ask You to take them out of the world, but to keep them from the evil one." You even taught them to pray, "Lead us not into temptation but deliver us from evil." To You dependency on the Father in the face of a fallen world is a good thing. I will imitate You and pray the same way. For myself, I find comfort in Your invitation, 'Come to Me all who are weary and heavy-laden and I will give you rest." Lord, I am heavy-laden about my son's sexuality, and I feel weary trying to figure out my role and words. I come to You this day for Your rest. Take my burden and grant to me a renewed strength. Help me obey Your Word that tells me, "There is no fear in love; but perfect love casts out fear . . . and the one who fears is not perfected in love." Mature me in love, dear Lord. In all of these things, I will trust You as I entrust my precious boy into Your hands. I will not doubt what You are doing, though I cannot see it. Now, enable me to act on the wisdom of what I have learned for the sake of my son and Your honor. In Jesus' name, amen. (John 17:15; Matt. 6:13; Matt. 11:28–30; 1 John 4:18)

Apply G.U.I.D.E.S. to His Sexuality

Let me turn a corner here. As we wrap up this chapter, let me assist you in talking to your son about his relationship with the opposite sex on a social level. Early on, most boys feel awkward about girls because they don't have the same relational skills that girls have. A boy can feel out of his league and flounders. Let's apply G.U.I.D.E.S to his understanding of women. Peter instructs husbands to "live with your wives in an understanding way . . . since she is a woman" (1 Peter 3:7). Your son is a future husband who needs to understand women.

Give: *Do I give something to help him know and relate to the opposite sex?*

Younger Boy:

There is an ever-growing list of books that address sexual topics. Based on the age and stage of your son, I would purchase some books on this topic and say to him,

> "As you become a man of honor, I want you to know God's design of boys and girls. I know you have seen some differences between boys and girls, and I want you to better understand God's purpose for this. For instance, God designed women with something very special. They care deeply about people. Many boys do as well, but I want you to recognize that one of the best ways to understand a girl is by understanding her concern about the people in her life."

Older Boy:

This is a delicate issue to address, but if you have conveyed to your son that you believe in him and are committed to doing everything you can to help him become a man of honor, then let him know you will spare no expense in protecting him from being victimized by pornography. For this reason you will provide parental protection software that monitors and motivates a healthy view of women, and protects him from a distorted view. You can let him know that what is portrayed in these pictures does not represent what the vast majority of women feel. Women care about people and relationships. In fact, it has been said that men use love to get sex; whereas, women use sex to get love. Love motivates women, and sadly, they can be misled. Teach him never to say, "I love you" to a girl in a deeply romantic way until he is seriously prepared to marry her. A man of honor prizes the expression "I love you." He never cheapens it for self-serving purposes. All of this underscores the why behind the protection software. The goal is to ensure a healthy view of women and sexuality. Those addicted to pornography end up with unhealthy ideas and practices.

Understand: *Do I understand his struggle with knowing and relating to the opposite sex?*

Younger Boy:

When he plays too rough with a little girl in his Sunday school class and causes her to cry, he may experience shame. Say to him,

> "I respect that you are getting bigger and stronger, but now you
> must learn as a man of honor not to wrestle like this with girls.
> God made you to protect girls, not fight with girls. See yourself as
> the protector, and you won't feel bad since you won't cause her to
> cry."

Older Boy:

When feeling awkward with and ignored by certain girls, do you tell him that you understand and respect why he is feeling embarrassed and humiliated? Do you divulge your respect for him and his desire to be a quality guy with great character that girls find attractive? Do you communicate that you respect that he is in a season to discern if these girls see character or just cuteness as the appeal?

Instruct: *Can I instruct him on how to know and relate to the opposite sex?*

Younger Boy:

> "When you are at school and you say or do something that hurts
> the feelings of a girl, as a man of honor here is what I want you to
> do. Look her in the eyes and say respectfully, 'I am sorry. Will you
> forgive me?' Maybe she shouldn't feel hurt and sad, but it is called
> 'going the extra mile.' Instead of telling her she ought not feel
> hurt, just apologize as a great warrior who says, 'I am sorry' when
> he knows that will make the other person's heart happy."

Older Boy:

When he reveals his difficulty in talking to girls, ask him,

"Can I honor you by inviting Kelly and Cheri for dinner to talk about the three things a girl wants a boy to know? These two college girls really like you, and they'd love to chat about this. You can get an insider's view. The plan is to have a meal, and they will do the talking while you eat and listen. Then you can be dismissed with no questions asked. They are coming next Tuesday regardless, but if you put your foot down, we won't have them bring up these three things, though it would be fun."

God's Word presents basic truths that a boy can understand. God calls the parent, not the kid down the street, to be the sex educator for your boy. God entrusts to you an understanding of His revelation to us about the foundational realities between men and women. Using a multitude of examples from Scripture, parents can have conversations like this with their children:

"In Genesis 1:24–27 we learn that God created them male and female. God made boys and girls differently, and that difference is for a wonderful purpose. What are some of the differences you see between boys and girls? Did you know God designed us differently to help each other? Each of us has a strength we bring to the other. What are some strengths a boy brings? What strengths do girls bring?

"God intends for a male and female to eventually marry. Though some do not marry, such as Jesus Himself, in Genesis 2:18–25 we learn that man and woman "shall become one flesh." Do you have a general idea what this means? God designed a man and woman to become one flesh in marriage. We refer to this as sexual intercourse. There is more to the marriage than sex, but this is where sex is to be enjoyed.

"In Genesis 1:28–31 we read, 'Be fruitful and multiply.' This means that God intends for a mommy and daddy to have children. God designed marriage for two people to enjoy the pleasures of sex and from that union to have children, the way mommy and daddy had you, for which we are so very thankful.

"In Psalm 139:14 we learn that every human being is 'wonderfully made.' When a husband and wife have sexual intercourse, the man brings what we call sperm, and the woman brings the egg. When the sperm penetrates the egg, a life is conceived. Then, a baby grows in the womb, as you did in mine. Each child is wonderfully made. You are wonderfully made.

"We read elsewhere, in Exodus 20:14, 'You shall not commit adultery.' Do you understand what that means? God intends for every husband and wife to stay together in their marriage. They are not to become one flesh with another person. Sexual intercourse is to remain the enjoyment between a husband and a wife, and neither is to have sexual intercourse with any other person. Because this is God's command, adultery hurts the heart of God.

"There is something else we must learn. In 2 Samuel 13:12, a woman tells a man, 'Do not violate me.' We refer to this as rape. Rape is when a man forces a woman to have sexual intercourse against her will. This is a violent act, when a man harms a woman in order to satisfy his sexual desires. Such a man is not an honorable man and he does not honor a woman.

"In 1 Corinthians 6:19–20 we learn that 'your body is a temple of the Holy Spirit . . . therefore glorify God in your body.' To glorify God in your body, you value that God made you a male, that you prepare yourself to be one flesh with a woman, that you will have the joy and responsibility to multiply yourself by having children, and you will bring about a child who is wonderfully made. To glorify God in your body, you will avoid adultery, rape, and anything that hurts the heart of God."

The Psalmist asks in 119:9, "How can a young man keep his way pure? By keeping it according to Your word." Let the Word of God guard and guide your boy. In fact, may I challenge you to memorize Psalm 119:9?

Discipline: *Should I discipline him when he is too knowledgeable of or relates in an unhealthy way to the opposite sex?*

Younger Boy:

"Even though you are six, you are becoming a man of honor. You need a reminder about young girls. There are guidelines, just as there are boundaries on a football field that you must not step over. For example, right now the Smiths are staying with us for several days, and their daughter, who is your age, was in the bathroom. You knowingly walked in on her. I had just looked at you and said, "Kathie is in the bathroom." Walking in on her embarrassed her as it embarrasses you. God made us to enjoy our privacy. So let's respect her privacy, okay? Thank you. But because you directly disregarded what I said, you need to go to your room for a time-out for ten minutes; then you need to come to me. I have a project for you to do."

Older Boy:

"God designed you with deep interest in girls. That interest can be good and enjoyable. However, with the many temptations one click away on the internet and iPhone, we need to come up with a plan to protect your honor as a blossoming man of honor. Temptation is real. You are not the enemy, but you can be the victim of the enemy. Not everyone on the internet has your best interests at heart. So dad will be talking to you about some filters that he uses. He seeks to be a respected man and wants the same for you. And let me say, women really, really respect men who guard their eyes and hearts. It makes them feel safe, secure, and loved. You are giving women a great gift. I bring this up because we found inappropriate sites on the search history on your iPhone. For the next week you lose iPhone privileges, and dad will be setting up the appropriate monitors."

Encourage: *Can I encourage him to keep developing knowledge of and relating to the opposite sex?*

Younger Boy:

Whenever a relative teases your ten-year-old by asking if he notices the girls at schools, your son gets really red in the face and turns shy. Later you can say to him,

> "God designed you to notice girls as he designed girls to notice boys. I noticed your dad and your dad noticed me. You are not alone with your inner thoughts about girls. That is normal. Uncle Fred was teasing you because he knows you are noticing as he noticed girls when he was your age. You are okay."

Keep the point short and sweet. This reassures him that he is okay and causes him to be more restful and confident.

Older Boy:

Though he was rejected by a girl and feeling as if no girl will ever be interested in him, honor him by saying that the character qualities he possesses will attract the right woman at the right time. Highlight the four or five characteristics in him that you know will attract a godly, wise woman to him. For example, Proverbs 19:22 states, "What is desirable in a man is his kindness."

Supplicate: *Do I pray about his knowing and relating to the opposite sex?*

Younger Boy:

In private with him, after he shared his interest in a girl at school, pray in the dark as he is in bed,

> "Lord, thank You that Brian shared about Michelle. I thank You that he sees such great qualities in her, like her kindness, honesty, and faith in You. Thank You that he observes these things. This is what honorable men do, and he is becoming that type of man."

Note: do not use prayer to mother him or send him an instructional message. Think more about honoring him as he seeks to honor God.

Older Boy:

Share with him:

> "I respect your desire to find the right woman. I continue to ask God to bring to you a godly, wise wife. I have always found comfort in what Jesus said about a husband and wife, 'What therefore God has joined together, let no man separate' [Matt. 19:6]. God fulfills a significant role in all of this. Though the Bible puts responsibility on the man to find a wife [Prov. 18:22], the Lord directs our steps. I am asking God to favor you. You will bring great happiness to the woman you marry. In fact, Deuteronomy 24:5 says, 'When a man takes a new wife . . . he shall be free at home one year and shall give happiness to his wife whom he has taken.' I know you will be this kind of man."

Ultimate Goal

The ultimate goal is to help your son understand Ephesians 5:33, where God commands a husband to love his wife and a wife to respect her husband. At Love and Respect Ministries, we seek to provide resources to enable this.

Here's a positive approach a mother can use with a more mature teen boy to motivate him to watch a Love and Respect marriage conference DVD and learn about love and respect:

"At this conference, you will learn that God designed you as a man of honor to live by an honor code. I see this in you big-time. Because of this, God calls you to navigate relationships with women in honorable and loving ways. This conference will give you tools that work with the opposite sex, whether it is with me, a girlfriend, or future wife. I want you to watch because this will greatly encourage you even though some of this won't apply until several years down the road. At the same time, some of this will apply at school on Monday. I know this is a sacrifice, but at the same time this is an investment in yourself. I believe in you and your future relationships."

By the way, this will help with your relationship with him. A mom said,

Several months ago, our church held a Love and Respect Conference. I encouraged my sixteen-year-old to attend. He did and took notes in his book and everything. I felt it was important for him as a young man to get an early start on understanding how he should treat me, a girlfriend, a future wife. He complained somewhat that it was boring at times to him, though he often repeats your jokes; however, he now constantly reminds me of his need for me to speak differently to him in my approach with him, and he responds positively when I point out how something he does feels unloving to me. I find that I have become much more conscious of how I say things to him, and when I fall short, he doesn't hesitate to point it out. He is much more sensitive to the way I interpret his lack of concern for something he does or does not do in regard to following rules as him not loving me enough to do the right things. Obviously, I know intellectually his love for me has nothing to do with his messing up, but it is how it makes me feel. He is much more understanding of that now, and I seem to frustrate him less.

In conclusion, few of us feel comfortable talking about sex. Who relishes the idea of informing a son about "knowing" a wife and understanding the sexual/romantic aspects of a relationship? Each of us, though, must remind ourselves that sex and romance in marriage are God's ideas. We need not be ashamed of what the Lord calls good. Though others promote lust and degrade women, a mother can indirectly counter this by leading the conversation in the direction that God intends. The fact is, someone will inform your son about sex and women. He will learn something. Will it be good and godly? Unlikely. This is your privilege and responsibility. Do not leave this to the boy down the street.

11

An Empathetic Look at the Motherly Objections to Respecting a Boy

Does the idea of using Respect-Talk strike you as questionable if not objectionable?

From listening to women over the years, I have heard several concerns about respecting males, which spills over onto sons. I have composed these criticisms below and offered answers with the hope this will ease the unsettled feeling about something not being right. My hope is that after you consider my responses, you will have a new vigor to apply Respect-Talk to the spirit of your son.

> Objection: "The Bible says love is the greatest. Love is all that matters. Love is enough for my boy. That's how I feel."

When the apostle Paul wrote in 1 Corinthians 13:13 that love is the greatest, he restricted the comparison to faith and hope. Of faith, hope, and love, love is the greatest. Paul did not have honor, respect, and glory in mind in this context. Why is this important to know? As God loves us throughout eternity, He glorifies us throughout eternity. As we love God throughout eternity, we reverence and glorify God forever. Therefore, we might say glory is respect on steroids.

How have some of us missed the importance of glory, honor, and reverence? When we have eyes for love, we will only see love in the Bible. When we do not have eyes for words such as *honor*, *respect*, and *glory*, we overlook these concepts. Admittedly, some have become more feminine in their outlook. Thus, one's outlook might cause an overlook. But we must know "the whole will of God," not just some of it (Acts 20:27 NIV). For example, theologians agree with the declaration of the Puritan catechism: man's chief end is to glorify God (1 Cor. 10:31) and to enjoy Him forever (Ps. 73:25–26). Yes, we are to love God and our neighbor as the first and second commandment, but we best love God by glorifying Him and enjoying Him forever. We best love a boy by respecting and enjoying him.

Objection: "My boy needs love. I will not neglect this need. I will not replace love with respect."

Boys need love and lots of it. I am not proposing that a mother stop loving and only do this respect thing. Think of it this way. A boy needs love like he needs water to drink, and he needs respect like he needs food to eat. A boy needs both. When mom only offers her love, she does not meet all of her son's needs. Water without food makes it impossible for one to survive. Love without respect makes it difficult for a boy to thrive. So I am not saying choose respect over love. For vital reasons, I am promoting the idea of increasing love by including respect, by adding Respect-Talk to mom's vocabulary. He needs to feel her respectful attitude toward him as a human being created in the image of God, not just hear her expressions of "I love you" toward the one who will, in her mind, always be her "cute, little boy."

Objection: "Because I love him, he should feel
respected. Love and respect are synonymous!"

I beg to differ with mom on this point. Respect differs from love. We respect our bosses, but we do not feel love for our bosses. We feel love for our teen sons, but we do not always feel respect for them. Actually, a mom can feel disrespect for her son all the while feeling deep love for him. An older boy knows the difference. Ask this son, "Does your mom love you?" He will reply, "Yes." Then ask, "Does your mom respect you?" He might answer, "No, not really. Not today."

Some contend that if you love a person, you will show respect, and when you respect a person you will show love, and to that I agree, but the concepts still differ. Though the left and right shoes are extremely similar, they are not the same. At many levels love and respect are extremely similar but they are not the same.

Objection: "Because I care, I get disrespectful.
My son won't listen to me otherwise. My
love is behind my disrespect."

It is impossible to argue that a mother's love can be behind her disrespectful treatment of her son.

First Corinthians 13:5 says that love "does not dishonor others" (NIV). It is a verse that is foundational to hear. Love does not show disrespect to another human being. It is not rude. It does not act unbecomingly. It is not ill-mannered. Such habitual disrespect is toxic, not healthy or loving.

That does not mean a mother agrees and approves of unacceptable and sinful behavior. It means that she confronts the unacceptable actions in a firm and truthful way but doing so under control and with respect toward the spirit of the other person—whether a son, husband, father, or male waiter.

Recently, as I exited a grocery store, a mother and grandmother entered the store with a boy around eight years old. As I glanced at them, suddenly they screamed and cursed at the boy in front of everybody. I looked at the boy to see what horrible thing he might be doing. He was ten feet away from them, on tiptoe, looking at the pastry section. He could smell the cakes and donuts. As I watched them all, I realized the adults found the boy disgusting in that moment. I am uncertain of what transpired earlier, before coming into the store, but what he did there for those five seconds paled in comparison to their verbal and emotional abuse. He responded by walking back to them. But I could tell he had shut down on them. His spirit did not connect with them. I am sure he closed off emotionally to protect himself from their verbal harpoons.

I have seen these scenes before in public, as have you. I am convinced that some of these women wish to appear to all that watch them as responsible, caring, and loving authority figures. They project that they are in charge and are mature adults. They view themselves as good parents, not like those permissive parents that let their kids run wild. I can almost hear their inner script: "Not mine! Not here!"

But their dishonor of this boy was unloving, not loving. All who gazed knew the truth. However, I wager that if we asked this mother and grandmother, "Would you say that you love this boy and are a loving mother and grandmother?" they'd say yes. No doubt, they could claim they are loving as evidenced by their discipline of the boy in the grocery store.

What about you? Do you give yourself a pass on your disrespect because you put this under the umbrella of your love for your boy? Do you confront him disrespectfully because you care?

What about your outbursts of anger? Galatians 5:20 states that "outbursts of anger" are sinful. Instead of referring to these outbursts as sin, should parents label them as loving rudeness? Would they maintain that their anger and disrespect are caused by the son who fails to be respectable?

I do not know of any goodwilled, tender mother who would argue against Galatians 5:20 to justify herself. Most mothers readily admit, "I went too far with my anger and disrespect."

Why are these gals so humble? First Corinthians 13:5 rings true to them. Love "does not dishonor others" (NIV).

Objection: "He causes my disrespect. I would not
be so disrespectful if he were more respectable."

Sarah and I learned at a certain point that our sons did not cause our
anger and disrespect. We now teach: "My response is my responsibility."
In other words, the boys revealed our decision to be bad-tempered and
rude. My boys did not cause me to be the way I was but revealed the true
me. My sinful reactions were not their fault, even though I rationalized
ways to blame them. This does not mean I should be unaffected by their
disobedience as though I were a robot. All of us will feel mad and sad.
However, my conscience told me about a line I should not cross. Being
mad is different from going mad. Being glum differs from calling my
son dumb. Sternness need not turn into screaming. Righteous indignation need not cross the line into sinful anger (Eph. 4:26). I knew what
Proverbs 29:11 states, "A fool always loses his temper, but a wise man
holds it back." My kids did not cause me to be a fool but revealed me to
be the fool. Ouch! Yes, a son needs to be respectable, but that's a separate
issue from a mom's choice to be disrespectful. A son may drive his mom
to the edge with his disregard and disrespect, but going over the edge is
her choice.

Objection: "Respect is not natural. It feels
counterintuitive. I don't even think about it. This is
not who I am. My mother tongue is love, not respect."

I agree that few mothers think about this respect stuff toward their boys,
and fewer still find it natural. Love-Talk is the mother tongue of mothers. God made mothers to love. But suppose a son has a need for respect
beyond mom's love? A mom needs to ask herself, *Is this about how I feel,
or is this about my son's need to feel respected for who he is as a human being
created in the image of God?* Sarah would say that many days she did not
feel like fixing meals for the kids, but she did it because she knew they
needed food. What she felt didn't matter. Because mothers love naturally,

I implore them to let that love oblige them to do what feels unnatural: meet their son's need for respect. The Bible supports that position. Philippians 4:8 says, "Whatever is honorable . . . dwell on these things." A mother should think about what is honorable to her boy. It is loving to think honorably.

Objection: "I don't really mean the disrespect. I love him. But there come moments when I have just had it with his disobedience."

A mother said,

> I have to vent. I cannot hold it in. I would not be honest or healthy. If I sound disrespectful, I really don't mean to. I feel better after the rant, and my son should know this. I just find his behavior is unacceptable and get carried away with some of my words.

Sarah and I empathize. However, at those moments, what does the boy feel? By way of analogy, can a dad say, "Look, when I am harsh and angry at my daughter, I really don't mean it. She should know that I am just upset and not take it so personally"? When mothers hear a dad explain himself this way, they are up in arms. He makes his daughter's need for love trivial and marginal. He excuses his loss of self-control. So, too, a mother must guard against trivializing and marginalizing her son's need to feel respected. Yes, he hurts, frustrates, and angers her, but giving in to the disrespect only exacerbates the problems between mother and son. Mom may not mean much by her disrespect, but it can steamroll her son. Mom's feelings take a backseat to what her son believes. "Well, Emerson, I have told my son that when I say disrespectful things, I don't mean those words, not really. I am not sincere." That's good, but hear this scripture: "Love must be sincere" (Rom. 12:9 NIV). A loving mom must not keep telling her son that she is not sincere about her disrespectful comments. He could question the genuineness of her love.

Objection: "He should not personalize all of this
as disrespectful. I am just trying to connect with
him and will provoke him to get him to talk."

When a mother wants to connect with her daughter, she will provoke her to get her to talk. The daughter may not like it, but she knows instinctively why mom goads her. Eventually, she opens up, and they talk about the stresses. Generally speaking, a daughter does not interpret the mother's disrespect as an end in itself. The daughter sees the disrespect as a loving means to get her to talk so both of them can feel better. She knows they will have a heated flare-up, but soon enough they will be talking heart-to-heart about their feelings, and mom will apologize profusely for her negative reaction and ask her daughter to forgive her. The daughter will forgive her mother, plus apologize for her moodiness and unwillingness to talk earlier. They hug and go about their business, feeling as if a hundred-pound weight has been lifted from their shoulders.

But it is not like this with a son. Does he feel that mom despises him as a human being? Does he think that she finds him inattentive, insensitive, and inept and, therefore, in need of a rude rebuke? Having said this, he knows that mom cares, and he knows that her bark is worse than her bite. He knows that he often deserves her fury. He also knows he can block her out and not personalize her ranting and raving. As a male, he can capably compartmentalize her criticisms, letting them roll off his back. But a moment comes when he cannot block the hurt. Mom's disrespectful words harpoon his heart, causing him to feel like he is dying. This can contribute to his finding ways of escape from her. He does not fear her physically; he fears her tongue. As she blurts out words of disdain that rock his world, he shuts himself down. He is light-years away from thinking she just wants to talk to make things better. No, he takes it as a personal attack on his character as a human being. He feels she intends to shame him for who he is.

I urge such a mother to realize that her son interprets the provocation as a challenge to his maleness and feels disrespected. He tends to interpret life through the respect lens. A boy personalizes conflict with mom to mean: "I am coming at you because I don't respect you, and I am using this conflict as an opportunity to tell you that I find you unacceptable and inadequate." This is why a mom needs to say to a boy, "I am not trying to be disrespectful. I just need to hear your thoughts on what is happening here that is dishonoring you." Note: do not confuse *thoughts* with *feelings* here, or *dishonoring* with *unloving*. Use the correct words to speak to his heart.

Or she might say it this way:

"How do I approach you on a couple issues that I need to address without your thinking I don't respect you as a young man? Help me speak the truth honorably to you without your getting angry and shutting down on me as though I only wish to dis you. Coach me. I want this to be a conversation among two people who have the other's best interests in mind."

Though a lengthy discussion may not ensue, the boy will relax more during the exchange since mom provides him information that enables him to rightly interpret her motive. She assures him that she is not using this dispute as an open window to poke her head out and yell, "I don't respect you!"

Objection: "I do not feel much respect for my son. It would be hypocritical of me to show respect when I don't feel it."

Are you a hypocrite when your alarm goes off at 6:00 a.m. and you get up even though you do not feel like it? We are never hypocrites for doing the right thing though we do not feel like doing it. That's called maturity.

Some moms think that if they do not feel any respect for their sons, then it would be wrong and dishonest to show respect. As long as they love and care, they think they should be able to honestly say, "I neither like you nor respect you."

But typically such feelings overstate the case, making things worse. A mother wrote:

> I am so ashamed of my son's behavior and his inability to walk away from blatant sin. I tell him I will always love him no matter what he does, but how do I resolve my lack of respect for him and his behavior? . . . He said, "You act as though I've been unfaithful to you." I told him I felt like the mother of Judas. So you see I have not handled this well.

Because of these feelings of disrespect, she overstated the case. Calling a boy Judas is comparable to a dad calling his daughter Jezebel. Maybe that's how a mother and father feel, but such words do not bring repentance and healing. Her son won't turn sweet on the heels of her sour description of him.

Add to the mix how God designed women to love and nurture. But when she feels distressed and unloved, disrespect oozes from her. This is why, in part, God commands wives to put on respect in Ephesians 5:33 and 1 Peter 3:1–2. They naturally feel and display disrespect when stressed. God's instruction protects wives from the tendency to act on feelings of disrespect. Of course, this is why a woman feels like a hypocrite when called to put on respect. She knows that she does not feel the respect in her heart. The problem is that she assigns the blame to her son's misbehavior, not to her nature. In her carnal and impulsive nature, she defaults to disrespect quickly and intensely but holds her boy responsible for these feelings. She needs to guard against this.

Objection: "Respect allows disobedience. I will not respect bad behavior. Respect-Talk gives him license to do whatever he wants to do. Only permissive parents do that kind of thing."

Unfortunately, as a society we think the showing of respect to undeserving people gives them license to do whatever they want. Some moms believe that the more respectful they are of their sons, the more lenient they must be toward their boys. To prevent indulging their sons via respectful treatment, these moms make a "logical" leap to, "I have to be disrespectful, or my son will disobey me. I must never let him think I respect his bad behavior."

So does this mean I promote the idea that a mother must let her boy slug his sister as a sign of respecting him and his violence? That's asinine. Putting on respect does not mean going along with whatever a son wickedly wishes to do. Respect entails boundaries. Mom must say no. Respectfulness demands truthfulness. What mom would say, "I respect my son so much I let him ride his Big Wheel on the highway since he begged me. I didn't want to be disrespectful to my little boy"? Respect does not mean a mom acquiesces.

The approach is simple, though not easy to do. Mom must respectfully confront bad behavior and firmly maintain limits on her son's selfish choices. This is about mom displaying a respectful demeanor as she respectfully confronts wrongdoing.

Who allows disobedience? A mother without a moral compass and strong backbone tolerates disobedience.

Objection: "Disrespect empowers me. I feel that if I am respectful, he will take advantage of me. If I am nice, he won't be. My disrespect makes him toe the line."

Respect is not about mom's being compliant and nice. That's not respect; that's enabling. Respect-Talk is tough. As love speaks the truth, so respect speaks the truth. Respect-Talk does not lack discernment about confronting, correcting, and enacting consequences, which I address in *Love & Respect in the Family*. Respectfully confronting a boy is a deterrent to that boy's taking advantage of mom. Long term, her respectful and truthful words empower her. On the other hand, a mom makes a mistake to think her disrespect makes her powerful. Some moms feel they must roll the eyes, sigh heavily, give a look of disgust, and say something like,

"Cheating and lying are wrong. You are a deceptive and dishonest person. People can't stand cheaters and liars. You repulse me. You are hopeless." In talking this way, a mom can feel empowered by her words. But this is not power; this is cruelty. Though such disrespectful words have a great deal of truth in them about the consequences of cheating and lying, the hyperbole shames the boy. Assassinating his character won't empower mom to prevent his misbehavior and inspire obedience. If anything, she inspires her son to be more cunning and underhanded to avoid her tongue-lashing.

> Objection: "Disrespect motivates him. My disrespect causes him to be more loving and respectful. It is the only thing that really works with him."

Disrespect does not motivate respect. Disrespect manipulates. Outward conformity is not inward receptivity. Contempt does not light a fire in a boy's heart to humbly adhere to the rules. Yes, yelling at a boy to stop yelling does work but only externally and temporally. Mom's disrespect does not elicit a boy's interest in being teachable.

Unfortunately, we are up against mom's experience, which tells her that disrespect works. This is why a mom chooses disrespect as her weapon of choice to motivate a son to do what she tells him to do. Sure enough, he obeys on the heels of her contemptuous rant.

For all that, mom's disrespect is not the cause of the boy's obedience. He obeys because he fears what comes next, after mom's disrespect. He thinks she is about to enact severe consequences that will make his life miserable. Wishing to avoid her retribution, he picks up his clothes, brushes his teeth, picks up the towels, turns off his lights, and jumps into bed. She, of course, erroneously thinks her contempt is the wonder drug.

Hebrews 10:24 instructs us to "consider how to stimulate one another to love and good deeds." I can say unequivocally, mom's disrespect does not stimulate her son to love and good deeds—not long-term.

Mull over the approach of authority figures, such as police and judges. Contempt is not necessary, and it is even counterproductive when dealing with criminals. Wise authority figures treat even felons with basic respect. They do not show incivility, bad manners, and insolence toward the law-breaker. That won't reform him. I agree that respect doesn't guarantee inner change, but rudeness never works. The best approach is a respect-ful manner with consequences that a boy feels. Mom needs to learn that her firm and respectful discipline spurs a boy to obey, if anything will. A demeanor of disgust and disdain does not deter disobedience, nor does it kindle within a boy a desire to lovingly respond to mom.

For self-reflection, do any of the following words describe a routine reaction to your son to get him to behave? Are you bad-mannered, impo-lite, discourteous, uncivil, offhanded, brash, short, offensive, insulting, derogatory, disparaging, abusive, tactless, undiplomatic, or uncompli-mentary? Since most women recognize the pain of these concepts when a man applies them to her, a son feels the same agony. No one is motivated by these traits.

Objection: "Disrespect is his punishment. My disrespect makes him feel bad for what he has done, and he ought to feel bad. He needs to learn a lesson."

A mom can convince herself that exhibiting disrespect punishes her boy. Yes, disrespect shames him, making him feel horrible over what he did wrong, but eventually he feels horrible about himself. He looks less at what he did and more at who he is. What human being both responds to habitual loathing and enjoys healthy self-esteem? Just because the spirit of a boy deflates on the heels of mom's contempt does not mean the punishment fits the crime. That's comparable to a dad's punishing his daughter by withholding loving affection to teach her a lesson. Hostility and contempt make a child feel rotten, warping his self-image.

As a mother, meditate on what Peter said about Jesus in 1 Peter 2:23: "When they hurled their insults at him, he did not retaliate" (NIV). Though Jesus seems beyond our example, Peter said: "Christ suffered for you, leaving you an example, that you should follow in his steps" (2:21 NIV).

The way of Christ for a mother does not include retaliation. Paying her son back in a tit-for-tat, vengeful way undermines a mother's imitation of Christ. Fighting fire with fire so it stops spreading in a forest may work, but in the family it only inflames and incenses. In addition, such punishment is punitive and vindictive, and no boy will open his spirit to his mom. Yes, mom must discipline, but that means her correction has a positive, futuristic goal to help her son get back on track, not get back at her son for getting off track.

Objection: "I need to be respected. As a mother I deserve respect. I am the parent. This is about my boy respecting me, not vice versa."

Yes, he ought to respect you. One of the Ten Commandments is to honor one's mother. I wrote the book *Love & Respect in the Family* to explain ways of bringing that to pass. However, every human being needs respect, not just mothers. We are all created in the image of God. God calls all of us to show respect no matter what. Peter wrote, "Show proper respect to everyone, love the family of believers" (1 Peter 2:17 NIV). Everyone means *everyone*. In chapter 2, I define respect as positive regard no matter what. This is unconditional respect. Unconditional respect means there is no condition, circumstance, or situation that can get mom to display disrespect and contempt toward the spirit of her son. She may not respect his behavior, but she can speak to him in a respectful manner about that which is not respectable. Unfortunately, once a mother believes respect must be earned, she gives in to the cultural opinion that if the other person does not deserve respect, then she does not have to show respect. That, combined with her belief that she deserves respect, leads to self-righteousness, anger, condescension, and judgment toward her son. These attitudes cause a boy to withdraw and close off. He won't emotionally connect with Pharisee Mom. Nor will he have a fond desire to show respect. The very thing mom demands, she diminishes. The good news here is that mom can see this as a mutual thing. "Son, we both need respect, and there are times neither of us deserves respect, but as we have conflicts, let's refrain from disrespectful attitudes and words toward each other. Deal?"

> Objection: "My respect makes me subservient.
> Showing my son respect would be honoring him as
> the parent. I would be surrendering my authority to
> him. That's a role reversal contrary to God's design."

When one human being shows respect to another, it does not catapult the recipient of the respect into an exalted and authoritative position. Mom's respect toward her son does not make him superior and her subordinate. That's important to realize; otherwise, a mother will subscribe to the false idea that her disrespect proves and ensures that she is in charge. Fact is, displaying disrespect toward a son causes him to look for ways not to follow her leadership, and look for ways to make plain his disrespect. Should a mom demand respect? Yes. But she does this by demonstrating respect. When she models respect she increases her moral authority to appeal to her son to be respectful.

A mother never loses her authority by speaking respectfully about the areas in which her son needs to submit to her parenting. Furthermore, her disciplinary actions, not her contemptuous speech, best motivate her son to obey.

> Objection: "Girls need respect. Boys are
> not special. This is gender bias."

Many of us are probably familiar with Aretha Franklin's song "Respect," but the truth is, Otis Redding wrote that song and released it in 1965, two years before Aretha adapted it to her female perspective of a confident feminist. Otis's version is of a desperate husband pleading with his wife for respect. He will give her anything she wants and doesn't care if she treats him wrong. Aretha changed it to "I ain't gonna do you wrong." Otis playfully said it is a song "that a girl took away from me."[1]

Yes, girls have a true need for respect, equal to that of boys, just as boys have a true need for love, equal to that of a girl's need. There should be no debate about this. However, I distinguish *true* need from *felt* need. Felt need means the way in which each feels about a situation. As we have mentioned, girls do not interpret circumstances in the same way as do boys, and vice versa. For example, research highlights what stresses teen girls and boys. Girls are more anxious during relational conflict. Boys react to challenges to their authority, which they interpret as disrespectful. Both can experience the same situation but interpret that event differently. And, yes, boys truly need love, but they tend to be more assured emotionally that others love them, as compared to many girls who tend to ask, "Do you love me?" or "Will anyone ever love me?"

Are there exceptions? Of course. But focusing on exceptions detracts from the bigger picture. Though women need respect, they lean toward love.

Objection: "I refuse to manipulate my son. This respect stuff is scheming and devious. This is not some formula to apply to get him to jump through hoops."

I agree fully. I preach all the time that this is not a formula. This is about meeting a son's need to be treated respectfully even when he disobeys. We are addressing the meeting of a son's need as an end in itself. By comparison, a dad is to love his daughter as an end in itself, not to get her to perform for his purposes.

The real test in determining your true motivations for respecting your son is this: Are you willing to treat your son with an attitude of respect during the times he refuses to be loving, respectful, and obedient in return? Those mothers who use Respect-Talk only to manipulate will quit applying it when they do not get the response they were hoping for.

Having said this, a dad's love for his daughter motivates her to respond as long as she detects dad's sincerity. So, too, mom's respect for her son motivates him to respond given he detects mom's sincerity.

Objection: "I will not feed male narcissism,
dominance, and superiority. I believe that is
the agenda here. A return to patriarchy."

"This respect stuff sends the wrong message to my son that men dominate. This would weaken me. I will not mislead my son into thinking men
have a right to dominate women." But does a mother's contempt prohibit
her son from thinking he can exercise mastery over women? There is no
evidence to support such a claim. And if she shows respect toward the
spirit of her son and tells him she speaks to him this way since he is becoming an honorable man, does this language cause him to wickedly rule his
future wife? Certainly no one would attempt connecting those dots.

12

FORGIVENESS

May I invite you to do two things? One, seek forgiveness. Two, give forgiveness.

Seeking Forgiveness

Before I address the need to seek forgiveness, let me say that many of you may not need to seek forgiveness.

You speak and show respect toward your boy. You not only love him, but also you honor him. However, you gravitate in your mind toward your inadequacies and failings, not your successes. Frankly, you are too tough on yourself, which is a plight of motherhood for too many. They see their shortcomings and beat themselves up. They worry about the possible damage they bring to their kids because of these foibles.

Are you such a mother?

If I could sit with you, I'd affirm the countless things you have done well. Were we to chat for a couple of hours, afterward you'd walk away feeling good about your mothering. I hope you have not taken what I wrote in this book and thrashed yourself based on your belief you have performed miserably. I feel bad that in my attempt to present a more comprehensive approach to Respect-Talk, some moms will feel guilty because there is bound to be something that puts serious seeds of doubt in their hearts. They will pass judgment on themselves as horrible mothers due to a few frailties and flaws. You are not a failure in school if you get all As and a B on your report card. In fact, that makes you a wonderful student. In the same way, don't be so judgmental toward yourself and your mothering. There is room for improvement in all of us.

Some of you mothers with older sons hate yourself when you did nothing wrong in the eyes of God toward your boy. You devoted yourself to your son as God intended, but your boy appears to have rejected your faith and values. Unfortunately, you concluded that you failed as a mother. Though you're self-loathing, you did not fail. We live in a culture that effectively persuades many of our kids that following Jesus is antiquated. Society broadcasts that secular living is for the intelligent, and believing in the Bible is for utter fools. The worldly elite believe conservative Christians are to be looked down on as peculiar, bigoted, unthinking, and hypocritical. The persuasiveness of the secular culture against the Christian faith is much stronger than it was when your parents were raising you. For this reason, this is not about your failings as a mother but the successes of a secular culture in turning your boy against your faith and values.

We have good news! We are praying along with you that as you apply the respect message, you will honor his deepest longings and motivate him to trust and follow Christ. There is no guarantee that he will follow, but you are not to hate yourself while he questions or strays. You must trust that the respect message is part of the antidote to the worldly influences that confuse him. Eventually, he will evaluate who is really authentic. As a mother who genuinely loves and respects her boy, you will be in the number-one seat of influence. Don't give up as though you have failed. You have not. Stay on message. And when you have fallen short, you can rebound by seeking your son's forgiveness.

How Can I Know If I Wronged My Son?

To jar your memory, is there anything that you have done or said that disrespected his deepest desires related to C.H.A.I.R.S.?

C: Did I disrespect his desire to work and achieve?

H: Did I disrespect his desire to provide and protect?

A: Did I disrespect his desire to be strong and to lead and make decisions?

I: Did I disrespect his desire to analyze, solve, and counsel?

R: Did I disrespect his desire for a shoulder-to-shoulder friendship?

S: Did I disrespect his desire to understand and "know" the opposite sex?

If not, rejoice! You are doing well. Relax.

If, though, your conscience felt convicted, then by all means, keep reading.

The Ground Rule

Here's the ground rule: seek your son's forgiveness only when you know for a fact that you were disrespectful. Sometimes a mom takes responsibility for what her son did wrong due to his selfishness and open defiance. But mom was not disrespectful; he was. However, if you are guilty of being disrespectful, simply say, "I am sorry. Will you forgive me for being disrespectful?"

Just saying, "I'm sorry" reveals how a mother feels, but it is only half the equation. How does her son feel? She will not know how he feels until she asks the question, "Will you forgive me?" She needs to hear his answer.

When a mother seeks forgiveness for having been disrespectful, he recognizes her sincerity. Whereas, if she were to seek his forgiveness for being unloving, he might feel that's a trick. Perhaps she is trying to get him to confess that he was unloving by confessing that she was unloving. Most boys see their mothers as very loving, but they do not always see them as respectful. That's why when she seeks forgiveness for being disrespectful, it gets his attention. He feels honored. I am not inappropriately parsing words here. In a boy's world there is a huge difference between the words *love* and *respect*. In most cases he is deeply moved in his heart and grants heartfelt forgiveness. Mom can experience a wonderful connection with him.

Seeking Forgiveness for Being the Offensive One

Some mothers resent the unloving and disrespectful reactions of their sons; but when studied more closely, the moms realize they inadvertently started the hurtful Family Crazy Cycle: without respect a boy reacts without love, and without love (and respect) a mother reacts without respect.

One major thing blinds mom. She does not see her contribution to her son's defensive reaction, which she feels is offensive, as being disrespectful. She knows she is trying to do the loving thing. Thus, in her opinion, her son should not feel disrespected. But a mom may not see that when she speaks from love she can *appear* very disrespectful. When women feel hurt and want to resolve the relational tension, they do so because they care, but the way in which they proceed appears contemptuous to men. Her face turns sour. She sighs. She rolls the eyes. She puts her hand on her hip. She scolds with her finger. And her word choice of disrespect can cause the leader of a motorcycle gang to wince. So instead of taking up offense, a mother needs to see her part and recognize that often her son's negative reaction is a defense against her derision. How sad that some mothers live for years resenting their sons' offensive reactions when the boys were only defensively reacting.

I ask mothers, "Just before your son reacted in an unloving and disrespectful way to you, did you say or do something that felt disrespectful to him?" They often readily acknowledge, "Yes, but he should know I didn't mean it. I was just so upset with him." Again, do not justify this but clear the air with,

"I am sorry. Will you forgive me for being disrespectful? That was not my intent. My intent was to address what happened, not belittle you. I need to tone it down. I am trying to help you become the honorable man I believe you to be. When can we talk about the tension between us in a mutually respectful manner?"

Boys Respond

A mother told me:

When [my adult son] was young I did not treat him with respect. Needless to say, I also didn't treat his father as I should have, either. When he began to go through some trials in his marriage he responded in ways that I did not approve of. I was very critical of him and did not respond to him in a respectful way. After reading your book I became convicted of my attitude toward him. I had learned the lesson regarding my husband but had not thought to apply it to my son. I wrote him a letter asking his forgiveness for treating him as I had, both as a young man and in the current situation. I am happy to say that he did forgive me and our relationship is better than it has been for many years.

Another mom wrote:

One day, I sat my seven-year-old down and said to him, "I'm sorry I haven't treated you like the man you are. I'm sorry that I've treated you like a little kid when you're not a little kid anymore." His shoulders visibly relaxed, and he agreed with my assessment of how things had been. I began to relate to him in a way that meets his need to be honored and respected, and I toned way down on the barrage of hugs and kisses. He responded by becoming more confident in general, and he began to treat others with more respect, rather than behaving aggressively toward them.

What About God's Forgiveness?

Should a mother seek God's forgiveness for her disrespect toward her son? After all, boys make far more mistakes than mothers, right? Shouldn't her boy be seeking her forgiveness and God's?

True enough. This, though, is not about comparing the mother to the son but about addressing the mother's relationship with Christ apart from her son. If she knows in her conscience that she crossed the line with her son, then she needs to also seek Christ's forgiveness. She can quiet her heart and express, "Lord, I am sorry. Will You forgive me for my disrespectful attitude toward my boy?"

As we have learned throughout this book, a disrespectful attitude in a mother toward her son is as sinful as an unloving attitude in a father toward his daughter. God expects us to be loving but also honoring (Rom. 12:10; 1 Peter 2:17). Disrespectful and dishonoring reactions constitute sin.

Appropriating Christ's Forgiveness

Okay, hold on to your sinking heart. I wish to make a very important point to every mother. Most women have a strong female trait: self-deprecation. Mothers blame themselves and move into personal shame on the heels of failing. For instance, if she feels no one is listening to her, maybe she explodes. She moves into attack mode and accuses everyone of failings, doing so with great disgust. A little while later she calms down, and regret floods her being. She may make the melancholy declaration, "I am a horrible mother."

What do some mothers do then? Some halt all reading of this book. Some pitch it into the garbage can. Others put it on a shelf. They remove Respect-Talk from their minds. They cannot stand the self-judgment they bring to themselves. They blame the book and mentally drift away from the topic of respect by preoccupying themselves with other things: volunteering, working overtime, shopping, caring for a family member, returning to school, singing in the worship band, or whatever. They suppress this truth about respecting their sons because it creates such anxiety and self-loathing.

However, that is not the way forward. The way forward is by appropriating the forgiveness that Jesus Christ extends and allowing the situation with her boy to deepen her confidence in Christ's positive view and love toward her.

Hear this story about a mother who recognized her faults but was able to forgive herself and turn around her relationship with her teenage son:

In the past I have made [my son] stand face-to-face with his older sister until he broke down and apologized, feeling like I finally broke him when he would cry or get furious. I wept at the conference at my huge mistakes and the wounds I have caused in my son. There has been a wedge between us, especially as he has gotten older (he's thirteen now). I have been, in a sense, on the Crazy Cycle with him. I came home ready to redeem the precious time I still have with him and show him respect and do life shoulder-to-shoulder with him. The day after the conference, I had to drive three and a half hours to pick him up from his grandma's. At the beginning of the conference, I was so excited and planned to spend the *entire* ride home telling him all that I had learned and how sorry I was for dishonoring him in so many ways. . . . He got in the car and announced he was going to sleep the whole way home . . . probably an attempt to protect himself from the fire hose of words I usually give him. So I said, "That sounds like a great plan. . . . I'm sure you are tired." And then I was quiet. Oh it was *hard*! But I wasn't sulky quiet. . . . I've done that before. I was just allowing him to BE. He lay there for a few minutes and then announced that he wasn't tired after all. We listened to the radio and just drove along. I didn't ask a single question the whole ride home! . . . Then he turned off the radio and told me stuff from like two years before, details and everything! We drove home this way, turning on the radio and just driving along and then him thinking of something and turning it off to tell me. When we walked in the house, he was skipping. And so was I. It really works! A few days later he was in the kitchen showing me his muscles . . . something he does on a regular basis . . . and I told him how truly amazing it was that I knew that he would die for me and would protect me if anyone tried to hurt me. He looked at me with such pride and love! . . . He was soaking up the respect! And I was getting love from my son! THANK YOU!

God's Forgiveness Is Total

The mother needing God's forgiveness is not an insignificant entity. Instead, she is an adopted child of God who needs to discover the extent to which Christ intends to help her as she responds to the light that he gives to her. She needs to welcome this light in humility and move forward with the confidence that Jesus Christ is going to honor her. Think of it this way: How can she expect her son to receive the light that she gives to him in order to enlighten, enable, and encourage him while she runs from the light of Christ in her own life?

She must trust what the apostle John penned in 1 John 1:7, "If we walk in the Light as He Himself is in the Light . . . the blood of Jesus His Son cleanses us from all sin." He then said in 1 John 1:9, "If we confess our sins, He is faithful and righteous to forgive us our sins and to cleanse us from all unrighteousness."

Regardless of your past failures, as you confess these in the light, Jesus Christ is reliable and good. He will wipe clean any wrongs from your record. From an eternal and judicial vantage point, it is as though you have never sinned in the eyes of God. Hebrews 10:17 states, "AND THEIR SINS AND THEIR LAWLESS DEEDS I WILL REMEMBER NO MORE." When you come confessing, "Lord, I have sinned again against You," it is as though He answers, "Again? I don't remember the last time."

I do not intend to suggest that God ceases to be omniscient. He will always know all things. But just as the court declares absolution of all wrongdoing for someone, so does God. In the court no one concludes that all memory of the past transgressions will now be removed from everybody's brain. People remember stuff. Instead, it means the court will not bring a penalty against the criminal. It will not be remembered legally, just as a wealthy aunt may not "remember" her niece by way of written documentation concerning an inheritance.

Of course, there are still earthly consequences. Imagine a bank robber who lost a leg during a car chase that resulted in a crash that killed three people. He must always suffer the loss of that leg and his remorse; but if the driver of the getaway car takes full responsibility for the incident, the robber will not incur a penalty for murder. In a greater way, our heavenly Judge absolves us from all wrongdoing in his record book. Yes, there may be earthly consequences but not eternal ones. Though it seems too good to be true, we are forgiven now and forevermore.

Accusations

Jesus never intends to shame you. Instead, He purposes for you to begin again. Proverbs 24:16 says, "A righteous man falls seven times, and rises again." The Lord forgives and expects you to stand up with your head up. Your problem is not the view that Jesus Christ has of you. Your problem is your view of yourself and the lies of the diabolical one. You need to recognize that the accuser of the brethren is Satan, not Jesus (Rev. 12:10). As with Eve, Satan whispers, "Hath God said?" (Gen. 3:1 KJV). Appropriating Christ's forgiveness by faith, while ignoring feelings of self-condemnation, is a tough row to hoe. Even so, you need to be able to say to the indictment of the devil, "Satan, I am far worse than you could declare but acquitted forever and ever by the blood of Christ."

Many stumble right here. They find it difficult to forgive themselves because of what they've done. For this reason a mother must mentally discipline herself to focus on what Christ did for her. We read in Colossians 2:13–14, "You were once dead because of your failures and your uncircumcised corrupt nature. But God made you alive with Christ when he forgave all our failures. He did this by erasing the charges that were brought against us by the written laws God had established. He took the charges away by nailing them to the cross" (GW).

This is not about what we have done but what Christ has done. We read in 2 Corinthians 5:21, "He made Him who knew no sin to be sin on our behalf, so that we might become the righteousness of God in Him." In other words, all of our badness in God's eyes was put into Jesus, and all of Christ's goodness was put into us in God's eyes. We refer to this as the imputation of Christ's righteousness to us. In the eyes of God, because of Christ's suffering for our crimes, we can no longer be accused and condemned by anyone, including ourselves and the devil. Romans 8:1 declares, "Therefore there is now no condemnation for those who are in Christ Jesus."

To the person who argues, "Oh, I could never forgive myself," I firmly object. If the Son of God intends to forgive you, who do you think you are not to forgive yourself? The Lord calls you to appropriate by faith, not by feelings, the forgiveness He has extended to you. He is God and you are not. He says He forgives all sin. Who are you to take issue with this? Do you have an element of carnal pride that works against accepting the fact that you are a sinner who needs forgiveness and who needs to forgive herself? Do you actually think you are good enough and powerful enough to pay for your own sins by refusing to accept Christ's forgiveness and thereby forgive yourself?

Again, there are natural and logical consequences on earth to our bad behavior. If you throw a dish at your boy that hits him in the head and leaves a scar, the scar *and* the nightmarish memory remain. However, when we grasp what Christ did for us on the cross, we realize that our sinful act will not be held against us at the Judgment. This is why we talk so much about grace and mercy. Grace is receiving something we don't deserve (the imputation of Christ's righteousness). Mercy is not receiving what we do deserve (condemnation for our unrighteousness).

Giving Forgiveness

Could a mother resent her son for failing her expectations and/or God's standards? Few mothers are filled with venom toward their boys, but let's be honest: as a boy gets older, he can act immorally or illegally, which deeply offends his mother. One day she detects indignation within herself and struggles to forgive him. Perhaps, for example . . .

C: He did not work or achieve as he should have. He lied or stole.

H: He did not provide or protect as he should have. He was seriously negligent toward another.

A: He was not strong, did not lead, and did not make decisions as he should have. He followed the wrong crowd, resulting in serious trouble.

I: He did not analyze, solve, or counsel as he should have. He put himself and others in serious jeopardy.

R: He did not do shoulder-to-shoulder friendship as he should have. He engaged in illegal activities with his friends.

S: He tried to understand and know what he should not have about the opposite sex. He got a girl pregnant.

Suppose one or several of the above transpired with your son. Do you feel extremely upset and offended? Do you find yourself mad about this day after day? Do you feel an animus toward your son that controls your opinion of him?

Forgiving, Forgetting, and Absolution

You need to forgive your son. By that I mean you need a forgiving spirit.

Unfortunately, many misunderstand the expression "a forgiving spirit." They think it means absolving a boy of all wrongdoing and moving forward as though nothing happened, as though mom has amnesia.

Many of us have heard the saying, "To forgive is to forget." That then begs the question, "If we have not forgotten, have we not forgiven?" Anyone with half a brain won't forget serious transgressions. For this reason, we need to learn that one can have a forgiving spirit while remembering the transgression. The Bible does not teach that if you forgive you will lose all recall.

Furthermore, one can have a forgiving spirit and still make the other person answerable for what he did wrong. Forgiveness does not demand exoneration. Let's take an extreme example. A mother can have a forgiving spirit toward her son who stole all of her jewelry and sold it to get money for his drug addiction. Her forgiving spirit does not prohibit her from contacting the police to inform them of what he did and bringing the full weight of the law to bear against her boy. (By the way, she remembers his wrongdoing the rest of her life. Her forgiveness does not entail forgetfulness.) Forgiveness does not necessarily mean she drops the charges either. She can have a forgiving spirit while visiting him in prison. A forgiving spirit does not preclude the enactment of serious consequences for lawlessness. There is no contradiction with a mother's forgiving spirit and having her son under lock and key.

She can say to her son,

"I have forgiven you totally, but my love and respect for who I believe you to be compelled me to do what was clearly best for you. The best option was to allow you to suffer the consequences of your wrongdoing and be placed in a rehab facility. I forgive you, but I am not for 'giving you' license to do that which will ruin the honorable man I see in you."

What About Trust?

Does a forgiving spirit mean a mother must trust her son? No. This is important since some boys guilt-trip their moms. "If you really have forgiven me, you will trust me and won't keep asking me what I am up to." Intimidated, mom turns quiet and docile to prove that she has forgiven and that she trusts her son. However, she does not have to prove anything. She did nothing wrong. Her son is the one who did wrong and needs to prove himself. If a mother interprets a forgiving spirit as demanding blind trust, she will turn angry, contentious, and contemptuous after he takes advantage of her for the fifth time.

The wisest pathway to walk is to have a forgiving spirit while remaining diligent to do what is best for the boy, not back away into silence and meekness because the boy says, "You don't trust me." A mom can reply,

> "I trust your spirit, but I do not trust your carnal flesh. I don't trust my own carnal flesh. Neither one of us must kid ourselves about our weaknesses. But this isn't about my trusting you; this is about your proving to me that you are trustworthy, and that comes by my verifying what you are doing. Trustworthy people can always verify themselves."

As President Reagan used to espouse: trust but verify.

The Bible on Bitterness and an Unforgiving Spirit

"But Emerson, I hear you. I can hold my son's feet to the fire along with a forgiving spirit. But honestly, I no longer want to be forgiving. I have lost the energy and incentive to let go of my resentment."

Another mom might declare, "I tried this forgiveness thing, and it didn't work. I have to be in a constant state of anger to remain strong and forceful." She concludes that her bitter attitude toward her son ensures that he does not forget that he offended her, guards against his hurting her again, and empowers her to motivate her son to repent.

Let me share two fundamental incentives God's Word reveals for letting go of rancor.

First, the Bible says in Hebrews 12:15, "See to it that no one comes short of the grace of God; that no root of bitterness springing up causes trouble, and by it many be defiled." Note that bitterness (an unforgiving spirit) does not eliminate trouble but causes trouble. In fact, a mother becomes defiled by her own bitterness. If you have ever had someone break into your home while you were gone and they went through your belongings and stole things, you know what it feels like to be defiled. In like manner, your bitterness breaks into your soul and defiles you. It also spills over onto friends and family members. As the text says, "by it many [are] defiled." Nothing good comes of an unforgiving spirit.

Second, long-term resentment subjects a mother to demonic attack and undermines her close fellowship with Christ. We read in Ephesians 4:26–27 "BE ANGRY, AND yet DO NOT SIN; do not let the sun go down on your anger, and do not give the devil an opportunity." Note that Satan takes advantage of prolonged anger. Paul referenced the same idea with the Corinthians. We read in 2 Corinthians 2:10–11, "But one whom you forgive anything, I forgive also; for indeed what I have forgiven, if I have forgiven anything, I did it for your sakes in the presence of Christ, so that no advantage would be taken of us by Satan, for we are not ignorant of his schemes." Again, an unforgiving spirit gives Satan access to us in a way that he would not have if we had let go of the resentment.

At the end of the day, before the sun sets, this is not about your son. This is about you giving permission to the devil to have a foothold in your heart. He cannot possess you, but he will oppress you. He will intensify your anger, undermine your relationships and reputation, and cause you to come short of receiving all the grace God intends to impart. I wouldn't mess with an unforgiving spirit.

See Your Son's Goodwill

Get in tune with your boy's goodwilled intentions. He may be thoughtless, but he is not mean-spirited. A mom wrote:

Remember how it felt to be stood up on a date? Well, how is it to be stood up on a lunch date by your own twenty-six-year-old son, and to top it off, he sees you four days later and doesn't mention it at all?

This is where I have to remember the goodwilled principle and really exercise obedience to be merciful and forgiving. He, as a man in my life, did not intentionally get up that Wednesday morning and decide that he wanted to hurt me and ignore his promise to dear old mom. I have to *choose* not to say what is going through my mind or plot some stinging rebuke to his next attempt at making this lunch date.

Your boy isn't trying to be unloving or disrespectful. Trust his heart. See his goodwill. This eases the hurt and removes the supposed offense.

This Is Ultimately Not About Your Boy

For the mother following Christ, God calls her to do what she does "as to the Lord." Jesus said that as we have done things to the least of these, we have done them to Him (Matt. 25:40). The great news is that everything a mother does toward Christ counts. This means seeing Jesus beyond the shoulder of your boy.

A mother e-mailed:

I was convicted by your teaching to always show respect for my four boys. I have been having immense struggles about obedience with my seven-year-old son. I have been burdened with a dislike for him as we engage in this Crazy Cycle. I don't want to be a part of it, but [I am] raising seven children, ages thirteen to four months, with a husband that travels at times. I start to lose my purpose in serving the Lord. Your message today was so freeing. I know he shows the ugliness in my heart. I was at my end, exhausted from my inability to break this cycle. I am going to look beyond him and see Christ. I am going to reflect on scripture to show Jesus' love for him. I am going to let God do the work to mold him.

In my book *Love & Respect in the Family*, I address that which I call the Rewarded Cycle. When a mother does what she does "unto" Christ, the Lord will say to her, "Well done!" We learn in Ephesians 5 and 6, which addresses marriage, parenting, and indentured servants, that Paul established a universal principle: "Serve wholeheartedly, as if you were serving the Lord, not people, because you know that the Lord will reward each one for whatever good they do, whether they are slave or free" (Eph. 6:7–8 NIV).

Nothing you do toward your son is wasted when you do it as to the Lord Jesus Himself. In fact, God intends to reward you throughout eternity. As you seek to revere Christ beyond the shoulder of your boy, you will approach your son with dignity and respect. Actually, showing a respectful attitude toward your son when encouraging him or disciplining him receives a boost when you envision Jesus with the eyes of faith standing beyond your boy.

As we end, please know that though you cannot control the ultimate outcomes in your boy, you can control your actions and reactions. You can seek your son's forgiveness and the Lord's, and you can have a forgiving spirit. You do what you do unto Christ beyond the shoulder of your boy. When you do these things, you touch the heart of the other Son in your life.

Appendix A

A Quick Start

For Those Who Feel Pressed for Time

Beyond "I Love You," Say, "I Respect You" (Without Superficiality or Manipulation)

Listen to these mothers who told me what happened when they used the word *respect*. As you read these testimonies, consider if you can do the same this week. This is the Quick Start recommendation.

A mom of adult sons recounted:

> In talking to my sons on the phone, I thought I would try out the respect thing. Instead of always ending our conversation with I love you, I said "I respect (I made it personal to their situations)." One son got quiet and then said, "Thank you, mom," which really touched my heart. Another son who is more distant from us emotionally and spiritually also got quiet and then said, "I love you," which he seldom says first or responds to when I say it. To me that was awesome. I expect new fruit in many areas and look forward to using these tools to bring healing to first myself and then others. God bless your ministry.

After using Respect-Talk with her college-age son, a mom reported:

[He] responded with shock, "Why are you saying you respect me?" But he started acting differently. I could hear in his voice and see in his e-mails he seemed to be more confident in his maleness. He's been so socialized about "love," it was like he was set free to embrace the need to be respected. His defensiveness in being an independent college student stopped.

A mom e-mailed:

My relationship with my twenty-two-year-old son improved overnight! Who knew that silence was so valued? That sitting side by side and simple changes in words could make such a difference. Now I tell him how much I appreciate him, and he tears up. Before, I told him I loved him and got back, I know, I know, I luv u too. Learning the right words to get my feelings across in a way they can be assimilated was so easy! I encourage everyone I know to watch your series. Thank you!

A mom chronicled:

I have spent a lot of my formal education studying psychology, counseling, and especially counseling children. . . . I was going to give the (respect) topic a little more thought and see if I could practice some things with my own four- and two-year-old sons before writing. I don't have any daughters, so I can't compare, but I need to share what just happened tonight before I forget. At bedtime we always do a lot of cuddling and singing and reading and praying. We always hug and kiss at the end and I *always* tell each of my boys that I love them. They always say, "I love you too, mom." Keep in mind they are four and a half and two and a half, so this is such a sweet time. They are so sweet. They tell me often that they love me and always say it back when I initiate it (I'm sure this won't always be the case).

Tonight my husband wasn't home, so I was putting them to bed by myself. At the end of our time, before I left the room, I was really close to my four-year-old, and I said, "Brendan, I totally respect you." He grinned from ear to ear and almost bashfully said, "Thank you." He is normally polite, so it's not like I've never heard "thank you" before, but in this context it kind of blew me away. I think I either expected a question like, "What do you mean?" or I expected him to just repeat it back to me. But he didn't. He just appreciated it. . . . . I intend to keep telling my boys that I respect them because I do. Thank you so much for your powerful ministry. I have already passed a lot of this information on to my sisters (the disrespecting men and male-bashing stuff runs pretty heavily in my family).

A mother wanted to see how her sons would respond to the concept of respect. She told me,

Aaron is a charmer—and a bit of a ladies' man (even at five and a half). It is not unusual for him to tell me (or any other female) that I am cute. I frequently tell him I love him, and he responds with "I love you too, mom." However, when I told him that I liked him, he said, "Mom, even when you don't let me do things that I want to do, I still love you." I felt that I got a more heartfelt response because he didn't just parrot back to me what I had said to him. I really think I was communicating in his language of respect, and he responded in mine (love). He has never initiated saying "I love you," and for it to come after I told him I liked him seemed significant to me.

Another mom said,

I decided to try your respect test with my fifteen-year-old son. Saturday night I sent a text message to my son that said, I Respect You—within moments he replied, Thanks, mom, why? I then responded to him with reasons why. He said, Totally random but thanks, mom. When I returned home and saw him, it was Valentine's Day, and I handed him a small box of chocolates, and he said, "Cool, just like your text over the weekend." My son is someone who never wants to talk to me (probably pretty typical of a fifteen-year-old male with his mom). I was totally amazed and will continue to show him the respect he needs. Thank you for your ministry—what a beautiful life-calling.

Mothers know the typical attitudes and responses in their sons. That's why when applying respect, some things seem so simple to the outsider looking in. But mothers know it is not common. That's why we continually hear moms say, "To me that was awesome. . . . He has never initiated saying 'I love you.' . . . It kind of blew me away. . . . I was totally amazed."

Let's hear from a dad who followed my instruction on Respect-Talk when it came to disciplining:

I have been amazed at the response from [my son] when my discipline to him includes using the words, "Son, I know you are a man of honor . . ." My son is far more open to understanding the discipline when I am sitting next to him shoulder-to-shoulder on the bed or on a walk, where we can both stare forward or down.

In regard to the Man of Honor statements, when my son and daughter get into a fight, I no longer ask him, "Why did you hit your sister?" but now I sit on the bed shoulder-to-shoulder and say, "Son, I know you're a man of honor, so I don't understand why you would hit your sister." Then I give him a minute to think about it before letting him know that it was unacceptable and that I would like him to learn from this lesson and act honorably in the future.

I tell everyone about the Man of Honor approach when disciplining boys that you told me about, and they all get it! I can tell you firsthand that it has changed the way I address issues with my son, and the results have been amazing, with much less unintentional shame and a much faster re-engagement process with the family after we have him sit alone and process the issue.

Mothers, listen to this dad and apply the same. This just works, folks.

Okay, mom, I want you to use the phrases: "I respect you" or "I appreciate you" or "I am proud of you." Maybe say when you are disciplining, "You are a man of honor, so help me understand why you did XYZ."

As you read the chapters of this book, I go more in depth, coaching you on how to communicate respect in six areas.

- "I respect your desire to work and achieve."
- "I respect your desire to provide, protect, and even die."
- "I respect your desire to be strong and to lead and make decisions."
- "I respect your desire to analyze, solve, and counsel."
- "I respect your desire for a shoulder-to-shoulder friendship."
- "I respect your desire for sexual understanding and 'knowing.'"

This is about character qualities related to these six areas. "I respect your decision to be honest . . . your diligence in doing your homework . . . your desire to share your toys with your friend . . . the way you encourage your teammates . . . your commitment to tithe to the Lord . . . your faithfulness in attending youth group." There is always a character quality a mother can affirm verbally, even if in other areas her son falls short.

Respect-Talk does not apply to physical features that have nothing to do with his character and desires. "I respect that you look so handsome. I respect your blue eyes." That's comparable to a husband saying to his wife, "I love you for looking so good to me." So will he stop loving her if she stops looking good to him? Will mom stop respecting him if he stops looking handsome?

Some words of caution when you do the Quick Start:

One: Always Speak What Is True.

One, always speak what is true. Do not make up something about respect. Never lie. Always find something about which you can speak truthfully and respectfully. Think before you speak because your son will detect deception. All moms perpetually look for some insight to get their son to change for the better. That's a good thing.

Because mothers feel motivated by love, combined with their worry and weariness, they try out this respect thing to see if it might work in helping their sons improve. For example, a mom glances at this book on the shelf at a bookstore, then puts it back on the shelf and heads home to try this technique on her son. She reads this "Quick Start" chapter and "gets it." That's not a bad thing.

But what I have encountered repeatedly is an odd mind-set. She heads home to try out this "respect thing" to see if it is true. By way of analogy, she reminds me of someone with a token in hand standing in front of a vending game. "Hey, the respect coin (saying 'I respect you') is in my pocket, and my boy is standing in front of me like a vending game. I may as well say, 'I respect you' and see if he does something loving. I want to discover if this is true. Maybe I will be surprised with something special. If not, I have dinner to prepare."

I say this tenderly, based on what some moms have told me. A mother can be naïve if not imprudent, superficial if not manipulative—all because she feels love and wants love, and other tactics haven't worked. As long as her motive is loving, she fools herself into thinking her methods are sanctioned.

But she is raising no dummy. Her son can detect that he is her guinea pig. Such actions by a mother equate to a step-dad insincerely telling his adopted daughter that he loves her so she will quit crying and he can watch the football game. Every mother I know gasps for air when a man deceitfully conducts himself like this. In her case, though, she doesn't blink an eye when she conducts herself in a comparable way, for two reasons: One, she believes the father is impure; whereas, she cares for her son. Two, a daughter is hurt by such actions; whereas, her son is oblivious—he is fair game to try this on. But when it comes to the respect subject, he is not unaware or unsuspecting. This may be a touching theory or a marginal matter to a mom but not to her son, who quietly tracks respect at the core of his being. Mothers need to tread carefully here. She must use "I respect you" with utmost sincerity and truthfulness.

Two: Don't Overuse the Phrase "I Respect You."

Men among men use the *respect* word less than women use the *love* word. Men do not go around saying, "I respect you," the way women continually express, "I love you." Men are more compartmentalized; whereas, women are more expressive-responsive. So don't overexpress the phrase "I respect you." In other words, I am not asking you to substitute "I respect you" for all the "I love you" statements you make every day.

Said too often, a boy will conclude that mom is disingenuous. He will detect that you are using a technique to get something from him instead of meeting a need in him. Too much cake makes anyone sick. As you read the chapters, you will learn when and where to use Respect-Talk. I provide you with many examples for younger and older boys. You will get the hang of this. Again, relax, but go slow at the beginning. Do not over-speak it.

Here's the good news about Respect-Talk. You might miss the exact moment to tell him you respect him because you were distracted or lovin' on him. However, later that day as you review the day's events and recall a missed opportunity, you can still go to him and say, "I was thinking about what you said earlier, that you told the truth. I really respect you for that." Then exit the room. Don't hang around to talk about it unless he immediately wants to talk about it.

Respect-Talk is not time-sensitive as much as it is fact-sensitive. Did he in fact say or do something that allows you to say, "I respect you"? If you recall a fact from two weeks back or two months ago, you can tell your son.

Whereas expressions of love among women give immediate feelings of connection between mother and daughter, boys process differently, generally speaking. It is the substance of the comment that touches them, energizes them, motivates them, and influences them more than the respect words causing a connection with mom—though there is a subsequent connection. That's why you have not failed your son when you express respect for him fourteen days later when you suddenly remember something. You did not miss a moment to connect with him since it isn't just about connection between the two of you.

In my marriage book, *Love & Respect*, love for a woman results in closeness, openness, understanding, peacemaking, loyalty, and esteem. Respect for a man results in greater motivation to work and achieve, provide and protect, be strong and lead, analyze and solve, be friends, and relate honorably. Generally speaking, love causes women to connect; whereas, respect causes men to act and be more loving.

Let me make a comment about what I call the Energizing Cycle: mom's respect motivates a son's love, and a son's love motivates mom's respect. A mother wrote:

> My husband and I have enjoyed reading *Love & Respect*. We are missionaries in West Africa and borrowed your book from another missionary. We wanted to share how your ideas worked with our three-and-a-half-year-old son. I wanted to tell my son a special thank-you for the good behavior he had shown in the last week. So I knelt in front of him and said, "I am so proud of the way you have done good listening, cleaning up, and helping." I was about to give him a hug when he said, "I love you so much" and gave me a kiss. I was amazed! *Love & Respect* works for children too!

There it is! A mother's respect motivates a son's love. Many moms believe that her love should motivate her son's love, and it does. But wait until she observes Respect-Talk motivating his love. Yes, you need to take this by faith. For now, just trust me. This works.

Three: Love and Respect Deposits Can Be Wiped Out by Serious Withdrawals of Disrespect.

Everyone knows we ought to communicate truth respectfully. What we don't pay attention to is the delivery. A mom, for example, can be right in what she says but wrong at the top of her voice. Her words of affirmation from yesterday are stolen today by her tone and loudness, which sound disrespectful to him today.

In marriages, I coach couples to ask themselves this question: "Is what I am about to say going to sound respectful or disrespectful?" In most cases we can figure it out if we *want* to figure it out. Of course, when we cannot discern the answer, we need only ask the other person, "Did that sound respectful or disrespectful?"

First, ask yourself after you spoke, "Did I say that disrespectfully to my boy?"

Second, if you do not know, ask your son. "Did I say that in a way that sounded disrespectful to you?" No mother intends to make respect deposits only to make larger withdrawals due to her disrespect. These two questions help her avoid bankrupting the relationship with her son.

Four: Just Relax.

Ask God to bring things to your mind and begin the marathon. Start jogging. This is not a hundred-yard sprint. You cannot "do this respect thing" to get it over with so you can go back to doing the love thing. This is not a one-and-done exercise. This is about a lifetime commitment to meeting a respect-need in your boy. Because you love him, you will meet his masculine need for respect, just as a father who respects his daughter will meet her need for love—month after month and year after year. Love and respect for a lifetime.

Ask Your Son, "Do You Want Me to Say, 'I Love You' or 'I Respect You'?"

Another Quick Start exercise is to have fun in discovering what your boy thinks. A mother told me:

> I had a wonderful conversation with my eleven-year-old son that same
> evening. We went to dinner and a movie together (a rare opportunity
> without his sister and dad). I asked him which was more important from

dad and mom: to be told that we love him or that we respect/value/are proud of him? He thought for moment and then definitely stated it was more important that we value him or prize him.

This is how he defined respect. I loved his expression to "prize" him (value him as a person). He added that when he was younger (six, seven, or eight) it was more important to hear that we loved him and to show him outward affection. Now that he is entering middle school, it is more important that we respect/trust him and allow him independence— he strongly disapproves of "nitpicking" mothers (sounds familiar to "nagging" wives).

Inform your son, as you ask him, that in choosing just one, you are not saying the other is less important. Let him know that this is just a fun little test and you are curious about what most uplifts him: "I love you" or "I respect you."

This allows some mothers to see firsthand a dimension in their sons that, heretofore, "in every respect" (pun intended) escaped their notice.

Let me insert that younger boys do not yet understand an abstract concept such as respect as a standalone. I asked my four-year-old grandson, Jackson, if he wanted to hear me say, "I love you" or "I respect you." He said, "I love you."

I then asked, "Do you know what *respect* means?" He said no. I then gave him this word picture: "When you put on a Superman outfit and are brave and strong, do you want me to say 'I love you for being Superman,' or 'I respect you for being Superman?'"

Immediately and with great energy he said, "Respect." He went from not knowing to knowing. He "gets it" with a concrete word picture. If boys do not understand the concept of respect, they will default to the word *love* since moms always use the word.

In asking the question some of you will be surprised by his answer. But don't act negatively surprised. You could make him feel that he ought not to feel this way. If he says "respect" but you give off an air of disapproval, such as rolling your eyes, you run the risk of him closing off to you out of fear. No boy wants his mother's disapproval. That feels disrespectful.

In our marriage conferences we address a husband's need for respect, and after that session hundreds of women turn to their husbands and say, "Is that really how you feel?" They cannot believe that what I said about their husbands is true, and they want their husbands to say, "No, that's not true about me." Instead, he meekly comments, "What do you think I have been trying to tell you all these years?"

Many wives write me in shock: "I had no idea that's how he felt." A mother can do the same with her tone and words when asking her boy. "Do you want love or respect from me? Surely not respect, right?" Her question is not a question but a demand. I say this tenderly, but a mom might not want to risk hearing her son say "respect" because deep in her heart she knows the amount of disrespect she has displayed.

Many women tell me that they have become contemptuous within the home. Exhausted, frustrated, hurt, and angry, a mom can take it out on the child who creates the most stress—who typically is a boy. Consequently, this information threatens and guilt-trips her. She covers up her fear and shame by rising up against her boy: "What? You want respect? What are you saying, that I am disrespectful? How can you say that?" She shuts him down. She knows of her rudeness and belittling but rationalizes it. She turns a special moment to peek through a window into her son's soul into a moment where he boards up his soul against her discourtesy and disparaging words.

Here's an incentive for not reacting this way. My wife, Sarah, addresses this in our conference. She asks, "Do you want your daughter-in-law to speak with habitual disrespect toward your son?" Not one mother wants this. For this reason, every mother needs to model what she may need to tell her daughter-in-law to do.

This mother needs to speak out of her credibility and reputation about how to treat her son respectfully, though he does not always deserve respectful confrontations. It is easier to be disrespectful when confronting his unrespectable behavior. She needs to be able to explain that Respect-Talk is not about a son deserving respect but about a woman learning to convey truth in a respectful manner.

Contemptuous speech never creates fond feelings of love and affection in the male soul. In chapter 2, "Understanding What Respect Looks Like to Boys," I define respect and how to show respect when a boy does not deserve it.

A father wrote to me:

> I have one other observation: we have two boys, ages ten and twelve. Since listening to the [Love and Respect] CDs, I have started to watch carefully how they interact with their mother. What I have noticed is that they have their own mini Crazy Cycles. When she speaks to them with what I think of as "that tone"—the condescending and disapproving voice—I see how it crushes them, and they soon show unloving and disrespectful behavior and vice versa. I pray that my wife will not only gain from this study for the benefit of our marriage but that it will also benefit her relationships with our two sons. I now counsel them daily to show mom love even when they feel she is being "too critical," as my twelve-year-old put it.

Some mothers trigger the Crazy Cycle: without respect a boy reacts without love, and without love (and respect) a mother reacts without respect. For this reason I ask a mom, "Is your son reacting in ways that feel unloving to you, and then you react in disrespectful ways?" Do you spin?

Many moms identify with the Crazy Cycle and want to stop it. Disrespect triggers a negative, unloving reaction from most boys, especially as they get older. Once mom decodes this dynamic, she can defuse it with the power of Respect-Talk.

Of course, this information generates questions. A mom asked,

> Do you have any information about the Crazy Cycle when it involves a mother/teenage son relationship? I know our sons are

men-in-the-making and that they need respect to become manly, but in so many ways they still need correction. Have you any suggestions as to how to correct an adolescent son without starting the Cycle spinning?

Yes. I cover this in the chapters of this book. For instance, I help a mom understand how to discipline with Respect-Talk in ways that motivate a son to be more loving and respectful. I show you how to confront, correct, and enact consequences toward a disobedient son without using disrespect as the weapon of choice.

Sarah had lunch with a friend. While they were seated at the table, the male manager visited with them. Sarah mentioned in the course of the conversation that I was writing a book on mothers and sons and the importance of a mother's speaking with respect. Blown away, this man painfully shared, "This is the problem my wife has toward our son. She is condescending and belittling to get him to obey. She says things to him that are emotionally killing him. He then reacts big-time."

Exactly! Disrespect triggers a son's unloving and disrespectful reaction. Though disrespect sometimes works to get him to clean up the mess the dog made, in the long run disrespect feeds the Crazy Cycle. It does not reduce the insanity.

Back to the question: "Do you want to hear 'I love you' or 'I respect you'?" What if a boy says "love"? Keep two things in mind. One, some boys will say "love" because they really want love, and that's okay. It is perfectly acceptable for a boy to express himself this way.

Philip, age nine, says to his mom, in response to her question about wanting love or respect, "Definitely love all the way. Can't live without it. The word means more to me. Just tell me you love me." She says, he "likes being told, 'I love you.' And he also says, 'I love you *so so* much.'" In our research, 17 percent of the males expressed their preference for love. I have no intention of trying to make a boy mouth something he does not feel. However, the research bears out that 83 percent of the men gravitate toward the need to feel respected.

Even so, I am not concerned about that boy who exclaims, "Definitely love all the way." Moms will love that boy naturally. It is a win-win. My concern resides with the boy who wants to feel a mother's respect and is ignored.

When asking the question, make sure your son does not say "love" just because he fears it will hurt you if he says "respect." He knows you love to love, and if he senses at any point you ask the question with the expectation that he will answer, "I love you," then he'll tell you what you want to hear. He does not want to be disrespected for differing with you.

Here is something you might want to do for extra credit. Say to your son, "I want you to feel free to say, 'Mom, I know you love me, but I feel like you are not respecting me.' I want you to tell me this when you feel this way. I may not change what I am saying, but I will try to say it more respectfully, okay?"

A mom told me:

> I make sure that he knows how much I value and respect his feelings, as well as the fact that he is willing to share those feelings. I've learned that even though he is only eleven, I still have to show him respect. I choose my words carefully. I never want him to feel belittled. I always am watchful that my words do not crush his spirit. When addressing my son, I make sure that he knows how important respect is when dealing with everyone.

Here is extra, extra credit: Ask your son, "What makes you feel respected, honored, appreciated, valued, or prized?" Some boys have never been asked or given permission to even discuss this desire. Some will puff out their chests and tell mom their answers. Most will reply, "I don't know." Most boys find it hard to describe what they feel about respect; whereas, a daughter can talk at length when asked, "What makes you feel loved?"

If your son cannot answer, do not conclude that this issue is insignificant to him. Not having a ready answer does not mean he finds the matter trivial. Boys are less expressive-responsive. To conclude he has no desire for respect because he does not readily talk about that desire is comparable to asking a teen boy about his interest in sex and observing him look down at his feet and say nothing. What person would conclude, "Oh, I guess my boy doesn't think about sex since he said nothing when I asked him about it"?

This is not about ceasing Love-Talk but adding Respect-Talk. Boys need both love and respect.

A mom e-mailed:

> I have only boys—three of them (three, five, and seven in age)! So I can only speak on the boys' side of things. They are too young to really verbalize which they would rather have, but I do know that . . . my oldest responds better with respect yet loves to be told we love him. I do notice when I say I'm proud of him for his behavior/actions, he swells up with pride (in a good way) and wants to know all the reasons why I was proud of him in the particular situation.

There it is: "he responds better with respect yet loves to be told we love him." Can a mother beat that combination? Two sides of the coin.

"Emerson, are you sure my love is not enough?" You can love him but not meet his need for respect. You can actually love your son but not be proud of him, and he interprets that as no respect for who he is as a person. Some mothers readily confess, "I love my son dearly but do not always like him or respect him, though I try never to communicate those negative feelings. Admittedly, he frustrates and angers me because he doesn't listen and obey me."

Interestingly, as the boy ages, he sees more of mom's true attitude than she sees in herself. "My mom loves me, but she is not proud of me." This explains a scene with an older boy when his mom says, "But I love you." He angrily reacts, "I know you love me. You tell me that all the time." Baffled and hurt, she cannot figure this out, until now. He needs to feel her respect.

Hear Your Son Again for the First Time

Due to selective listening, I invite you to hear your son again for the first time. This is another immediate action step you can take.

With some boys, you will hear them using Respect-Talk as though for the first time. You will realize you never paid attention to this because it wasn't relevant to you. You speak Love-Talk and hear Love-Talk. You do not speak Respect-Talk, nor do you hear it.

I received an e-mail from a mom who heard my presentation on a boy's need for respect:

> I know you're working on your book about boys and respect. I'm sitting next to my boy, who's playing the computer game *Fate*. All of a sudden, he said, "Mom, I am respected now!" In the game, you have a respect level score that gets higher the more you play well. My boy reached the level of . . . "Renown."

Because of what I had taught her, she listened with new ears and looked with new eyes. A lightbulb came on for her. Before this, his comments would have passed her like a ship in the night. Oblivious. However, this time what she heard him say provided a glimpse into his masculine soul, and this insight thrilled her. It registered with her that she was onto something epoch-making.

What if a mother retorts, "That game proves nothing other than some meaningless fantasy residing in that boy's head"? Her rejoinder is comparable to a dad saying that his daughter's dollhouse is nothing other than some meaningless fantasy residing in that girl's head. No, these are the early bubbles—evidence of an underground spring, soon to flow into a creek and then a river. The boy is becoming a man as the girl is becoming a woman.

I urge moms to listen carefully. Your son speaks through a blue megaphone, and you need to put on blue hearing aids because your pink hearing aids operate at a different frequency.

Why might a mother not hear what her son is saying about respect? In psychology it is called "selective exposure." She tends to hear what she listens to. She does not see what she does not look for. Most mothers want their sons to be more loving. Continually she urges him to be more sensitive, to say, "I am sorry," to look the other person in the eye, to ask how he is doing, and to be nice. The list of loving attitudes and actions she expects lengthens. She filters almost everything through the love-grid. She selectively pays attention to Love-Talk.

In addition, she loves her boy and serves him each day, and she longs for him to respond to her and be grateful. She looks intently at whether or not he values all that she does for him since a quality son will appreciate his mother. Because love dominates her thinking, she does not look for respect stuff.

Selective exposure means a mom can put on blinders, which prevent her from seeing anything but love. A horse with blinders sees only straight ahead. He cannot see the whole world around him. Blinders are great to prevent a horse from being spooked. Blinders on a mother, however, prevent her from seeing her son's need for respect. This is not a good thing.

A mom told me:

[I have a] nine-year-old son. I received the cutest hand-written Mother's Day card this week, and you would be amazed what the first line of the card read: "I appreciate you because you are respectful." The rest of the card talked about being thankful for doing his laundry and how I am good at math, but the respect comment was on the top.

This boy revealed something about himself to his mom. This mom wrote to tell me that she almost missed it because she wasn't listening for it. But when she did pay attention, his note exploded with meaning to her in a way that would have passed her.

A question for you: If your son complimented you for being respectful, what would have been your thought prior to learning about respect? What would you think now?

Decide Right Away Against the Quick Quit

It is so easy for me to guilt-trip mothers without trying.

Their sensitivity and love are so intense that the mere hint that they have failed to speak with Respect-Talk (or worse, have used disrespect) shuts them down with shame and guilt.

For instance, watch how guilty I can make you feel. You say to me, "Dr. E., can I just tell my son that I didn't mean it when I spoke disrespectfully?" I reply, "This is the same comment a wife makes about her husband on the heels of her disrespect of him. She will tell me, 'My husband should know that I didn't mean it.'"

Okay, here is where I hammer you. "I agree that you didn't really mean it with your son. However, the nursery rhyme—'Sticks and stones can break my bones, but words can never hurt me'—is a lie. By way of another analogy, did you know that in the law there is a category called 'involuntary manslaughter'? For example, a driver unintentionally hits a pedestrian who darts out into the street, and she runs over him and kills him. She had no malicious intent, so the courts give her mercy, and she is neither fined nor sent to jail. But she still killed the man. Though the analogy is drastic, many mothers have no evil intent when being disrespectful. But a handful of mothers are emotionally killing their sons nonetheless."

Okay, do you feel like a rotten mother, a man-slaughtering woman? Some mothers immediately put themselves into that camp of mothers. They may have excelled in so many other arenas but have fallen short in this way. The failure overwhelms all of her successes.

Because of a mother's sensitivity, guilt overwhelms her due to her incredible concern to be a good and loving mother. But here is what I find peculiar: she suddenly bolts for the door to get out of this "respect room," for a few gals subscribe to the notion of "out of sight, out of mind." It is here a few moms shut down. Instead of standing at the starting line to begin this exciting marathon, they exit the race. They decide against a Quick Start. They decide for a Quick Quit.

They walk off the track, never to return. To ease their guilt, they wall off what they envision as my pointing finger. They imagine me waving it in their faces, screaming, "Shame on you!" They interpret good news about their sons as bad news for them.

But hear me: *you are not a bad mother who has killed the spirit of your son.* I gave the manslaughter illustration as a mere metaphor to make the point that we can have goodwill and no malicious intent, but we can still hurt our boys. But you have not killed your son. So take a deep breath.

Truth is, your son knows your loving heart; and you will learn how quickly men forgive, drop it, and move on.

In chapter 12, I address the importance of seeking forgiveness for past disrespect.

Now, though, I want you to see how quickly your Respect-Talk brings healing to the hurt your son feels. Think of your response to your husband after he hurt you. How quickly does your spirit soften and move toward him to connect when he says in humility, "I am truly sorry for my unloving reaction. Will you forgive me? I was wrong"?

Every wife I know nearly melts. Love-Talk heals the hurt. The language of Respect-Talk that I teach in this book will touch the heart of your son in matching ways. Respect-Talk only consists of a few vocabulary words, so do not expect this to be a yearlong language course.

But you must not shut down on me. Shutting down is easy because there is no one out there who is saying to you what I am saying. You can position yourself next to the loudspeaker that is blasting this message: "Love your son by telling him he needs to be more loving . . . more loving . . . more loving . . . like you!" The decibels resonate so loudly, they drown out my small whisper from a hundred feet away: "Let me teach you about Respect-Talk."

You no longer hear me, and then you turn to your BFF and say, "I just heard this guy say my son needs respect." She snaps back, "What? Respect your son? He needs to respect you. That's ridiculous. Your son needs to respect your love and be more loving, just as my boy needs to learn the same. This isn't about what we need to do as mothers; this is about what our sons need to do. Turn up the loudspeaker. Our boys need to hear they need to be more loving."

Added to this, some moms say to themselves, *I feel bad enough about myself as it is. I do not want to feel worse. I cannot handle one more thing right now. I do not have the energy to take on this respect stuff.* One such mom would drop the whole topic to maintain inner equilibrium, to feel good about herself as best she can.

In a week or two, if no one reminds you, you will put out of your mind the mother tongue of your son. You do the Quick Quit. You turn your full attention back to Love-Talk—every time. Love-Talk is your mother tongue, to which you default. This is why I recommend "Emerson's 21 Days of Inspiration in Applying the Respect Message" (Appendix E). I invite you to embark on this worthy journey—to keep Respect-Talk front and center in your thinking and not shut down due to some nightmarish scenes of disrespect. Let me inspire you with a reminder over twenty-one days.

"But, Emerson, I have really been rude—no, beyond rude. Surely I have failed my son and ruined him for life. I don't ride a broom, but I have 'witched' him!" You have not failed or ruined him. It is never too late, even if the son is seventy-five and you are ninety-five.

Would a seventy-five-year-old daughter forgive her ninety-five-year-old dad who said, "I have failed you. I have failed to love you. I have hurt you deeply, and I can only hope you would forgive me. Will you forgive me? I have been the fool who neglected to love you, a precious gift to me from God. Oh, how I hurt over the pain I inflicted on you. I have asked God to forgive me. I only hope you can find it in your heart to forgive me"?

Given this man is sincere, the daughters I have met find a cataclysmic shift takes place in their souls. So, too, a mom can recover with her son; it is never too late, and this book will guide you through this recovery. But you must choose to come out of the dark into the light. You must not dart away from this Quick Start. You must do the Quick Start recommendations, then keep reading the book for the path to follow. You can also sign up for my e-mails for twenty-one days of inspiration (see Appendix E). It is a bright, new day! Heaven sings!

Right Now, Ask God to Help
You Discern and Apply

In hearing this message about respect, I believe for some of you this is both an answer to prayer and a call to prayer.

Along with you, I believe that God is very interested in your mothering influence on your boy and always hears your prayers on his behalf. I also believe that He intends to reveal new truth to you about respect toward your boy. May I invite you to continue to pray but also to pray with new requests for ways to show your son respect?

The apostle James tells us that we have not because we ask not (James 4:2 KJV). Let's ask!

A mother wrote:

> I could not sleep this morning. I was praying and asking God what I must do. Our situation at home is not what I know it could be. I share some of the same testimonies of the mothers from your writings on respecting sons. I was specifically reflecting on one son's behavior last night. I believe God led me to read your insights in His perfect timing. I will be stopping now to spend quiet time with the Lord. I believe that God has answered my cries for help in this very emotional situation.

Another mom wrote:

> [In 2009] I finished the Love and Respect seminar. I went with the intention of improving my marriage, yet as I sat there, I kept reflecting on the deterioration of what used to be a very close relationship with my eighteen-year-old. Before the series, I just couldn't figure out what

was causing the distance between us. It was respect. My son desper-
ately needed respect, and I didn't know how to show it. I knew how to
show love but not respect, especially when my son was doing the typical
eighteen-year-old behaviors, such as putting off chores. How was I to
correct bad behavior and still show respect?

I went home and prayed that the Lord would show me how, and
He did! Instead of nagging about things that my son had done wrong, I
used a gentle tone to tell him how putting off chores made me feel, as if
he didn't care about my feelings or needs.

As she gave voice to her side of the equation, she let him know that
her words were not expressed with the purpose of disrespecting him but
to show him the power and influence he had in their relationship. She conveyed to him that she needed his strength and help. He stepped up to the
plate.

She commented, "Our relationship took such a drastic turn that within
three months we were as close as ever!"

A mother shared with me, "I begin the day asking God to open my
eyes to ways He can show respect through me; then I become proactive,
and the reactive episodes seem to diminish. . . . I have eight children, ages
twenty-eight down to eleven."

May I invite you right this moment to pray this prayer?

Lord, You know how comfortable I am with expressing my love to my
son. It is who You made me to be: one who loves. However, You know
how foreign this Respect-Talk sounds to me. Yet as I listen more deeply,
I am hearing a ring of truth. Though I cannot wrap my mind around all
that I am learning, I can see that my son needs respect. There really is a
man in my boy. Honor and respect energize and motivate him. Though
I wish he could remain my precious, sweet baby, You have designed him
as a male who needs respect. As difficult as this is for me, he must never
remain mommy's little boy.

In Genesis, You announced that a son is to leave his father and mother and cleave to his wife. No son is to cleave to his mother. He is to move toward independence, and I sense now that my respect, not just my love, contributes significantly to his healthy development and departure. I accept this; no, I welcome this as Your plan. Though I hope never to degrade or ignore this truth, help me in a culture and era when so many oppose respecting a man and some promote contempt. Let me not come under their influence. Instead, You be my influence.

Teach me what respect looks like to the boy You have gifted to me. I need You to help me do what is best for my son. I offer myself to You with the request that You guide me in meeting my son's need for respect. As I read this book, direct me to examples that fit my son. He and I both need your encouragement in this. And forgive me for those times of disrespect. I am sorry. But, more importantly, grant to me the power to change so I do not keep returning to You for forgiveness, though You always forgive, and for that I give You thanks. Most important, as I end this prayer, beyond respecting and honoring my son, may I reverence and honor Your Son. In His name I ask these things, amen.

During the first twenty-one days after reading this book, you can receive inspiring e-mails from me. (Learn how to sign-up in Appendix E.) Though difficult days come and doubts and discouragements control us more than we desire, God still calls us to look to Him as Jesus looked to the Father. God calls us to entrust ourselves and our sons into His hands. Though a mother cannot control the ultimate outcomes in her son, she can ask God to help her control her actions and reactions to her son. She can ask God to provide opportunities for her to act respectfully in ways that touch the heart of her son. She can ask God to help her stop her disrespectful reactions when such behavior deflates and defeats her son. Though her son may not appreciate her respectful demeanor as he ought during this age and stage, there is One Son who does—the Son of God. Nothing a mother does in trust and obedience toward Jesus is wasted. Everything counts. Everything matters to Him.

Appendix B

A CHECKLIST

Apply G.U.I.D.E.S. to His Six Desires: C.H.A.I.R.S.

The thing I love about moms is that they hunger for examples. But is it possible to give so many examples that a mother feels overwhelmed? Possibly. So let me say up front, I am providing two templates: G.U.I.D.E.S. and C.H.A.I.R.S. These serve as checklists. G.U.I.D.E.S. is a mother's side of the equation—the side God calls her to do as a parent. C.H.A.I.R.S. is a son's side of the equation—the desires God put in her son.

Have you ever watched a pilot as he sits in the cockpit? He goes through a checklist quickly to make sure he has covered the essentials before taxiing out to the runway. G.U.I.D.E.S. and C.H.A.I.R.S. enable you to check yourself and your son—quickly.

How do G.U.I.D.E.S. and C.H.A.I.R.S. interface? G.U.I.D.E.S. is God's call on mom as a parent that enables her to apply Respect-Talk. C.H.A.I.R.S. is God's design of boys and the desires He has placed within the DNA of a boy. Let me make some brief comments that explain C.H.A.I.R.S. and how to use Respect-Talk. See this as an appetizer.

As you quickly review these concepts, they should trigger in your mind opportunities to use Respect-Talk with your son as you go about loving him. My hope is that you will become familiar with the basic ideas behind G.U.I.D.E.S. and C.H.A.I.R.S. so that during an episode with your son, you can quickly think about how to respectfully apply *Giving*, *Understanding*, *Instruction*, *Discipline*, *Encouragement*, and *Supplication* to your son's Conquest, Hierarchy, Authority, Insight, Relationship, or Sexuality. Please do not be intimidated. If nothing comes to your mind, do not worry about it. But I believe you'll be amazed. You will find yourself saying, for example, "Oh, this is an area in which I need to Understand (U) his need for respect related to the Insight (I) he just offered his sister and me about why a bee will not sting unless threatened. I can say, 'Johnny, I respect your insight on bees. Thanks for sharing.'" Simple enough. Or "I need to Encourage (E) him with my respect related to the Conquest (C) he is pursuing in graduate school to find work in Alaska to study the oil pipeline. I can say, 'Josh, I respect this pursuit and your passion. Few young men have this kind of vision.'"

There are as many exciting ways to use Respect-Talk as there are boys, and these two acronyms open up dozens of doors. These serve as keys to the heart of a son. These two checklists provide sufficient information to enable you to apply Respect-Talk to the soul of your son. Remember, he is worth it.

Do not be overwhelmed by this information any more than when you look at a book with thirty-six recipes and feel flooded, as if you are drowning in data. As a book of recipes is a delightful resource to present a lovely meal on any given day, see what you read here as equipping you to feed your son a nourishing comment today and a differing nutritive comment two days from now. Do not feel deluged but delighted with these tasty tidbits. During the tougher moments with your son, see Respect-Talk as a spoonful of sugar that helps the medicine go down.

Let me show you how G.U.I.D.E.S. applies to C.H.A.I.R.S. Enjoy these three dozen morsels. When one of these areas strikes a chord, turn to the chapter where I address that aspect. Presto!

Giving: To show my respect, does my son need me to Give (G) resources related to C.H.A.I.R.S.?

- My Giving related to his Conquest: Can I give something to help him work and achieve?
- My Giving related to his Hierarchy: Can I give something to help him provide and protect?
- My Giving related to his Authority: Can I give something that will help him to be strong and to lead and make decisions?
- My Giving related to his Insight: Can I give something to help him analyze, solve, and counsel?
- My Giving related to his Relationship: Can I give something to help him develop shoulder-to-shoulder friendships?
- My Giving related to his Sexuality: Do I give something to help him know and relate to the opposite sex?

Understanding: To show my respect, does my son need me to Understand (U) his exasperation and anger related to C.H.A.I.R.S.?

- My Understanding related to his Conquest: Do I understand his struggle with working or achieving?
- My Understanding related to his Hierarchy: Do I understand his struggle with providing or protecting?
- My Understanding related to his Authority: Do I understand his struggle with being strong, leading, and making decisions?
- My Understanding related to his Insight: Do I understand his struggle with analyzing, solving, or counseling?
- My Understanding related to his Relationship: Do I understand his struggle with developing shoulder-to-shoulder friendships?
- My Understanding related to his Sexuality: Do I understand his struggle with knowing and relating to the opposite sex?

Instruction: To show my respect, does my son need me to Instruct (I) related to C.H.A.I.R.S.?

- My Instruction related to his Conquest: Can I instruct him on how to work and achieve?
- My Instruction related to his Hierarchy: Can I instruct him on how to provide and protect?
- My Instruction related to his Authority: Can I instruct him on how to be strong and to lead or make good decisions?
- My Instruction related to his Insight: Can I instruct him on how to analyze, solve, or counsel?
- My Instruction related to his Relationship: Can I instruct him on how to learn to develop shoulder-to-shoulder friendships?
- My Instruction related to his Sexuality: Can I instruct him on how to know and relate to the opposite sex?

Discipline: To show my respect, does my son need my Discipline (D) since he is not as disciplined as he ought to be related to C.H.A.I.R.S.?

- My Discipline related to his Conquest: Should I discipline him when he is too inactive or lazy?
- My Discipline related to his Hierarchy: Should I discipline him when he is too uncaring or fearful?
- My Discipline related to Authority: Should I discipline him when he is too unruly or bossy?
- My Discipline related to his Insight: Should I discipline him when he is too unteachable or foolish?
- My Discipline related to his Relationship: Should I discipline him when he is too unfriendly or isolated?
- My Discipline related to his Sexuality: Should I discipline him when he is too knowledgeable of or relates in an unhealthy way to the opposite sex?

Encouragement: To show my respect, does my son need my Encouragement (**E**) related to C.H.A.I.R.S.?

- My Encouragement related to his Conquest: Can I encourage him to keep on working and achieving?
- My Encouragement related to his Hierarchy: Can I encourage him to keep on providing and protecting?
- My Encouragement related to his Authority: Can I encourage him to keep on being strong, leading, or making good decisions?
- My Encouragement related to his Insight: Can I encourage him to keep on analyzing, solving, or counseling?
- My Encouragement related to his Relationship: Can I encourage him to keep on developing shoulder-to-shoulder friendships?
- My Encouragement related to his Sexuality: Can I encourage him to keep developing knowledge of and relating to the opposite sex?

Supplication: To show my respect, does my son need my Supplication (**S**) (prayers) related to C.H.A.I.R.S.?

- My Supplication related to his Conquest: Do I pray about his working or achieving?
- My Supplication related to his Hierarchy: Do I pray about his providing or protecting?
- My Supplication related to his Authority: Do I pray about his being strong, leading, or making good decisions?
- My Supplication related to his Insight: Do I pray about his analyzing, solving, or counseling?
- My Supplication related to his Relationship: Do I pray about his developing shoulder-to-shoulder friendships?
- My Supplication related to his Sexuality: Do I pray about his knowing and relating to the opposite sex?

Appendix C

DAUGHTERS, ADULT WOMEN, AND MOMMY ISSUES

What About Daughters?

D oes the culture really understand boys? Generally speaking, the mind-set is all about teaching boys how to treat girls. A mother wrote:

> Two of my children are attending an essay class. Last week they were told to write an essay titled, "How Should a Gentleman Treat a Lady?" or "How Should a Lady Treat a Gentleman?" . . . everyone chose the first option. My daughter, without being prompted, offered an explanation: "There is more material available to answer the first question."

Because girls exercise greater sensitivity and empathy, the thinking is to stay on boys to teach them to be sensitive and empathetic.

Here's what we do not observe. Women and girls react with great disrespect when feeling unloved. When females feel a brother is not sensitive and empathetic, they can verbally lash out in ways that cause the hair on a cat's back to stand up. Though a girl feels vulnerable, the female tongue does not sound vulnerable to a boy. Her tongue can be venomous.

What is our response to girls? Do we coach them on "How Should a Lady Treat a Gentleman?"? No. We tend to give a pass to girls other than saying, "You shouldn't say those things." There is no serious consequence. Because we know girls speak out of hurt and will soon enough apologize, we let them remain in that pattern for years. Added to this problem, the boys do not cry but steel themselves against their tongues. The boys appear arrogant, angry, or indifferent. We deduce the boys need even more rebuking. We hand them the essay "How Should a Gentleman Treat a Lady?" Inside the boys can be dying, but who cares? As a culture we gravitate toward how to treat a lady but not a man, thinking if we can exhort men, all will be well. But as I say, "The key to motivating a person is to meet that person's deepest need." If we do not teach girls about the power of their disrespect and how that shuts down the heart of a boy because it undermines his need as a human being, we will not motivate the boy to hear us when we coach him on how to conduct himself toward women. When he feels dishonored and unjustly treated, he will pull away. When he feels we respect his heart, he becomes teachable.

Daughters who are aggressive toward younger brothers really need coaching. A mother informed me:

I have even been teaching my older daughter to respect her brothers. I just told her today that it is detrimental for her to hit, hold, or push a boy. I watch my boys rear up in anger within seconds when restricted or pushed in frustration. My husband and I do not allow this behavior, but it does happen enough.

One mother made the adjustment:

So many times when my daughter shares frustrations with the males in her life, whether it is her twin brother, her dad, or boys at school, I am able to say, "Hey, let me help you try to see the issue the way they see it," or "Here is why they may come across like that." She is always interested to hear about the differences in men and women.

What happens when a sister makes a respectful gesture? A mother wrote:

Thank you soooooo much for speaking to the children on how love and respect apply to them. At one point in the conference, Katie (the dominant choleric) leaned over to Daniel (the quiet phlegmatic—and younger) and just hugged him and apologized for being harsh and not respecting him as a man and brother. I know I saw his shoulders puff out. Priceless. Quiet Daniel was most talkative and loved the lists Sarah covered.

Girls, when coached, will get it because of their sensitivity. A mom told me, "One of my daughters was really treating my son badly—bossing him and speaking to him like she speaks to our dog—and she has had a total turnaround for which I am so thankful." Girls can understand C.H.A.I.R.S. when it is explained to them.

I love what this mom said to her eleven-year-old daughter. Having attended the Love and Respect Conference, the mother said,

I began explaining the simple things we had learned. As I told her some of the different ways boys react than girls, she squealed, "Mom, you would not believe it. In social studies, you should see the boys act out some of the things we talk about in class. They pretend to blow each other up; they are *so* weird!" I replied, "Not weird, just different." A light went on in her precious head. We are changing the thinking of the next generation. How exciting to be able to pass these truths down to our two daughters and two sons.

A mother wrote me of her concern:

We need to change the message we send to daughters. My parents certainly taught me independence and competition . . . even with boys. We were built on the mantra "Anything boys can do, girls can do better."

Beating a boy was a victory and a celebration. These lessons make sense as a means to protect our daughters from hurt, but perhaps a better lesson and model is the idea of love and respect. A young woman who grows up ready to compete for power with a man will struggle to submit to the man of her heart.

She highlights an important truth about respect. But is teaching respect comparable to teaching a girl to submit? No. Both Paul and Peter began their discussions of marriage with direction to wives, regarding submitting to their husbands (Eph. 5:22; 1 Peter 3:1), but they referred to meeting a husband's need for respect (Eph. 5:33; 1 Peter 3:2). It dawned on me one day that a wife submits to her husband's need for respect just as a husband submits (Eph. 5:21) to his wife's need for love. Mutual submission is possible when understood to be the meeting of the other's deepest need. For this reason, mothers need to frame respect as something other than being a doormat. This is not about the girl being less than the boy and being walked on. That's never the way of Christ and is a perversion of the biblical meaning. This is about meeting a boy's need. This concept of submission, first and foremost, that a woman appears respectful even when upset and confrontational, has revolutionized the thinking of many women. It is positive and proactive.

What About Mothers, Sisters, and Female Friends?

Women talk about their children. Constantly. Some female friends may downplay this message of a boy's need for respect. They will object for any number of reasons, which we set forth in chapter 11. I want you to remain true to what you now believe about respect. Women influence women. Your female family members and friends are not mean-spirited, but some do not like or respect men because of earlier hurts. The disappointment has been so severe they now protect themselves by spewing out contempt. Thus, a conversation about respecting boys can meet with resistance. Instead of debating, ask for their feedback to discover what they feel and why. Ask them to share their opinion in response to these questions:

Can a mom conclude her love should be enough for her son? What if a boy truly needed something from his mother beyond her love? What if he needed far more respectful treatment?

Can a mom appear far more disrespectful to her son than she intends? Can she appear more disrespectful than she appears loving?

What does a boy feel when he concludes his mom does not like or respect him as a human being?

Can a boy know his mother loves him but see that as less important to him than if his mom respects him?

What if a boy needed to feel respected for who he was apart from his performance? Could a mom miss this need? If she misses this need, is it no big deal since she thinks the boy must be egotistical?

Does a mom really love her son if she thinks the boy should feel respected because of her love?

Can a mom love her son yet react in ways that feel hugely disrespectful to her son?

Can a mom fail to see her disrespectful reactions since she is so upset with her son's behavior? Can she inadvertently be disrespectful, just the opposite of what her boy needs?

Can a mom not see the extent to which she reacts negatively in ways that feel disrespectful to her son since her daughter does not feel that way?

Can a mom overlook the signs and signals given to her by her son for respect? What would it look like for a boy to reference his need for respect?

Can mom's disrespect explain why her son withholds his affection from her?

Can a mom observe her boy change and not know why because she does not recognize that he interprets her as loving him but not respecting or liking him?

If these women find their curiosity piqued, let them read this book. The good news is that this book provides the insight to prevent a mother from neglecting her son's need.

Mommy Issues

Mothers from families with only women feel ignorant about respect toward men. A mom wrote:

> I am a first-grade teacher and a mother of a four-year-old boy. During your conference, you spoke about the differences between little girls and little boys several times. Hearing you talk about the differences between boys and girls (not wrong, just different) was so helpful to me. I come from a long line of girls (all aunts and sisters, and my dad passed away when I was a child), so I do not have a lot of experience with little boys. I love my son so much and appreciate him for his energy, humor, and overall boyness. However, I want to make sure that I am doing all that I can to parent him as a boy should be parented. . . . My question is, can you point me in the direction of some good resources to equip me to be a better mother to a wonderful young man and a better teacher to many young men?

I hope this book will be a wonderful resource for this goodwilled mother.

Another husband wrote: "My wife never had any siblings, and so she does not understand the nature of boys." It is one thing to lack knowledge of men; it is another to be openly contemptuous toward men and boys. A woman wrote, "I was raised by a very strong single mother, and I grew up with her and her friends talking about men like they were just useless lazy creatures. To me, whatever boys can do, girls can do better." Another told me, "I have two sons, eight and almost seven. . . . I don't know why it took me so long to understand the heart of a male. But I can shed some light on this. I came from a very broken home. All I saw were strong, domineering, bullying types of women or very passive-aggressive [ones]. Not a great model for me to raise sons." Still another commented:

To be honest, if it weren't for my boys, I wouldn't be "dealing" with any man right now. I have a horrible view about men. . . . As you can tell from my negativity, I really don't have much hope in love and respect, and I am not really optimistic that your resources will change my perspective or my attitude. I haven't lost all hope, though, or I wouldn't be trying your resource.

Most women are not mean-spirited; they just never saw respect for men modeled. A mom e-mailed:

I am raising two boys, and in this time I can certainly bless them with the knowledge God presented through the two of you this past weekend. I realized while sitting there that growing up, I never witnessed a woman in my family treat a man with respect. Thus, I had no examples, but I surely do not want my boys to be with women who will disrespect them as men.

Some of you are clueless about this because no one explained any of this to you. However, do not move into shame. See this as a special moment to gain insight that can make a huge impact. See this as a moment in which the Lord is answering some of your prayers about your relationship with your son.

Mommy's Marriage

God calls wives to put on respect toward the spirit of their husbands (Eph. 5:33; 1 Peter 3:1–2). However, when a wife feels disrespect for her

husband, it can spill over onto her son. A woman shared, "I also am raising two boys ages nine and four, and my lack of respect for their father as
well as other men is sure to damage their self-respect as growing men. I
love my boys very dearly and do not want to harm them in this way. I want
them to grow as strong, loving, respectable, godly men, and I will have to
show them this."

Some wives have awakened to the impact that their disrespect toward
their husbands has on their sons. A woman wrote:

> I recently read your book and wish it had been written twenty years
> ago. My husband and I have three grown sons. For the first time I real-
> ize why they often reacted so negatively when I disrespected their dad.
> As I look back at times of verbal disrespect toward my husband, I now
> understand why my sons would at times visibly wince and come angrily
> to his defense. They understood what I did not. Respect is vital to men.
> I hope you will explain to the women at your conferences that a wom-
> an's lack of respect toward her husband has negative effects not only on
> him but on the other "men" in the house as well. I am making a point of
> praising and respecting my husband in front of our sons, and all four of
> them are standing taller!

A mom wrote to me:

> I know the Lord has forgiven me for my past disrespect, but my heart
> hurts so deeply that my words were the cause of so much emotional pain
> to my husband and sons, and I didn't even realize it. Even though I said
> other kind exhorting words to them . . . they just heard it as complaining,
> and it didn't matter. Using the right word is so vital. Women need to
> wake up and realize the way society responds to our men is wrong.
> We're harming our men, without even knowing it.

Sadly, some moms show disrespect toward their husbands because
they feel their husbands fail to be loving and sensitive to their sons.

However, the boy does not feel as the mother feels. A woman told me, "We saw your seminar on DVD, and it helped a lot. . . . The other day my husband walked into the kitchen and didn't say good morning to my son. I said, 'Can't you say good morning?' My son replied, 'Mom, he nodded his head—that's good enough.'"

Consumed with helping her husband be more loving toward their son, she ends up being disrespectful to both of them. This testimony illustrates the goodwill of the mother but also that she has an expectation of how things ought to be. She can quickly criticize when a husband falls short of that standard. In this instance, the son defends his dad, feeling his mom's critique was presumptuous, inaccurate, and unfair.

A son wrote to me about a sad memory. During the burning of their home, his mother showed contempt toward her husband, his dad, in front of the whole family:

I remembered a scene from 1965. The farmhouse in which my mother grew up caught fire and was gutted. My mother said, "The house would not have burned if my dad had been there." My mother did not know at the time she made the statement that her father was at the scene when the house was gutted. She had so much confidence in her father that she believed that he could have prevented the house from being gutted, even though he was nearly seventy-nine years old at the time. My point is that my mother *never* exhibited that kind of respect for our father in front of us children.

Nearly forty years later he still recalls the level of disrespect his mother showed his dad. A son feels disrespected by his mother's disrespect for his father, just as a daughter feels unloved by her father when he treats her mother unlovingly.

Mommy's Unrealistic Expectations

An adult son communicated with me:

In asking about how the love-respect issue relates to mother-son relationships, I really wasn't talking about the early years or even the teen years. I am almost embarrassed to say it, but I'm talking about three sons who are in their thirties. More often than not we, thirty-year-old sons, are on the Crazy Cycle with mom. We know she loves us because she genuinely does so much for us. And we love her. I think what it boils down to is we are still the priority in her life, as we were when we were children. That leads to disappointment for her when we don't meet her expectations of what she expects the mother-adult son relationship to be (thus, she feels unloved), and then she loses her temper or gets jealous when we don't give her a fair share of our time (thus, we feel disrespected). When we hop on the Crazy Cycle, we keep hearing the same issues from years ago, over and over and over again. I could go on and on. Our family appears to be the "perfect" family to everyone else—three pastors involved here—but our relationship continues to be strained. I am very interested to know how Love and Respect, which is God's directive for man and wife, applies to mom and adult son.

Moms must hear the heart of this adult son. Jesus said that a son shall leave his father and mother and cleave to his wife. A mom must accept the sequence of three phases: first phase, she controls the tots; second phase, she counsels the teens (she cannot control them 24/7); and third phase, she casts off her sons. According to Jesus, a son leaves. He tends to exercise greater independence. For this mother to carry on as she does with her three godly, wise sons only pushes them away from her emotionally. She must stop thinking about her love-needs and concentrate on their respect-needs—the other side of the coin. When she does this, they'll be more affectionate and connected. How can mothers miss this? That's comparable to a father demanding that his daughter respect him all the while spurning her need for his love.

Appendix D

TELL US YOUR STORY

Write to us at boys@loveandrespect.com. Let us hear how you applied Respect-Talk to your son.

Many ask, "What about fathers and daughters?" Girls need a daddy's love. I welcome your questions, comments, and stories related to fathers and daughters. Write to me at girls@loveandrespect.com.

Appendix E

EMERSON'S 21 DAYS OF INSPIRATION

IN APPLYING THE RESPECT MESSAGE

E-mail us at mom@loveandrespect.com to request the regular thoughts and reminders on the Respect Effect.
For example:

- What If My Boy Isn't Responding to My Respect?
- What If My Son Does Not Have Self-Respect?
- How Do I Accurately Rate Myself in Showing Respect to My Son?
- In What Ways Can My Husband Help Me Interpret My Son?
- How Do I Invite My Husband to Instruct My Son to Show Respect?
- What About My Disrespectful Feelings Toward My Husband?
- What If My Husband Isn't Loving or Respectful?
- Will an Uncontrolled Outburst of Disrespect Ruin the Relationship with My Son?
- I Fear Being Disrespectful Without Knowing It. What Should I Do?

- When I Feel Tired and Hurt, What Do I Do Again?
- How Do I Not Teeter-Totter Between Hostility and Appeasement?
- Do You Have Some Prayers That I Can Pray? I Need God's Help.
- How Do I Respond to Other Women Who Object to This Idea of Showing Respect to Sons?

Bonus Chapter

"THE REAL REASON TO PARENT GOD'S WAY" FROM LOVE & RESPECT IN THE FAMILY

What does this mean for us? The Family Rewarded Cycle visual on page 183 stated: "A parent's love regardless of a child's respect . . ." I want to expand on this to say a better statement is "a parent's love unto Jesus Christ and his child regardless of a child's respect . . ." As parents, we must parent "unto Jesus Christ," regardless of the choices our children make. Parenting God's way means that we parent unto Christ even though our children fail to be who we hope they can be.

How do we parent unto Christ? In these Family Rewarded Cycle chapters, I hope to show you that I am not talking about ethereal spiritual jargon. To parent unto Christ means an entirely different approach. It means to be Christ-conscious in all we do with and for our children—this is God's highest call to parents.

Does the Bible tell us to "parent as unto the Lord"? In Colossians 3:15–24, Paul instructed all believers to be conscious of Christ as present with us in daily living. We are to "let the peace of Christ rule in [our] hearts . . . and be thankful [to God]" (v. 15). We are to "let the word of Christ richly dwell within" us (v. 16). And, whatever we "do in word or deed," we "do all in the name of the Lord Jesus, giving thanks through Him to God the Father" (v. 17).

Briefly put, we are to do what we do and say what we say "as unto the Lord" (for example, Ephesians 5:22 KJV). I prefer the King James translation of "as unto the Lord" or, in some other passages, "as to the Lord" because it is a stronger way to express the idea that all that we do should be done, not just "for" the Lord but "unto" Jesus (Matthew 25:40 KJV). The Lord is actively present. In the total context of Colossians 3:15–24, Paul applied this powerful truth to marriage and family life (especially vv. 18–21). In all of life, and particularly as spouses and parents, we are to rise above horizontal living and be in touch with the vertical relationship we have with our heavenly Father through Jesus Christ our Lord. We are to do what we do "as to the Lord" (v. 23 KJV) because "it is the Lord Christ whom you serve" (v. 24). By the way, in a parallel passage—Ephesians 5:18–6:9—the same truths are set forth. This is no small matter.

To parent "as to the Lord" actually means that in a most profound way this book on parenting has very little to do with children. In a sense, our kids are secondary. This book is not about child-centered parenting but about Christ-centered parenting. Though we are conscious of our children and love them more than our own lives, as we apply G.U.I.D.E.S. 24/7, we are to be more conscious of Christ than we are of our children. Beyond the feelings of our children, we are to have a reverent regard for the feelings of Christ, the One we desire to please in the ultimate sense.

In fact, Scripture tells us to love Christ more than we love our kids. Jesus said, "He who loves son or daughter more than Me is not worthy of Me" (Matthew 10:37). Yes, we concentrate on the kids in parenting since that is inescapable, but we focus more on Christ in parenting since that is incomparable.

But if we are to confidently go about our parenting as to the Lord, we must be very clear on who we are in Him. Mentally and emotionally we must seize and hold dear the truth about our eternal value to the Lord. For example, we need to hear the word of Christ concerning our worth. "Look at the birds of the air, that they do not sow, nor reap nor gather into barns, and yet your heavenly Father feeds them. Are you not worth much more than they?" (Matthew 6:26). Each of us must recognize God's forever view of us and the incalculable value He places on us. Most important, does our value to God really affect our marriage and our parenting?

When I weigh the words Jesus used to describe what He has done for me, I am stunned. He has ransomed me, forgiven me, given me eternal life, loved me, and He has prepared a place for me (Matthew 20:28, 26:28; John 3:16, 15:9, 14:2). In letting the Word of Christ richly dwell within me, I catch a glimpse of His gracious acceptance, eternal endorsement, and priceless valuation of me. I invite you to comprehend the same—right now. And remember, none of this is merited. We do not earn any of Christ's unwarranted gifts but can only receive them and let all these truths affect the way we parent.

To not understand that our significance and true identity are in Christ and not in our children puts us in danger of being discouraged, as was the mother who wrote:

> One of my problems is that when the kids misbehave or don't act as I think they should, then I feel it is such a reflection on me and an extension of me. I suppose it is a pride thing or part of my personality, but do you have any suggestions because this seems to be what wears me down and then paralyzes me, and I feel defeated. Does this make sense?

Her comments make perfect sense to Sarah and me. We have been there. Sarah recalls our very first year of parenting: "I wanted Jonathan to be perfect in the nursery at church. Sadly, he wasn't perfect at three months old, and he cried every Sunday, and I felt like a failure."

As funny as this nursery episode sounds now, it is symbolic of what we felt as parents as the years went on and the matters became more serious. As our children grew, they did what children do—acted imperfectly.

Our motive for wanting perfectly behaved children was pure (we wanted to protect them from the consequences of bad choices), but when their behavior caused us to question our worth as parents and even our worth as Christians, we became deeply discouraged. On the heels of many wrong choices made by our children, Sarah and I sat sadly and quietly as we wondered where we had gone wrong. How did we fail to help our children make the right choices? What was wrong with us as parents? Why couldn't we guide them better during their testing and temptations?

There were some dark evenings when we had to deal with these woeful feelings, as many parents must. Would we let these situations conquer us and cause us to stop parenting God's way, as we wallowed in self-pity? The good news is that such reflection put us in a position not only to look for ways to improve our parenting but, more importantly, to face off with our identity in Christ. As we confessed our failures and defects to God, we allowed Him to remind us of His love, that He is for us, and that He will work all things together for our good.

If we allowed our kids' unruliness, irresponsibility, and sinfulness—all "normal" behavior that we were trying to correct—to define our true identity . . .

- our sense of self-worth would go up and down based on how "good" our kids were at all times. For us to feel good about ourselves, our children had to perform well. Obviously this was not fair to us—and certainly not to them.
- we would be making them responsible for our sense of peace, instead of letting the peace of Christ rule in our hearts.
- we would be letting their words about us determine how we felt about ourselves, instead of trusting the words of Christ to determine our sense of self-worth.

As the days passed, Sarah and I humbly let the Scriptures create a new script in our hearts and minds, and so must you. What is your inner script? Have you come to grips with your position in Christ? Do you realize that you have worth because He says you have worth, not because of anything you (or your kids) do or do not do?

As I talk to parents across the country, I find a lot of people who feel defeated as parents because of how their kids behave (or have turned out). What I am about to share with you will not only refresh your soul personally but also enable you to parent as God intends—or at least make better progress in that direction.

You Are "Worth Jesus to God"

All of us who believe in Christ as Savior have a "passport to heaven," so to speak, which says, "Because of Jesus Christ, this is a forgiven, accepted, approved, made righteous, made perfect, adopted child of God." As Jesus is *the* Son of God, we are adopted sons and daughters of God. We are in God's family never to be forsaken. This is our true identity. We are beloved children of God—children for whom He has never-ending feelings of compassion. Will we believe that God feels this way about us even when we do not feel this way about ourselves? We must! This is what faith means.

Do you get this? Do you comprehend what it means to be "beloved by God," a refrain used dozens of times in the Bible about all believers? It took Sarah and me some time at first to grasp this truth (and we are still in the process, to some degree), but when we did, it tremendously affected the way we parented. God's truth was there for the dark moments. We had to accept and believe what all Christian parents must believe: we are worth Jesus to God! The Bible declares: "For you have been bought with a price" (1 Corinthians 6:20; 7:23). What price? "You were not redeemed with perishable things like silver or gold . . . but with precious blood, as of a lamb unblemished and spotless, the blood of Christ" (1 Peter 1:18–19). We were bought with the blood of Christ. His life for our life.

Please join Sarah and me in saying: "Yes, I *am* worth Jesus to God. When God says I have worth, *I have worth*!"

I am well aware that in the daily grind of life, our feelings counter and undermine our trust in our true worth to God. But once we know our worth to God, we cease trying to derive our worth from our children. Yes, today they give us reasons to rejoice, and tomorrow they may cause heartache and sorrow, but at no time do they determine our value and importance as redeemed human beings. As believers in Christ we bring our identity to our parenting; we do not derive our identity from our parenting.

As one mother told me, "Our children can't heal our wounds; only God can." She realized how unhealthy her attitude toward her kids was when she expected them to create a healthy self-image in her. She realized she had been trying to hold them accountable for her well-being. She had been requiring them to act obediently to shore up her sagging self-esteem.

One more biblical promise confirms that we are worth Jesus to the Father: our eternal inheritance. "Therefore you are no longer a slave, but a son; and if a son, then an heir through God" (Galatians 4:7). But what does "heir" mean? "The Spirit Himself testifies with our spirit that we are children of God, and if children, heirs also, heirs of God and fellow heirs with Christ" (Romans 8:16–17). There it is! "Fellow heirs with Christ"! "All things belong to [us], and [we] belong to Christ; and Christ belongs to God" (1 Corinthians 3:22b–23).

I have given you this short course on the believer's worth in the eyes of Abba Father to demonstrate that Christian parents have a living, divine document—the oracles of God—that tells us who we are in His eyes (Hebrews 5:12). As we work at parenting each day, we must believe God's truth, even when we do not necessarily feel it.

We must believe that a biblical self-image gives Christian parents a controlling peace during the daily trials—a very practical benefit to us and our kids. So when the dog chews the corner of the couch, our toddler falls down the stairs and breaks an arm, or our teen wrecks the car, we can walk with the assurance of knowing that somehow in only His sovereign wisdom God is always working all this together for the good of those who love Him (*memorize* Romans 8:28). No, we do not expect perfect peace all the time; there will be frustrating and fatiguing days. However, if we but ask, moments of God's peace will soften the sharp edges that may form on our demeanor, which could cut and damage our children.

We parent as unto Christ because of our identity in Him, but we also parent unto Jesus for one more reason. An eternal reward awaits us, and nothing compares to this eternal reward. Paul intended all believers, including parents, to know "that from the Lord you will receive the reward of the inheritance. It is the Lord Christ whom you serve" (Colossians 3:24).

"Well Done, Good and Faithful Servant!"

All Christian parents will one day stand before the Lord at the judgment seat of Christ (2 Corinthians 5:10; Romans 14:10). Our parenting will be part of this judgment. We will not be judged for our children's conduct toward us but for our conduct toward our children. We will hear His humble and true evaluation of our actions and reactions toward our kids. Hopefully, we will hear, "Well done," and receive the Lord's reward for our godly actions and reactions in the parenting process.

This is why it is so important that our parenting should be more unto the Lord than toward our kids. In the words of our Lord in Matthew 25, "Truly I say to you, to the extent that you did it to . . . even the least of them, you did it to Me" (v. 40). And as Paul put it in Ephesians 6:7–8: "Serve wholeheartedly, as if you were serving the Lord, not men, because you know that the Lord will reward everyone for whatever good he does" (NIV). Paul was saying that whatever we do as to the Lord, we will receive back from Him, and that certainly includes parenting (which he addressed a few verses earlier in Ephesians 6:4). Everything you do as a mom or dad counts, even if your child ignores you. This is what the Family Rewarded Cycle is all about. God never ignores you!

Parents who feel discouraged can suddenly catch the truth that what they do matters to God; *nothing is wasted*. Putting on love toward a disrespectful child counts to God even if the child refuses to appreciate the love. These seemingly fruitless efforts matter to God because this is the kind of service He rewards. In other words, when our children refuse to respond to us but we still love them, the Lord rewards us as parents.

What are the rewards? We get some of them on earth, but we get an incredible reward in heaven. Jesus wants to say, "Well done, good and faithful servant! You have been faithful with a few things; I will put you in charge of many things. Come and share your master's happiness!" (Matthew 25:23 NIV). What would some of those "few things" be? Surely they include what Paul described as God's call to parents, which we studied under G.U.I.D.E.S. When you make a decision to parent God's way, the dividends are without end. Jesus is offering you a bargain. Do a few things on earth in this life and get many things forever in heaven.

Have you ever thought about what it will mean to "share your master's happiness"? It will be joy without measure. Think of your graduation day, wedding day, birthdays, children's birthdays, summer vacations, promotions, retirement, good times of all descriptions. What if every hour of every day you experienced the glory and joy of all these events at once in their fullest intensity? When you "share your master's happiness," the intensity will be trillions of times greater.

Envision the scene as believers ascend into heaven and stand before Christ. To a parent He says, "Well done. You've put on love toward your disrespectful child. I watched. You are about to be rewarded for every act of love."

As Christ-following parents we have the privilege of living with the end in mind, which is doing Christ's will and hearing His, "Well done, good and faithful servant." This is about pleasing Christ by the way we parent. In other words, parenting is a tool and test to deepen and demonstrate our love, reverence, trust, and obedience toward Jesus Christ.

But how do we stand the test? How does all this work in the daily battle? The next three chapters will deal with these questions. First, we need to ask His help to do the impossible—*unconditionally* love our kids.

ACKNOWLEDGMENTS

My appreciation to the hundreds of mothers who e-mailed to me their stories of applying respect to their sons and the incredible effects it had on the spirit of their boys, so much so that the mothers felt strongly about contacting me and telling me about the Respect Effect!

My deep gratefulness to my wife, Sarah, who prayed constantly while I wrote this book that God would use this message to encourage mothers in the same way He had spoken to her heart as well as touch the hearts of boys everywhere.

My thanks to Matt Baugher and his W Publishing Group staff at HarperCollins that served editorially in the final stages of this book. I especially value Matt's words after he read the manuscript, which I hope will be the experience of every person: "I am pleasantly floored by the power and impact of this manuscript."

My salute to Kevin Harvey, who did what he does well: rearrange words, sentences, and paragraphs so the pieces of the puzzle fit better together (or should it be "fit together better"?).

NOTES

Chapter 1: Why This Book?

1. Shaunti Feldhahn, *For Women Only: What You Need to Know About the Lives of Men* (Colorado Springs: Multnomah, 2004), 17.

2. Louann Brizendine, *The Female Brain* (New York: Doubleday, 2006), 34–35.

Chapter 2: Understanding What Respect Looks Like to Boys

1. Lauren Mackenzie and Megan Wallace, "The Communication of Respect as a Significant Dimension of Cross-Cultural Communication Competence," *Cross-Cultural Communication* 7, no. 3 (2011): 11.

2. Bernd Simon, "Respect, Equality, and Power: A Social Psychological Perspective," *Gruppendynamik und Organisationsberatung* 38, no. 3 (2007): 309–26.

3. Louann Brizendine, *The Female Brain* (New York: Doubleday, 2006), 1.

Chapter 4: Seeing the Man in the Boy

1. Dannah Gresh, *What Are You Waiting For? The One Thing No One Ever Tells You About Sex* (Colorado Springs: WaterBrook, 2001), 4.

2. Louann Brizendine, *The Female Brain* (New York: Doubleday, 2006), 15–18.

3. Shaunti Feldhahn, *For Women Only: What You Need to Know About the Lives of Men* (Colorado Springs: Multnomah, 2004), 17.

Chapter 5: Conquest

1. Tony Perkins, "2016 Field: The Doctor Is In!" *The Patriot Post*, last modified May 5, 2015, http://patriotpost.us/opinion/34993.

Chapter 7: Authority

1. Louann Brizendine, *The Female Brain* (New York: Doubleday, 2006), 34–35.
2. Deborah Tannen, *Talking from 9 to 5: Women and Men at Work* (New York: William Morrow Paperbacks, 2001), 167.
3. D. Leyk, et al., "Hand-grip strength of young men, women and highly trained female athletes," *European Journal of Applied Physiology* 99, no. 4 (2007): 415–21.

Chapter 8: Insight

1. Online Etymology Dictionary, s.v. "sophomore," http://www.etymonline.com/index.php?term=sophomore.

Chapter 9: Relationship

1. Oxford Dictionaries, s.v. "rapport," last modified October 3, 2015, http://www.oxforddictionaries.com/us/definition/american_english/rapport.
2. Deborah Tannen, *Gender and Discourse* (New York: Oxford University Press, 2003), 88–99.

Chapter 10: Sexuality

1. Rachel Sheffield, "Hooking Up, Shacking Up, and Saying 'I Do,'" The Witherspoon Institute, *Public Discourse*, September 10, 2014, http://www.thepublicdiscourse.com/2014/09/13765/.
2. Juli Slattery, "Understanding His Sexuality," *No More Headaches* (Carol Stream, IL: Tyndale, 2009), retrieved from www.focusonthefamily.com/marriage/sex-and-intimacy

/understanding-your-husbands-sexual-needs/
understanding-his-sexuality.

3. Shaunti Feldhahn, *Through a Man's Eyes: Helping Women Understand the Visual Nature of Men* (Colorado Springs: Multnomah, 2015), 32–33.

4. Ibid., 33–34.

Chapter 11: An Empathetic Look at the Motherly Objections to Respecting a Boy

1. *Wikipedia*, s.v. "Respect (song)," last modified October 3, 2015, https://en.wikipedia.org/wiki/Respect_(song).

About the Author

EMERSON EGGERICHS, PhD, is an internationally known public speaker on the topic of male-female relationships and family dynamics. Dr. Eggerichs presents to live audiences around the country in his Love and Respect Conferences, based on more than three decades of counseling, as well as scientific and biblical research. This dynamic and life-changing conference is impacting the world, resulting in the healing and restoration of countless relationships.

Well-known as a dynamic speaker, Dr. Eggerichs has spoken to audiences across the spectrum, including NFL owners and coaches, PGA players and their spouses at the Player's Championship, the New York Giants, the Miami Heat, members of Congress, and Navy SEALs. But most honoring to him was being invited by the military brass to speak to troops in the Middle East.

Dr. Eggerichs has a BA in biblical studies from Wheaton College, an MA in communication from Wheaton College Graduate School, an MDiv from the University of Dubuque Theological Seminary, and a PhD in child and family ecology from Michigan State University. He has authored several books, including the *New York Times* bestseller *Love & Respect*, and most recently, *Love & Respect in the Family*.

Before launching the Love and Respect Conferences, Dr. Eggerichs was the senior pastor of Trinity Church in Lansing, Michigan, for almost twenty years. Emerson and Sarah have been married since 1973 and have three adult children. He is the founder and president of Love and Respect Ministries.

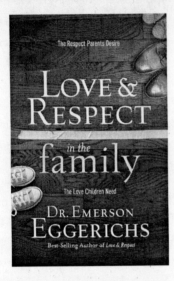
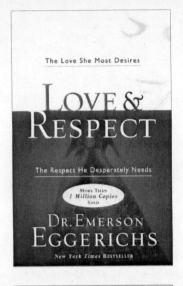
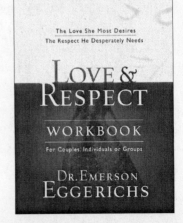

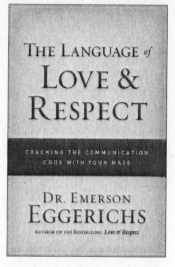

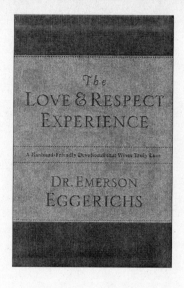

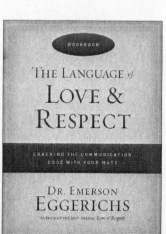

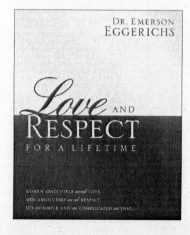